CW00410734

LUFTWAFFE
SECRET PROJECTS
FIGHTERS 1939-1945

Midland Publishing
Limited

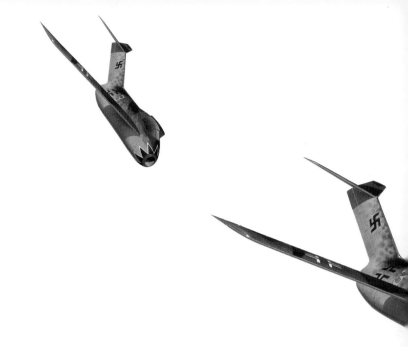

Photograph on half-title page:
Western and Soviet knowledge of aerodynamics received a huge boost as German
technology was examined upon the collapse
of the Third Reich. For example, the unfinished Messerschmitt P.1101 was shipped
to Bell at Buffalo in New York State, for examination. From these studies came the Bell X-5,
the world's first variable geometry aircraft.

Illustration on title page, opposite:
The Focke-Wulf Ta183 could well have
entered Luftwaffe service early in 1946 and
taken up the much-respected mantle of its
piston-engined predecessor, the Fw 190.
From a specially commissioned painting for
the dust jacket by Keith Woodcock GAvA.

LUFTWAFFE
SECRET PROJECTS
FIGHTERS 1939-1945

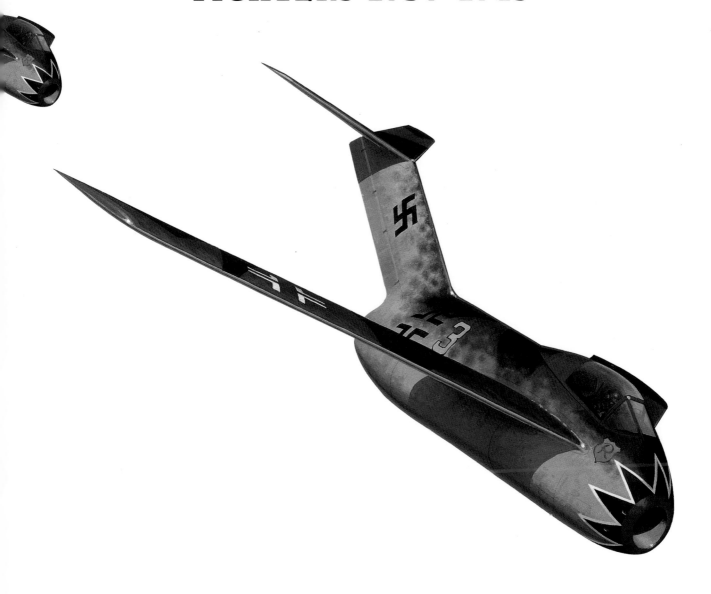

Walter Schick and Ingolf Meyer

Contents

Preface

This work documents secret fighter development in Germany between the years 1939 and 1945. It does not attempt to describe those technical dead ends and emergency solutions which were the product of the final desperate months. Despite their sometimes incorporating excellent ideas and detail design features, they were quickly overtaken by the advent of more effective ground-to-air rockets or were rendered redundant by radical changes in the post-war situation.

What it does cover are the fighter aircraft with high-compression piston engines or with the new turbojet powerplants, some featuring highly advanced aerodynamics, which anticipated much of the latest state-of-the-art aviation technology of the years following the Second World War. (Rocket-powered types are not included, being very much a study in their own right.) Aircraft with swept, crescent or delta wings, with and without tails, aircraft made of wood, aluminium, steel and even synthetics! A great deal of what was to be seen in the world's major air forces in the 1950s and 1960s originated during the war years on the drawing boards of German designers. It must be said, however, that the political leadership of the Third Reich failed to grasp the practical potential offered by these significant advances. Very few of the fighter designs described here reached the production stage or were under construction by the war's end.

In pointing the way ahead for the future of both military and civil aviation Germany's designers were to prove so valuable, saving the victorious powers enormous amounts in research and development costs. To this day the subject has lost none of its fascination.

The authors' primary aim has been to portray – by means of illustrations and a thoroughly researched text – the wide variety of ideas and concepts made possible by the use of new technologies. Numerous cutaway and detail drawings, wind tunnel photographs and illustrations of models serve to show that, in most cases, it was not a matter of visionaries or dreamers being driven by a sense of panic at the impending collapse, but rather of highly motivated designers and scientific engineers producing work, often under the most difficult of circumstances, which was, in effect, no less than the 'second great step' in the history of aviation technology: the transition from conventional piston-engined fighters to the modern high performance jet fighters of the post-war era.

The colour illustrations are intended to represent how these designs might have looked had they been built and entered service – in other words, pure fiction, but fiction based very much on established fact.

The text, supported by detailed specifications, supplements and amends much of what has been published in the past. It is the result of many years' collecting and research which was only possible by, and with, the help of many experts and enthusiasts at home and abroad. The end product is a technical documentation which dispenses for the most part with any form of inference or speculation.

Our thanks must go, above all, to Eddie Creek, Jeff Ethell, Gerhard Roletschek and Hanfried Schliephake. We are also especially indebted to Dieter H Herwig, Theodor Mohr, Willy Radinger and Günter Sengfelder, who have made their expert knowledge available to us throughout and who selflessly provided much of the documentary and photographic material which made this work possible.

Walter Schick
Ingolf Meyer

English language edition
January 1997

6

Introduction

The 1930s paved the way for an important and radical change in aviation technology. One of the milestones along the route to today's modern civil and military aircraft was the so-called 'Volta' Congress, which took place in Rome between 30th September and 6th October 1935 and at which the delegates, among them the world's leading aerodynamicists of the day, turned their attention to the question of high speed flight. Here they discussed for the first time the possibilities of flying at or above the speed of sound. The scientists soon came to the unanimous conclusion that this target could not be achieved with the powerplant combination of piston engine and propeller which had been the norm to date.

It was at this conference that a young scientist from the Aerodynamic Experimental Institute at Göttingen propounded his idea for the reduction of drag in high speed flight. For the first time Dr Adolph Busemann made reference to the swept wing, whose efficiency he had proven by purely mathematical means. But at that time few took notice of him ...

In April 1937, after much lengthy and diverse preliminary research across international boundaries, the first functional jet engines were run in Germany and Great Britain. Even before this date Junkers and BMW had each begun work on a modern axial-type turbojet powerplant out of which would eventually evolve the Junkers Jumo 004 and BMW 003 jet engines, both produced in large numbers. Initially neither the state, nor, it must be said, the parent companies, provided these developments with the kind of support which would have permitted their rapid realisation.

The same held true for aerodynamics. It was not until 1939 that research into swept wings began in Germany on any large scale. The drawbacks in Busemann's discovery soon became apparent. The experimental institutes and the industry's own research departments then made great efforts to find solutions to the problems; particularly that of a swept wing's behaviour in low speed flight. All sorts of special shapes and planforms resulted: crescent wings, delta wings and variable-sweep wings.

Ideas for aerodynamics such as boundary layer fences, leading-edge flaps and boundary layer control were put forward. Wind tunnel tests proved their effectiveness. On today's modern high performance aircraft such features have become a matter of course.

At the beginning of 1944, as part of their research into the optimum arrangement of the major components of a high speed aircraft, Junkers succeeded in discovering an aerodynamic regularity which today, as 'area rule', forms a basis for supersonic aircraft design.

These new aerodynamics, together with the new powerplants, had, by the war's end, laid the foundations for modern supersonic fighters. They also went hand in hand with the introduction of new methods of construction, the use of new materials, the employment of the most modern radio and radar technology, the provision of new emergency and rescue systems and, not least, the introduction of new, revolutionary weapons.

In Germany the result of all this concentrated and costly research work was an explosion of new project activity unequalled in the history of aviation; an explosion that was fuelled even further in 1944 by the lifting of all patent protection.

Almost anything seemed possible. Targets which the designers could only dream of just a few years earlier were now suddenly within easy reach; so near and yet, because of the political and military situation of the times, so far.

The multiplicity of projects underlines the leadership weaknesses within the Reichsluftfahrtministerium (RLM), but also highlights the industry's own uncertainties about the correct course to follow.

On top of that the designers themselves, perhaps understandably, could not resist the temptation to investigate every avenue, explore every possibility offering the remotest chance of achieving the feasible or the practicable.

Even under different circumstances, only a few of these projects would have attained series production. But much of the work committed to paper in Germany in 1945 signposted the way to the future.

The authors have taken the vast majority of technical and other data in this book from works' files or from official documents of the RLM. They have made limited use of post-war reference sources, and then only to extract information of a confirmatory or plausible nature, or which originated from participants in the events described.

All data have been recorded to the best of the authors' knowledge and only after a thorough study of all available documentary evidence. Contemporary terminology has been used as far as possible to reflect the 'feel' of the times.

A word of explanation on the calculated performance figures used throughout the book: performance values given in numbers must always perforce represent one moment of one particular flight, at a certain weight and with a known engine output at a certain altitude. More correctly, an exact representation of performance could only be illustrated by means of charts and diagrams. As a rule, therefore, the figures quoted must be taken to indicate only the parameters of the performance envelope. However, flight tests and practical results achieved during later (postwar) trials of aircraft of similar configurations and capabilities have served to show that the figures projected by German designers mirrored reality to a fairly accurate degree.

Many documents, and thus much of the knowledge of the subject, either disappeared in the chaos of the final weeks of the war or, for whatever reason, were destroyed during the years that followed. Much has survived, however, some albeit only partially, scattered in official archives or private collections throughout the world.

The authors therefore offer the following as an endeavour, which makes no claim to be either completely free of errors or definitive. They would thus welcome any corrections or additional information from readers. Their declared aim is to bring clarity to a decisive period in the history of aviation technology.

Dipl-Ing Walter Schick

Introduction written for the German-language edition. Walter Schick died in 1995, aged 47.

Glossary

Abteilung 'L' – Department 'L', the Lippisch design department within the Messerschmitt company.

APZ Automatischer Peilzusatz – automatic supplementary direction finding equipment.

AVA Aerodynamische Versuchsanstalt – Aerodynamic Experimental Institute.

AWG Auswertegerät – plotting device.

BK Bordkanone – fixed aircraft cannon.

BMW Bayerische Motorenwerke – Bavarian Engine Works.

DFS Deutsches Forschungsinstitut für Segelflug – German Research Institute for Sailplanes.

Dipl-Ing Diplomingenieur – literally diploma-ed engineer, equivalent to Diploma of Engineering.

Doppelreiter Literally 'double-rider', wing fuel fairings.

DVL Deutsche Versuchsanstalt für Luftfahrt – German Aviation Experimental Institute.

E Entwurf – project.

EF Entwicklungsflugzeug – development aircraft.

EiV Eigenverständigungsanlage – crew intercom.

EHK Entwicklungshauptkommission – Main Development Commission.

ESK Entwicklungssonderkommission – Special Development Commission.

ETC Elektrische Trägervorrichtung für Cylinderbomben – electrically-operated carrier device for cylindrical bombs.

EZ Einheitszielvorrichtung – standard sighting device.

FDL Ferngerichtete Drehringlafette – remotely controlled barbette.

FHL Ferngerichtete Hecklafette – remotely controlled tail barbette.

Fl-E Flugzeugentwicklung – Aircraft Development Department within the TLR.

Flitzer Literally Dasher or Whizzer, single-seater jet fighter.

FuBl Funk-Blindlandeanlage – radio blind-landing equipment.

FuG Funkgerät – radio or radar set.

FZG Fernzielgerät – remote aiming device/bombsight.

General der Jagdflieger Air Officer Commanding fighters.

Generalleutnant Luftwaffe equivalent to Air Vice Marshal (RAF) or Major General (USAAF).

Generalmajor Luftwaffe rank equivalent to Air Commodore (RAF) or one-star General (USAAF).

Generalstab General Staff.

GM-1 Nitrous oxide.

Gruppe Luftwaffe equivalent to Wing (RAF) or Group (USAAF).

IFF Identification, friend or foe.

Jägerstab Fighter Staff.

Jumo Junkers Motorenbau

LFA Luftfahrtforschungsanstalt – Aviation Research Institute.

MG Maschinengewehr – machine gun; later also cannon.

MK Maschinenkanone – machine cannon.

MW 50 Methanol-water mixture.

NJG Nachtjagdgeschwader – night fighter group.

Obergruppenführer SS rank, equivalent to Lieutenant General.

Oberleutnant Luftwaffe rank equivalent to Flying Officer (RAF) or 1st Lieutenant (USAAF).

Oberstleutnant Luftwaffe rank equivalent to Wing Commander (RAF) or Lieutenant Colonel (USAAF).

OKL Oberkommando der Luftwaffe – Luftwaffe High Command.

OMW Otto Marder Works

'Otto-Jäger' Piston-engined fighter.

P Projekt – project.

PeilG Peilgerät – direction finding set.

Pulk Luftwaffe term for USAF bomber box.

Pulkzerstörer Heavily armed anti-bomber aircraft.

Rb Reihenbildkamera – automatic aerial camera.

RfRuK Reichsministerium für Rüstung und Kriegsproduktion – Reich's Ministry of Armament and War Production.

RLM Reichsluftfahrtministerium – Reich's Air Ministry.

Rüstsatz Field conversion set.

SC Splitterbombe — fragmentation bomb.

Schräge Musik Luftwaffe term for oblique upward-firing armament (literally oblique or jazz music.

SD Splitterbombe, Dickwand – fragmentation bomb, thick-walled.

Technisches Amt Technical Office (of the RLM).

TL Turbinenluftstrahl-Triebwerk – turbojet engine.

TLR Technische Luftrüstung – Technical Air Armaments Board.

UKW Ultrakurzwelle – VHF.

Volksflugzeug People's (ie the Nation-State) Aircraft.

Volksjäger People's Fighter.

Volkssturm Germany's equivalent to the British home guard.

WNF Wiener Neustädter Flugzeugwerke – aircraft works.

W/nr Werk nummer – construction (or airframe serial) number.

Zerstörer Heavy fighter, literally destroyer.

ZVG Zielflugvorsatzgerät – homer attachment device.

Notes

Manufacturers

The Reichsluftfahrtministerium (RLM) adopted a series of (mostly) two-letter prefixes to act as design or manufacturer codes for aircraft. These mostly consisted of one upper and one lower case letter (eg Fw) but there were a handful of exceptions which used all capitals (eg BV).

The RLM list of manufacturers/design offices is as follows:

Al	Albatros
Ao	AGO-Flugzeugwerke
Ar	Arado
Ba	Bachem
Bf	Bayerische Flugzeugwerke
Bü	Bücker
BV	Blohm und Voss
DFS	Deutsche Forschungsanstalt für Segelflug
Do	Dornier
FA	Focke-Achgelis
Fh	Flugzeugbau Halle
Fi	Fieseler
FK	Flugzeugbau Kiel
Fl	Flettner
Fw	Focke-Wulf
Go	Gothaer Waggonfabrik
Ha	Hamburger Flugzeugbau
He	Heinkel
Ho	Horten
Hs	Henschel
Hü	Hütter
Ju	Junkers
Ka	Kalkert
Kl	Klemm
Me	Messerschmitt
NR	Nagler-Rolz
Si	Siebel
Sk	Skoda-Kauba
Ta	Tank
WNF	Wiener-Neustädter-Flugzeugbau *
ZMe	Zeppelin/Messerschmitt
ZSO	Zeppelin/SNCASO

* – also Wn but WNF used in preference to avoid confusion with w/nr.

This brings us to the inevitable 'chestnut' of 'Bf' or 'Me' for Messerschmitt's earlier designs. This work is very much a study of official documentation and RLM nomenclature has been adhered to.

For the RLM the transition from 'Bf' to 'Me' occurs between the unsuccessful Bf162 Jaguar (whose number was subsequently allocated to the He162 Volksjäger) and the Me163 Komet. The 'Me'155 (see Chapter One) avoids the issue by having been transferred at a very early stage to Blohm und Voss.

Then there is the 'grey area' of projected developments of 'Bf' types (eg the Bf109G) initiated after the change to 'Me'. This is tempting (eg Me109H) but since later operational variants of the '109 retained the 'Bf' prefix (Bf109K circa 1944-45) this work has standardised on all Messerschmitt types below the RLM number 162 being prefixed 'Bf' and all those from 163 and upwards being prefixed 'Me'.

Measurements

All German aircraft measurements etc are given in decimal (or SI – Système International d'Unités, established in 1960) units, with an Imperial (of British FPSR – foot, pound, second, Rankine) figure second. This is reversed in the few cases where UK or US-built aircraft are quoted.

The following notes may help:

aspect ratio   wingspan and chord expressed as a ratio. Low aspect ratio, short, stubby wing; high aspect ratio, long, narrow wing.

ft   feet – length, multiply by 0.305 to get metres (m). For height measurements involving service ceilings and cruise heights, the figure has been 'rounded'.

ft²   square feet – area, multiply by 0.093 to get square metres (m²).

fuel   measured in both litres/gallons and kilograms/pounds. The specific gravity (sg) of German fuel varied considerably during the war and conversions from volume to weight and vice versa are impossible without knowing the specific gravity of the fuel at the time.

gallon   Imperial (or UK) gallon, multiply by 4.546 to litres. (500 Imperial gallons equal 600 US gallons.)

hp   horse power – power, measurement of power for piston and turboprop engines. Multiply by 0.746 to get kilowatts.

kg   kilogram – weight, multiply by 2.205 to get pounds (lb). Fuel load frequently given in kilograms.

kg/m²   kilograms per square metre – force, measurement of wing loading, multiply by 0.204 to get pounds per square foot.

km/h   kilometres per hour – velocity, multiply by 0.621 to get miles per hour (mph).

kP   kilopascal – force, for measuring thrust, effectively a kilogram of static thrust. Present day preferences are for the kilonewton (kN), one kN equalling 224.8lb or 101.96kg.

kW   kilowatt – power, measurement of power for piston and turboprop engines. Multiply by 1.341 to get horse power.

lb   pound – weight, multiply by 0.454 to get kilograms (kg). Also used for the force measurement of turbojet engines, with the same conversion factor, as pounds of static thrust.

lb/ft²   pounds per square foot – force, measurement of wing loading, multiply by 4.882 to get kilograms per square metre.

litre   volume, multiply by 0.219 to get Imperial (or UK) gallons.

m   metre – length, multiply by 3.28 to get feet (ft).

m²   square metre – area, multiply by 10.764 to get square feet (ft²)

mm   millimetre – length, the bore of guns is traditionally a decimal measure (eg 30mm) and no Imperial conversion is given.

mph   miles per hour – velocity, multiply by 1.609 to get kilometres per hour (km/h).

Luftwaffe Secret Projects –
Fighters 1939-1945

© Walter Schick and Ingolf Meyer 1994, 1997

Design concept and editorial layout
© Midland Publishing Limited
and Stephen Thompson Associates.
Edited by Ken Ellis

First published 1994 in Germany by
Motorbuch Verlag, Stuttgart.

Translation from original German text
by Elke and John Weal,
with additional thanks to Tony Buttler,
Martin Derry, Jay Miller and John Weal
for their inputs.

English language edition published 1997 by
Midland Publishing Limited
24 The Hollow, Earl Shilton
Leicester, LE9 7NA, England
Tel: 01455 847815   Fax: 01455 841805

ISBN 1 85780 052 4

Worldwide distribution (except Nth America):
Midland Counties Publications (Aerophile) Ltd
Unit 3 Maizefield, Hinckley Fields
Hinckley, Leics. LE10 1YF, England
Tel: 01455 233747 Fax: 01455 233737
E-mail: 106371.573@compuserve.com

North America trade distribution by:
Specialty Press Publishers & Wholesalers Inc.
11481 Kost Dam Road
North Branch, MN 55056, USA
Tel: 612 583 3239 Fax: 612 583 2023
Toll free telephone: 800 895 4585

All rights reserved. No part of this publication
may be reproduced, stored in a retrieval
system, transmitted in any form or by any
means, electronic, mechanical or photo-
copied, recorded or otherwise, without written
permission of the copyright owners.

Printed in Hong Kong
via World Print Limited

Chapter One

Piston Engine Zenith

During the early years of the Second World War Luftwaffe Commander-in-Chief Hermann Göring and his Secretary of State for Air, Erhard Milch, had done more to hinder rather than to help the development of new aircraft types. German aircraft manufacturers therefore often had little other option than to try to adapt existing, frequently unsuitable, types to meet the ever-growing demands of the war in the air. This usually entailed the fitting of more powerful engines and improved armament. Such measures, however, did not always deliver the hoped-for results and all too frequently caused the Luftwaffe a whole host of other problems. (By the war's end, for example, there had been close on 100 different variants of the Messerschmitt Bf 109 alone, the exact number of sub-types being almost impossible to determine!)

In the latter half of 1941, after the lifting of what had, since the beginning of 1940, been a virtual ban on development, several new projects did begin to appear. Due to the time lost in the interim, however, progress was very slow. As neither the Bf 109 nor the brand new Focke-Wulf Fw 190 in their standard versions were proving effective above a height of

Focke-Wulf Fw 190, standard fighter of the Luftwaffe, here in 'A-8 fighter-bomber guise.

10,000m (32,800ft), the Luftwaffe's foremost priority now was for a high altitude aircraft capable of combating high flying reconnaissance machines and bombers.

In the spring of 1942 the Reichsluftfahrtministerium (RLM – the Reich Air Ministry) took the first steps towards solving this problem, thereby initiating a development phase which would, by its close, see a significant increase in the service ceiling of piston-engined fighters and particularly of specialised high altitude fighters such as the Tank Ta 152H and the radical Blohm und Voss BV 155.

German efforts subsequently concentrated on producing a fighter aircraft superior to the Anglo-American types, with increasing emphasis being placed on jet-powered designs. But at no time did they lose sight of the development and construction of high performance piston-engined machines. Towards the closing stages of the war, on 18th September 1944, Generalstabsingenieur Robert Lucht, head of the main design and development commission, put forward the following for discussion:

On the basis of the aforementioned advantages and disadvantages, the single-engined pusher-propeller 'Otto' (ie petrol-driven) fighter, which can perform the role of the Do 335 at approximately half the cost, is very economical for use against bombers at all heights.

It is equally suitable for deployment against enemy 'Otto' fighters at all altitudes.

Thanks to its endurance the 'Otto' fighter is the type most suited to protecting any given area of airspace. And due to its economical cruise capability, the 'Otto' fighter performs better at all heights in bad weather and blind-flying conditions than would a jet-powered aircraft. Furthermore, it is the most suitable fighter for operation in greater numbers when circumstances call for massed formations.

In our opinion, and in the light of the above, the 'Otto' fighter at its most advanced stage of development with pusher propeller is indispensible for aerial defence duties above and behind the front lines. And thanks to its being less susceptible to ground fire, it also lends itself to use in the fighter-bomber and ground attack roles.

Lucht also pointed out that the piston-engined fighter possessed much better flight characteristics when taking off and landing than did the jet fighter. The latter was, in fact, extremely vulnerable at such times and required the protection of the former. In addition, there would, be insufficient jet engines available within the timescale envisaged, and the engine manufacturers could not switch production from piston to jet overnight.

The representatives of the two companies producing jet engines in any meaningful

Messerschmitt Bf 109G, standard fighter of the Luftwaffe. Illustrated is a 'G-10 variant, in reconnaissance fighter markings.

numbers took a very different view and dismissed these arguments entirely. Arado Director Professor Walter Blume, who was convinced of the versatility and development potential of his Ar 234, wrote on 2nd November 1944:

...that to increase the speed of 'Otto'-engined aircraft requires more time and expense in every way. This is because, with 'Otto' engines, it is a matter of fighting for a percentage increase in the output and performance of every one of their component parts, with very little end result to show for all the work involved.

This typically technical response to Lucht's explicitly military problems underlined the differences between the technical possibilities and the military necessities; differences which at times had most unfortunate consequences for Germany's aerial rearmament.

At a meeting of the main design and development commission on 19th/20th December 1944, Prof Messerschmitt rejected the 'Otto' fighter entirely. Except for the Bf 109, its variants and further developments, he would be involved in no more fighter projects powered by the piston engine. But at the same session Generalmajor Ulrich Diesing, head of the technical rearmament department and thus Milch's successor in the office of Director General of Aircraft Procurement, refused to place all his bets on the 'jet card'. His view was that this 'still held too many risks and uncertainties of a tactical and technical nature.' Not unnaturally, the representatives of those firms working on piston-engined projects agreed with this assessment.

But the era of the high performance piston-engined fighter was finally drawing to a close. On 22nd February 1945 Göring decreed that only those projects powered by jet propulsion were to be developed further. Certain individual concepts first projected by German designers did engender interest elsewhere; in

France, for example, where not only was the Sud-Ouest Narval naval fighter the product of an original Focke-Wulf design, but where a whole range of German high performance engines was also built. Nor has to date the pusher propeller lost any of its importance for fast piston-engined aircraft.

Studies and New Designs

FOCKE-WULF

In the early summer of 1941, in other words before the Fw 190 had even entered service, the Bremen factory was already intent on improving the design. Among other reasons, this was due to the problems encountered with the BMW engine and the unsatisfactory performance of the new fighter at high altitude.

This led to the study of 1st August 1941: 'Design and performance of single-seat fighters with powerplants still under development'. In this study the design department, headed by Dipl-Ing Mittelhuber, researched the following combinations:

– Fw 190 with BMW 801 E.
– Fw 190 with DB 603.
– Fw 190 with DB 614
  (DB 603 with twin supercharger).
– Fw 190 with BMW P.8019.
– A single-seater with Jumo 222; enlarged Fw 190 airframe.
– A single-seater with BMW 802; a largely new design based on the Fw 190.
– A single-seater with BMW 803; a completely new configuration with central fuselage and twin tail booms.

From this comprehensive work, Mittelhuber drew two fundamental conclusions, which were to have a significant influence on further fighter development at Focke-Wulf:

On the basis of the given conditions, the engine performance, and with it the weight and size of the airframe, increase to such an extent at speeds above approx 760km/h (472 mph) that it appears necessary to select a different type of powerplant and to fit jet engines in the fighters.

And in respect of high altitude fighters: *...if, therefore, for tactical reasons, high service ceilings are required for such fighters, then the best solution in terms of performance and weight is to provide two-stage superchargers for the engines. Both wing size and span are determined by the highest permissible landing speed and the minimum requirements regarding aircraft manoeuvrability.*

In recognising these principles Focke-Wulf ensured the success of their Ta 152 and thus avoided going off on the wrong tack as happened with both the Messerschmitt P.1091 and the Blohm und Voss BV 155.

Focke-Wulf single-seater with BMW 802

24th June 1941

Crew	Pilot in armoured pressure cabin

Powerplant (Specification of 9th June 1941)
One BMW 802 with 1,939kW (2,600hp) take-off rating. This was an air-cooled 18-cylinder twin-row radial engine with three-speed, single-stage supercharger capable of delivering 1,193kW (1,600hp) at 12,000m (39,000ft). The engine was housed in a BMW-designed low drag cowling and drove a 3.8m (12ft 6in) diameter four-bladed variable pitch propeller. An alternative (not included in the study) was a BMW P.8011 with 2,088-2,163kW (2,800-2,900hp) take-off rating. This was a BMW 802 with two exhaust gas turbines enclosed in an aerodynamic engine cowling and driving two contra-rotating propellers. The data below have been taken from the study and refer to the BMW 802 version.

Dimensions

Span	12.50m	41ft 0in
Wing area	26.0 m²	279.8ft²
Aspect ratio	6 : 1	
Length overall	11.30m	37ft 0in
Height overall	3.80m	12ft 5in

Weights

Empty equipped	4,475kg	9,865lb
Take-off	5,400kg	11,904lb
Max wing loading	208kg/m²	42.6lb/ft²
Weapon load	max 500kg (1,102lb) bomb load or	
	2 x 300 litre (65.9 gall) jettisonable fuel	
	tanks. Optional, one carrier for 50kg	
	(110lb) bombs under each wing	

BMW 802 18-cylinder air-cooled radial engine without its aerodynamic cowling.

Just how realistic this concept was is illustrated by the Chance Vought F4U Corsair which was developed slightly earlier (the XF4U-1 prototype first flown 29th May 1940) and which, in dimensions, weight and engine power, proved very similar to this Focke-Wulf design. In contrast to Germany, however, the USA had sufficient numbers of radial engines available within this rating range. The Corsair illustrates just how close to field conditions the calculations of the German engineers actually came. While the F4U-4, with a Pratt & Whitney R-2800-18W Double Wasp (take-off rating: 1,827kW/2,450hp) reached 443mph (714km/h) at 26,000ft (8,000m), the speed calculated by engineer Voigtsberger at Focke-Wulf Flugmechanik for this design was 725km/h (450mph) at 8,000m.

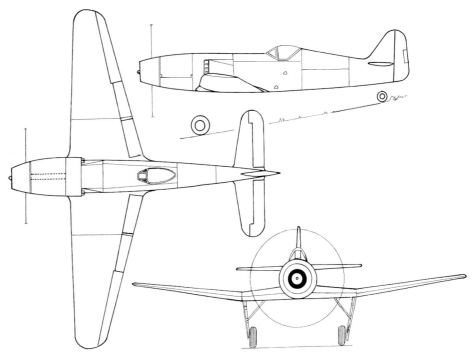

Focke-Wulf single-seater with BMW 803

24th June 1941

In contrast to the other designs of this study, which were all derived to a greater or lesser extent from the Fw 190, the basic layout of this project was influenced by the Fw 189 Uhu (Owl). After Focke-Wulf revised this proposal in 1943, it formed the basis for the design of the single-jet Flitzer (Dasher or Whizzer), drawings of which were first made in December 1943.

When the design department revised this project two years later, the cooling system was completely redesigned. In place of the fuselage annular radiator and fan, tail boom drum radiators were installed. In a second version the two radiators were combined into one unit located in the nose.

Crew	Pilot in armoured pressure cabin

Powerplant   (Specification of 15th May 1941)
One BMW 803 liquid-cooled 28-cylinder four-row radial engine in the 2,984kW (4,000hp) rating class. Emergency rating at 3,100m (10,200ft): 2,928kW (3,925hp); with two 3.2m (10ft 6in) diameter three-bladed contra-rotating propellers.

Dimensions

Span	13.20m	43ft 4in
Wing area	35.0m²	376.7ft²
Aspect ratio	4.98 : 1	
Length overall	13.80m	45ft 3in
Height overall	3.20m	10ft 6in

Weights

Empty equipped	6,325kg	13,944lb
Take-off weight	7,500kg	16,534lb
Wing loading	214kg/m²	43.8lb/ft²

Performance

Max speed	730km/h at 9,000m	453mph at 29,500ft
Initial rate of climb	18.9m/sec	62ft/sec
Service ceiling	11,200m	36,750ft
Time to 8,000m	9.5 minutes	
Time to 10,000m	15.7 minutes	
Endurance	1.5 hours at 9,000m	

Armament
Four 20mm fixed forward-firing MG 151 cannon in forward fuselage, provision for two larger calibre cannon, plus two to four machine-guns installed in the wing-roots. One 250 or 500kg (550 or 1,100lb) underwing bomb carried below each tail boom or two 300 litre (66 gallon) jettisonable fuel tanks.

BMW 803 28-cylinder liquid-cooled radial engine.

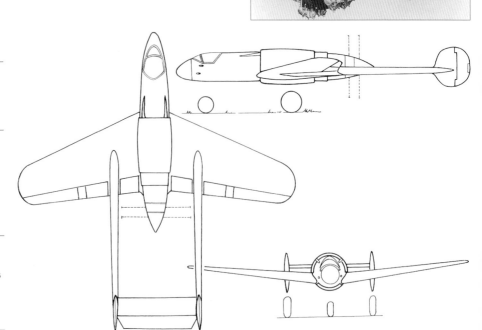

Focke-Wulf fighter with BMW 803, second version

April 1943

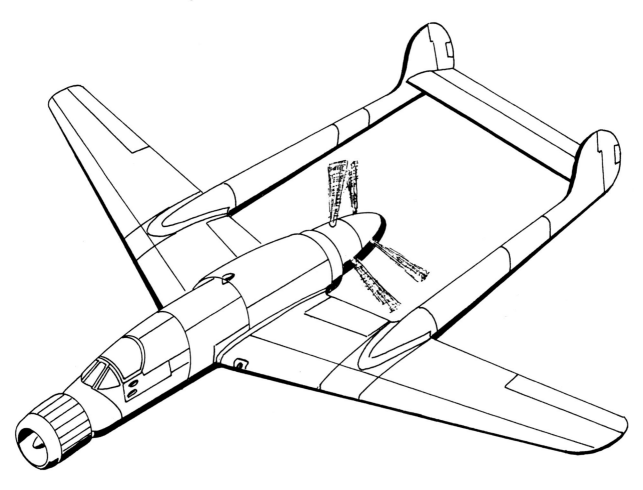

Crew	Pilot in ejection seat in pressure cabin

Powerplant

One BMW 803 liquid-cooled 28-cylinder four-row fuel-injected radial engine in the 2,984kW (4,000hp) rating class with two 3.8m (12ft 6in) diameter contra-rotating variable pitch propellers.

Dimensions

Span	15.50m	50ft 9¼in
Wing area	40.0m²	430.5ft²
Aspect Ratio	6.0 : 1	
Length overall	13.70m	44ft 11in
	14.30m	46ft 10½in
	(with nose radiator)	
Height overall	4.70m	15ft 5in
	(propeller arc)	

Weights

Loaded	8,500-9,000kg	18,738-19,841lb

Performance — No details available

Armament — Two 20mm MG 151/20 cannon and two 30mm MK 103 cannon in forward fuselage to left and right of cockpit.

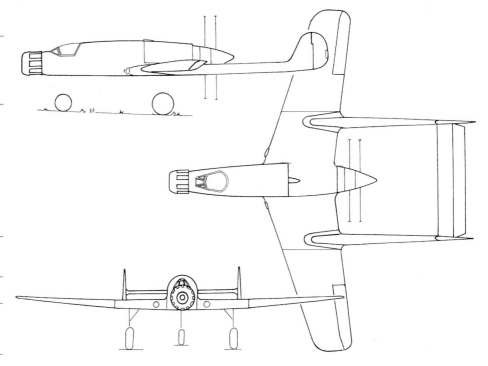

Focke-Wulf fighter with BMW 803 and wing radiators

April 1943

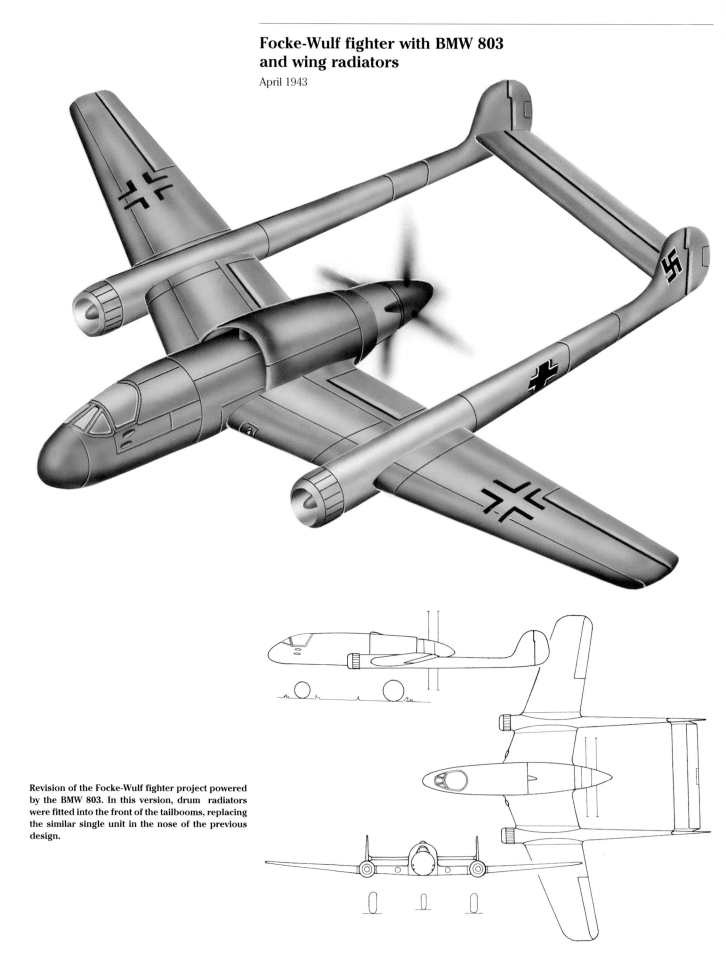

Revision of the Focke-Wulf fighter project powered by the BMW 803. In this version, drum radiators were fitted into the front of the tailbooms, replacing the similar single unit in the nose of the previous design.

Focke-Wulf fighter and fighter-bomber with Jumo 222C/D

22nd October 1942

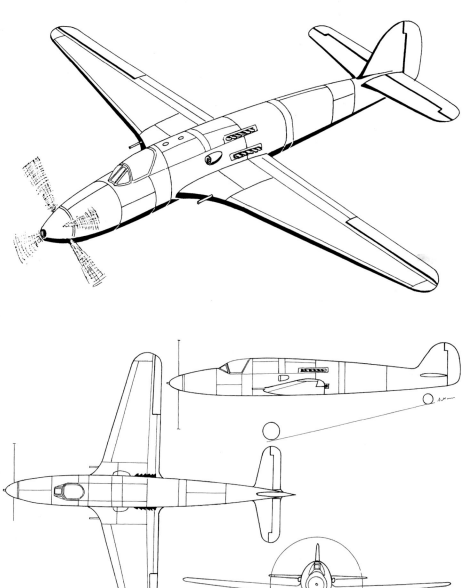

Powerplant

One Jumo 222C/D liquid-cooled four-row radial engine with 2,238kW (3,000hp) take-off rating; a geared extension shaft driving the 4.39m (14ft 5in) diameter propeller.

Dimensions

Span		11.50m	37ft 8½in
Wing area		22.3m²	240ft²
Aspect ratio		5.93 : 1	
Length overall		12.40m	40ft 8in
Height overall		4.05m	13ft 3½in

Weights

Empty equipped	(1)	4,301kg	9,481lb
	(2)	4,339kg	9,565lb
Take-off	(1)	5,290kg	11,662lb
	(2)	6,328kg	13,950lb
Max wing loading	(1)	237kg/m²	48.5lb/ft²
	(2)	284kg/m²	58.1lb/ft²
		(1) = fighter, (2) = fighter-bomber	

Performance

Although no performance data are available, a max. speed of about 750km/h (466mph) at 5,000–6,000m (16,000–19,700ft) may be assumed.

Armament

One 30mm MK 103 engine-mounted cannon firing through the propeller hub plus two 30mm MK 108 wing cannon. Or two 20mm MG 151 cannon in fuselage plus four 20mm MG 151 cannon or four 30mm MK 108 cannon in wings. Or two 30mm MK 103 cannon in fuselage plus four 20mm MG 151 cannon or four 30mm MK 108 cannon in wings. As fighter-bomber, one 1,000kg (2,204lb) bomb under the fuselage or two 500kg (1,102lb) bombs under the wings.

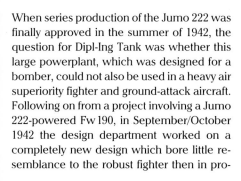

When series production of the Jumo 222 was finally approved in the summer of 1942, the question for Dipl-Ing Tank was whether this large powerplant, which was designed for a bomber, could not also be used in a heavy air superiority fighter and ground-attack aircraft. Following on from a project involving a Jumo 222-powered Fw 190, in September/October 1942 the design department worked on a completely new design which bore little resemblance to the robust fighter then in pro-duction. The powerplant position showed similarities to the American Bell P-39 Airaco-bra and P-63 Kingcobra fighters.

In addition to a fighter project with two BMW 801Fs, several other proposals for a fighter with the Jumo 222A or 'C, some based on the Fw 190, had been made by mid-March 1943. Unfortunately, only data sheets survive as evidence of this work. When the Jumo 222 was again shelved in the summer of 1943, these plans too were consigned to the files.

Towards the end of hostilities, when the Jumo 222 was re-instated yet again and given top priority, new and aerodynamically greatly improved projects for high performance fighters utilising this engine and other heavy powerplants such as the Argus As 413 and the Daimler-Benz DB 603N were on the drawing boards.

HENSCHEL

The name of this company is associated primarily with locomotives and lorries. But in 1933, with the launch of the re-armament programme, this group also entered the aviation field, building an aircraft factory at Berlin-Schönefeld. In aviation circles the name 'Henschel' immediately brings to mind assault aircraft (Hs 123 , Hs 129) and reconnaissance machines (Hs 126). Less well-known are the Hs 124 heavy bomber, the Hs 127 fast bomber and the Hs 128 and Hs 130 high altitude aircraft, not one of which, however, advanced beyond the prototype stage. The chief designer, Dipl-Ing Friedrich Nicolaus, was always trying to envisage likely military and technical developments and to offer the RLM proposals for future roles and specifications. But this way of looking at things met with little understanding.

As Nicolaus himself commented in October 1946:

However much this was understood by some experts at the RLM, little enthusiasm to assume responsibility in such matters was shown by the directorate of the Technical Office, which simply awaited the requests of the operational staff [of the Luftwaffe – Authors].

And the latter did not make their wishes known until the very moment that the military situation dictated that the aircraft, or powerplant, or weapon, needed to be readily available. The equipment of front line units therefore lagged considerably behind their actual requirements.

Such was the mentality which the whole of the German aircraft industry had to fight against. The results are all too well known.

The Henschel works drew up detailed plans, and provided full performance data, for various single-seat fighter projects, all of unconventional design. Specifically these were:

– P.75 of 1941, a 'canard' with pusher engine.
– P.130 of 1944, a tail-less heavy fighter
– with pusher engine.
– P.135 of 1945, also a tail-less fighter powered by a jet engine.

Henschel P.75

1941

Powerplant
One Daimler-Benz DB 613A/B liquid-cooled 24-cylinder coupled engine, take-off power 2,611kW (3,500hp), with two 3.2m (10ft 6in) diameter contra-rotating propellers driven via an extension shaft.

Dimensions (in part reconstructed)

Span	11.30m	37ft 1in
Sweep	16° at 0.25 chord	
Wing area	28.4m²	305.7ft²
Aspect ratio	4.5 : 1	
Length overall	12.20m	40ft 0in
Height overall	4.30m	14ft 1in

Weights (estimated)

Loaded	7,200–7,500kg	15,873-16,534lb

Performance

Max speed	790km/h at 7,000m	490mph at 23,000ft
Service ceiling	12,000m	39,000ft

Armament
Four 30mm MK 108 cannon in the nose

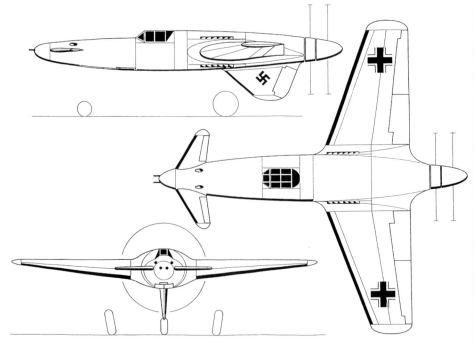

This design for a military aircraft, still relevant today, featured a configuration which gave rise to intensive discussions in a number of countries in the years before the war. Several prototypes entered flight testing prior to 1945 (eg the American Curtiss XP-55 Ascender and the Japanese Kyushu J7W1 Shinden). But the actual breakthrough did not come about until the advent of the modern jet engine of the present day.

In addition to its aerodynamic novelty, the Henschel concept offered the opportunity of housing a battery of heavy weapons in the nose. The cross section of the fuselage and the method of its construction was ideal for the wide, heavy powerplant, which consisted of two DB 603s coupled together and which was located close to the machine's centre of gravity. The ventral tail surfaces acted as a keel to protect the propellers against ground contact.

Wind tunnel tests with a scale model gave very favourable results. The project reached the stage which would have permitted an immediate start on detailed construction drawings, but these never materialised.

Despite recommendations from the RLM technical branch, the Luftwaffe cancelled all further work on the project, giving as the reason, 'The pilots would never be able to get used to having the propeller at the back and the tail at the front'.

Flight tests would, of course, had to have proven whether such a heavy 'canard' could meet the requirements of a fully operational fighter, particularly the manoeuvrability so necessary in a dogfight.

Henschel P.130

1944

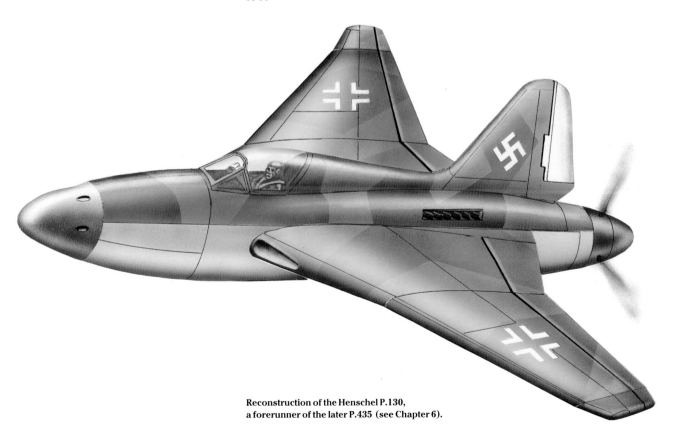

Reconstruction of the Henschel P.130,
a forerunner of the later P.435 (see Chapter 6).

MESSERSCHMITT

Messerschmitt (Lippisch) Me 334

Early 1943

This paper proposal from Alexander Lippisch was one of the very few such designs whose aim was to convert a fast jet aircraft to piston power. But Lippisch had good reasons for so doing: the Me 163B V1 had been waiting since May 1942 for delivery of its rocket engine from Messrs Hellmuth Walther. But the difficulties experienced by Walther's Kiel works seemed to be endless, and Lippisch had perforce to seek alternatives. So, alongside the projected jet-powered Lippisch P.20, he also drew up plans for a piston-engined version.

With the successful maiden flight of the Me 163B powered by its intended rocket engine in June 1943, further work on the piston-engined proposal was no longer necessary.

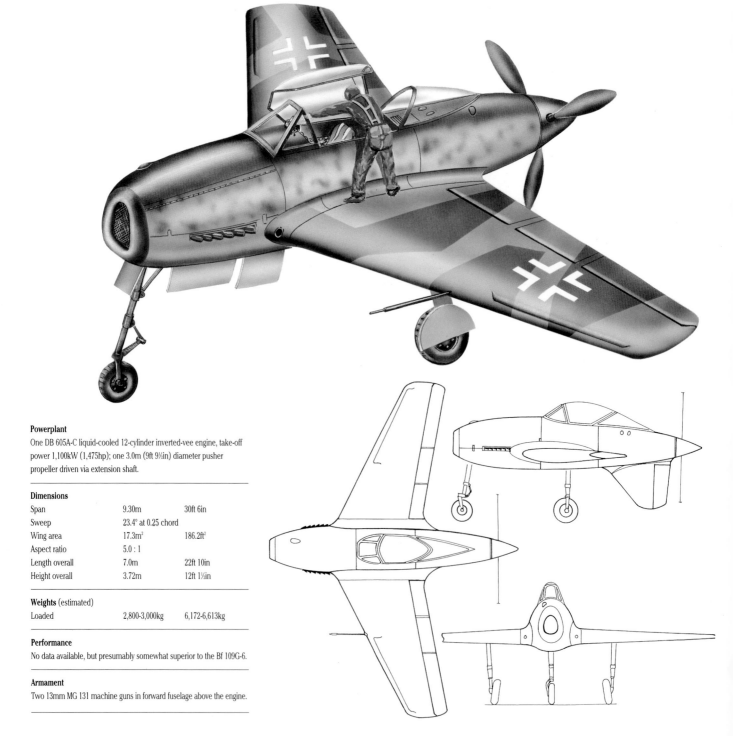

Powerplant
One DB 605A-C liquid-cooled 12-cylinder inverted-vee engine, take-off power 1,100kW (1,475hp); one 3.0m (9ft 9⅛in) diameter pusher propeller driven via extension shaft.

Dimensions

Span	9.30m	30ft 6in
Sweep	23.4° at 0.25 chord	
Wing area	17.3m²	186.2ft²
Aspect ratio	5.0 : 1	
Length overall	7.0m	22ft 10in
Height overall	3.72m	12ft 1½in

Weights (estimated)

Loaded	2,800-3,000kg	6,172-6,613kg

Performance
No data available, but presumably somewhat superior to the Bf 109G-6.

Armament
Two 13mm MG 131 machine guns in forward fuselage above the engine.

High altitude fighters

Such aircraft are those capable of operating at altitudes of between 14,000 and 16,000m (45,931 and 52,493ft). For this purpose they feature specialised equipment, usually consisting of: a special powerplant, a pressure cabin, and aerodynamics suited to their operating altitude (eg increased wing area).

The ideal solution is, of course, an aircraft which possesses an almost equally good performance at all altitudes.

At the beginning of 1942, and at the insistence of the Luftwaffe, the Technische Amt (the RLM's Technical Office) began seriously to consider the viability of a high altitude fighter which would be capable of intercepting the fast de Havilland Mosquitos, which were appearing in ever-increasing numbers and which were now overflying Reich territory, sometimes at almost unapproachable heights, with near impunity. Berlin was equally perturbed about enemy engine developments which were providing Allied airframe manufacturers with a steadily growing supply of supercharged, high altitude powerplants.

In contrast, German attempts to develop a similar high altitude engine verged on the chaotic as, at the RLM's instigation, any and every scheme which offered even the remotest possibility of success was taken under consideration. These schemes ranged from emergency solutions (eg GM-1 nitrous oxide injection) to the most complex and expensive installations (eg engines with completely separate supercharger units). It is hardly surprising that the development of a high altitude fighter resulted in similar confusion and, at times, outright mistakes.

In 1942-43 it was uncertain whether the problem could be solved by the use of jet aircraft; the behaviour of a turbojet engine at any sort of altitude was simply unknown. Such information did not become available until tests by Junkers early in 1945.

The advantage of the piston engine was that its performance could, to a large degree, be sustained at altitude by the use of superchargers or oxygen injection (GM-1). German high altitude fighter development was therefore based on types successfully flown or on those currently under construction.

MESSERSCHMITT

At a meeting held at Augsburg on 20th May 1942 the RLM instructed both Messerschmitt and Focke-Wulf to begin development of a specialised high altitude fighter. At the same time the Technische Amt required a carrier-borne single-seat fighter with a good high altitude performance for service aboard the aircraft carrier *Graf Zeppelin* then under construction. Messerschmitt were not fully unprepared for this task. The company was able to fall back on long-term work already under way on the Bf 109T shipboard fighter and, above all, on their proposal for a 'Special Carrier Fighter Bf 109ST' developed from the Bf 109G. Designated in-house as the Me 409, it was planned to produce the Bf 109ST in three variants; version 'A powered by the DB 605, version 'B with the DB 628 high altitude engine and version 'C with the Jumo 213.

Development work, carried out in parallel with the Me 262, Me 163, Me 209 and Me 309 was understandably somewhat slow. Nevertheless, in the course of 1942 the design was allocated the RLM type number 8-155, with the carrier version being designated Me 155A and the high altitude fighter, now to be land-based, becoming the Me 155B.

The abandonment of work on the German aircraft carrier programme at the beginning of 1943 resulted in the cancellation of the Me 155A project. Work on the Me 155B, however, was to be continued – albeit without any great priority – both at Augsburg and at the SNCAN (Société Nationale de Constructions Aéronautiques du Nord) factory in Paris.

Messerschmitt Bf 109H

The Bf 109H V54 'interim high altitude fighter', 'DV+JB', werk nummer (w/nr – constructor's number) 15 708, first flew on 5th November 1943. But the construction of the second prototype, the Bf 109H V55, heralded the end of the programme for Messerschmitt. Developments at Focke-Wulf, which would result in the Ta 152H, and the unsatisfactory outcome of their own flight tests, led to the cancellation of all further work in the late summer of 1944.

Messerschmitt 'Me'155B high altitude fighter

4th February 1943

Daimler-Benz DB 628 high altitude engine.

Crew   Pilot in pressure cabin

Powerplant

One Daimler-Benz DB 628, take-off power 1,100kW (1,475hp). Power at fully pressurised altitude (12,000m – 39,000ft) 820kW (1,100hp)

Note: The Bf 109 V54, powered by the DB 628, was flown in May/June 1943 and achieved altitudes in excess of 15,000m (49,000ft) without any great difficulty; the powerplant revealed no problems at all.

Dimensions

Span	13.00m	42ft 7in
Wing area	21m²	226ft²
Aspect ratio	8.0 : 1	
Length overall	9.60m	31ft 6in
Height overall	4.10m	13ft 6in

Weights

Empty equipped	3,276kg	7,222lb
Loaded	3,858kg with 400 litres fuel	
	8,505lb with 90 gallons fuel	
Max wing loading	184kg/m²	37.7lb/ft²

Performance

Max speed	708km/h at 12,000m	
	440mph at 39,000ft	
Speed at ground level	508km/h	315mph
Initial rate of climb	17m/sec	55ft/sec
Service ceiling	14,100m	46,000ft
Time to 12,000m	16.7 min	
Endurance	1¼ hours at 6,000m (19,500ft) at cruise	

Armament

One MG 151 engine-mounted cannon, plus two MG151 cannon in wing roots.

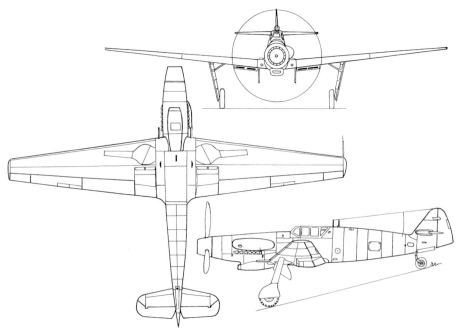

The RLM was not altogether satisfied with these figures; the departmental official overseeing the project enquiring verbally whether the expected achievable altitudes could not be improved upon. At this stage in the proceedings questions should perhaps have been raised as to the whole point of such a requirement. But in July 1943 Messerschmitt was nothing if not flexible and so, with the P.1091, he proposed instead a costly programme, based upon the Bf 109/Me 209, which would entail the step-by-step development of a high altitude fighter (with the secondary role of high altitude bomber) capable of operating at a height of 17,000m (55,750ft)!

The purpose of Stage I (the developed Bf 109H) would be rapidly to produce an aircraft, developed from the Bf 109G, which would in turn, during Stages II and III, undergo further development into the special high altitude fighter ultimately required.

As the Messerschmitt company was already more than overburdened by important war production, in August 1943 the RLM transferred the 'development work' to Blohm und Voss, who were to undertake the practical design of Stage III – the BV 155. Messerschmitt sensibly retained responsibility for the production of Stage I. No work was assigned to Stage II.

Blohm und Voss BV 155,
first version

Summer 1994

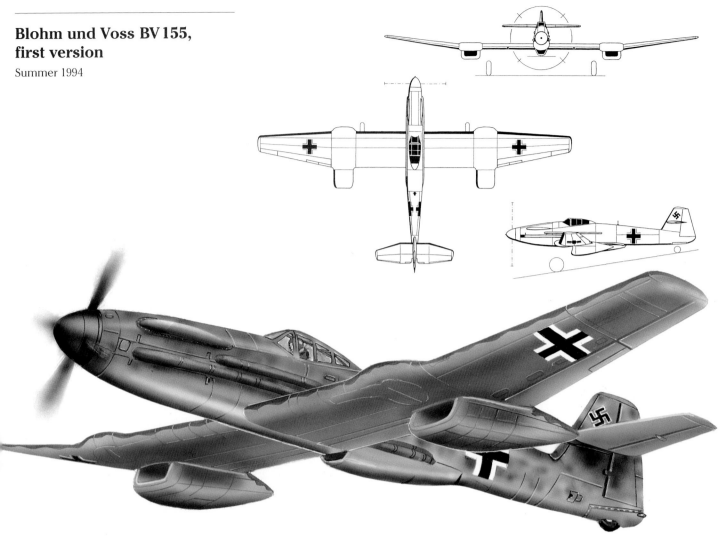

Stage III, which had been taken over by the Hamburg-based Blohm und Voss company as RLM number 8-155, was subject to a certain amount of design change at the hands of Dr Richard Vogt. These modifications were mainly to the profile and static construction of the wing. With Dr Vogt's alterations to the design accepted, detailed construction work could begin. It was completed towards the close of 1944, by which time the aircraft had been re-designated as the BV 155B. Due to various circumstances and difficulties, however, the maiden flight of the first of three planned prototypes did not take place until 8th February 1945. The short test programme which followed highlighted the problems with the extensive cooling and radiator layout which had already been foreseen.

BV 155 (either the V2 or V3) at the Royal Aircraft Establishment at Farnborough, October/November 1945.

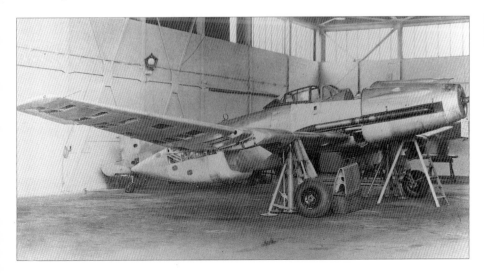

Blohm und Voss P.205

July 1944

Immediately after Blohm und Voss' taking over Project 1091, the layout and arrangement of the radiators became a topic of heated discussions between Hamburg (BV) and Augsburg (Me). With Project BV P.205 Dr Vogt proposed a solution which saw the thoroughly unpopular wing radiators disappear into the fuselage.

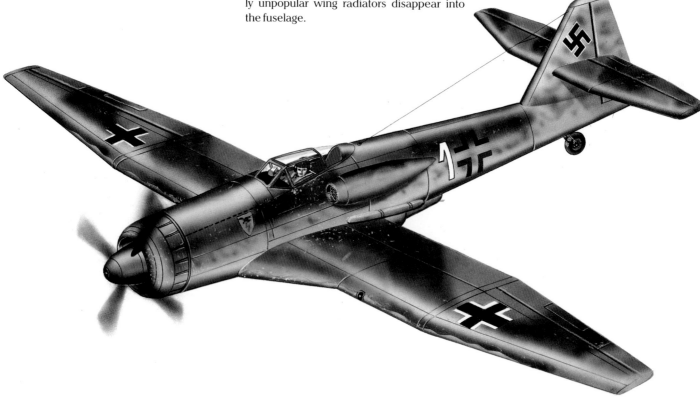

Crew   Pilot in pressure cabin

Powerplant
One Daimler-Benz DB 603V, take-off power 1,275kW (1,710hp), plus Hirth TJKL 15 exhaust gas turbocharger.

Dimensions

Span	18.65m	61ft 2in
Wing area	37.0m²	398ft²
Aspect ratio	9.4 : 1	
Length overall	12.10m	39ft 8in

Weights

Loaded (approx)	6,200kg	13,668lb
Max wing loading	162kg/m²	33.2lb/ft²

Performance
Max speed (approx) 700km/h at 16,000m 434mph at 52,500ft
No further data available, but the performance of the P.205 should have been only slightly inferior to that of the BV 155C.

Armament
One 30mm MK 108 engine-mounted cannon, plus two 20mm MG 151 wing-mounted cannon.

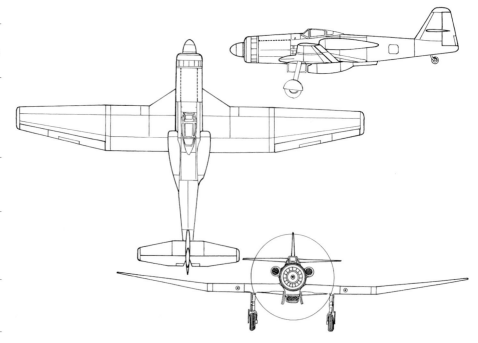

Blohm und Voss BV 155C

1944

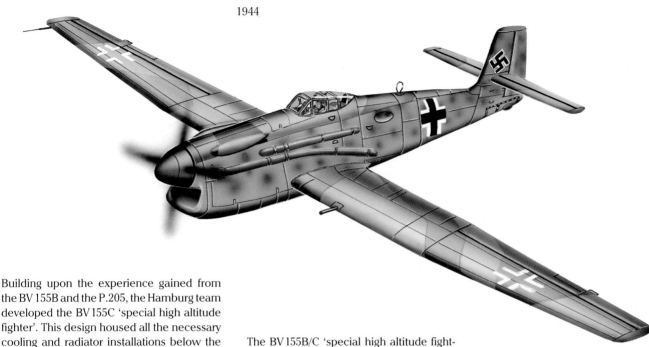

Building upon the experience gained from the BV 155B and the P.205, the Hamburg team developed the BV 155C 'special high altitude fighter'. This design housed all the necessary cooling and radiator installations below the engine compartment, which meant that the wings could be kept aerodynamically very clean. Although a delivery schedule called for the construction of 27 examples of this aircraft commencing 25th December 1944, by the war's end the programme had not progressed beyond the completion of a single mock-up.

The BV 155B/C 'special high altitude fighter', developed out of the P.1091/Stage III, was an aircraft whose operations anywhere below 12,000m (39,000ft) would have made very little sense. And as there was no hard evidence to suggest that the enemy would be overflying Reich territory at altitudes of 13-15,000m (42,600-49,000ft) in the foreseeable future, the intention was for the BV 155 to be developed up to the point where, if the necessity arose, it could quickly be put into series production. In the light of the above, it is hard to counter the argument that, where there was no apparent urgency, the RLM and Luftwaffe forged ahead with all speed, but in areas where the need for immediate re-equipment had reached crisis levels, there was nothing but hesitation and delay.

Crew   Pilot in pressure cabin

Powerplant

One Daimler-Benz DB 603U, take-off power 1,710hp (1,275kW), plus Hirth TKL 15 exhaust gas turbocharger; 3.7m (12ft 2in) diameter four-blade propeller.

Dimensions

Span	19.05m	62ft 6in
Wing area	35.8m²	385.3ft²
Aspect ratio	10.14:1	
Length overall	12.05m	39ft 6in
Height overall	4.17m	13ft 8in

Weights

Empty equipped	5,682kg	12,526lb
Loaded	6,384kg	14,074lb
Max wing loading	178.3kg/m²	36.5lb/ft²

Performance

Max speed	700km/h at 16,000m	
	434mph at 52,500ft	
at ground level	430km/h	267mph
Service ceiling	16,830m	55,200ft
Time to 16,000m	31.6 min	

Armament

One 30mm MK 108 engine-mounted cannon, plus two 20mm MG 151 wing-mounted cannon. Provision for a camera installation.

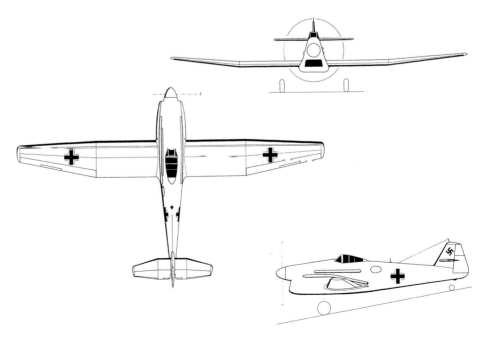

DORNIER

Dornier P.273
high altitude fighter
4th May 1943

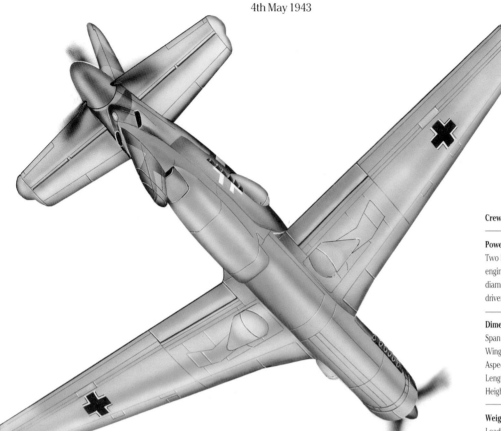

Crew	Pilot in ejector seat in 'high altitude chamber'

Powerplant

Two Daimler-Benz DB 603G liquid-cooled, 12-cylinder inverted-vee engines each rated at 1,417kW (1,900hp) for take-off; 3.5m (11ft 5in) diameter tractor propeller, 3.3m (10ft 9½in) diameter pusher propeller driven via extension shaft.

Dimensions

Span	18.00m	59ft 0in
Wing area	45.5m²	489.7ft²
Aspect ratio	7.1 : 1	
Length overall	13.70m	44ft 10in
Height overall (approx)	5.00m	16ft 4⅞in

Weights

Loaded	9,100kg	20,061lb
Max wing loading	200kg/m²	40.9lb/ft²

Performance

Max speed	835km/h at 8,700m	518mph at 28,500ft
Operational altitude	14,000-16,000m	46,000-52,500ft

Armament

One 30mm MK 103 cannon firing through the forward propeller hub, plus two 20mm MG 151 cannon in forward fuselage above the front engine. This project was resuscitated in 1944 as the 'B-4 high altitude heavy fighter version of the Do 335, only to be abandoned again in favour of the less costly Focke-Wulf Ta 152.

On 16th January 1943 Dornier had received instructions to build the Do 335 Pfeil (Arrow). There was the danger, however, that this aircraft - intended as a 'very fast bomber' - could fall victim to a change in strategy and tactics. In order to pre-empt this, Dornier looked for alternative roles. Upon the completion of the mock-up on 18th April 1943, and with construction about to begin, the design department put forward the proposal, designated P.273, for a high altitude fighter version; a requirement for which was the subject of much discussion at the time. Compared to the Do 335 this project featured a greatly increased wingspan, but was otherwise very similar to the basic model.

FOCKE-WULF

Performance-enhanced Focke-Wulf Ta 152H
1943

Focke-Wulf Ta 152.

In response to the RLM contract of 20th May 1942 for the production of a high altitude fighter, Focke-Wulf began by converting an Fw 190A into a test-bed for the proposed Fw 190B and 'C. As a second step the design department, led by Prof Kurt Tank, then developed the Ta 153, a 'fighter for high altitudes', which likewise stemmed from the Fw 190 and which, on 17th August 1943 and in a slightly revised form, was designated Ta 152. Similarities between Focke-Wulf's progress and Messerschmitt's development of the Bf 109H and the Me/BV 155 are clearly apparent. After extensive development and testing, Focke-Wulf were successful with the Ta 152 and, in the 'H version, were finally in a position to provide the Luftwaffe with its long-awaited high altitude fighter. But the aircraft, which was superior to all Allied machines at altitudes above 10,000m (33,000ft), was built in only small numbers and did not see service in its intended role.

Focke-Wulf Ta 152 high altitude fighter with Jumo 222E and laminar wing
Early December 1944

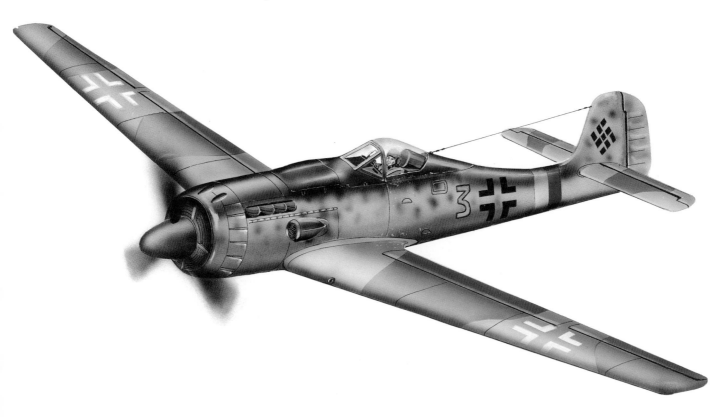

The use of a more powerful engine and a laminar wing profile, enabled Prof Tank to offer the Ta 152 in an improved version. It was apparent that, despite the high standard already achieved, the aircraft had scope for a great deal more technical development and the design was still far from the end of its potential.

Crew   Pilot in pressure cabin

Powerplant

One Junkers Jumo 222E 24-cylinder four-row radial engine, take-off power 1,865kW (2,500hp), with two-stage supercharger, MW 50 injection system and Junkers VS-19 3.6m (11ft 9½in) diameter four-blade propeller. The Jumo 222E engine could be replaced by a Jumo 222A.

Dimensions

Span	13.68m	44ft 10in
Wing area	23.7m²	255.1ft²
Aspect ratio	7.9 : 1	
Length overall	10.77m	35ft 4in
Height overall	3.75m	12ft 3¼in

Weights

Empty equipped	4,618kg	10,180lb
Loaded	5,815kg with 794kg fuel	
	12,819lb with 1,750lb fuel	
Max wing loading	245kg/m²	50.2lb/ft²

Performance

Max speed	740km/h at 12,000m	459mph at 39,500ft
Initial rate of climb	22.0m/sec	72ft/sec
Service ceiling	15,000m	49,200ft
Max endurance	2.02 hours	
Max range	1,290km at 10,500m	801 miles at 34,500ft

Armament

Two 20mm MG 151 in fuselage, plus two 20mm MG 151 in wing roots, or two 20mm MG 151 in fuselage, plus two 30mm MK 103 in wing roots. Provision for Rüstsatz (field conversion kit) ETC 504 for bombs and fuel.

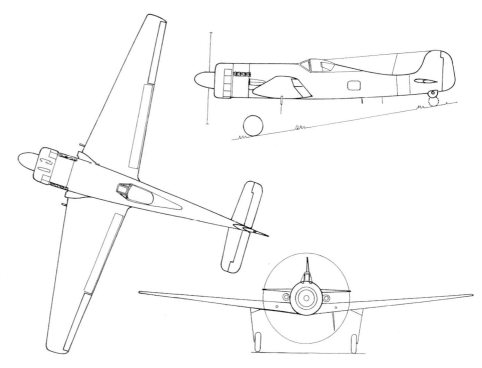

Heinkel P.1076 fighter and high altitude fighter

Autumn 1944

As a further development of their He 112, the design which had lost out to the Bf 109 V2 in the pursuit fighter competition of early 1936, Heinkel built the impressive He 100. On 30th March 1939 the He 100 V8, powered by a Daimler-Benz DB 601/M 159 engine, set a new world air speed record of 746.606km/h (463.932mph), which shortly thereafter was just bettered by the Me 209's 755.138km/h (469.233mph). But even this most promising and aesthetic design still failed to win for Ernst Heinkel a contract from the RLM for large-scale series production.

Heinkel He 100.

However, when the Heinkel firm was later given specifications by the RLM for a piston-engined fighter which was to combine speed with an excellent high altitude performance, Siegfried Günter turned back to the He 100. He produced an improved proposal possessing even better aerodynamic qualities, with only the supercharger air intake disrupting its otherwise perfectly smooth surfaces.

The advanced surface evaporation cooling system taken, and further developed, from that of the He 100 obviated the need for either fuselage or wing radiators. In the light of the quality and experience of the Heinkel company, it is safe to assume that, had this project been carried through to fruition, it would have resulted in one of the fastest propeller aircraft ever to have been built.

Three proposed versions of the P.1076 have been identified, including one powered by the DB 603N and featuring an increased wingspan.

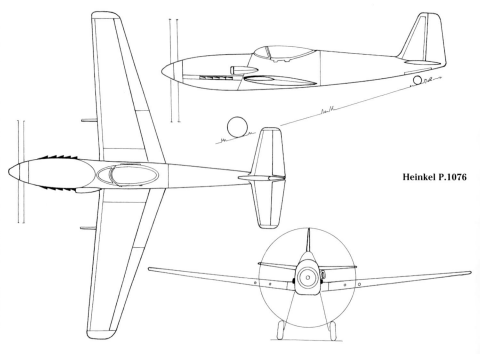

Heinkel P.1076

Heinkel P.1076

Powerplant

One Daimler-Benz DB 603M twin-supercharged engine, take-off power 1,361kW (1,825hp), take-off power with MW 50 injection: 1,566kW (2,100hp); or one Junkers Jumo 213E with two-stage, three-speed supercharger, take-off power 1,305kW (1,750hp), short-term boost with MW 50 injection: approx 1,566kW (2,100hp); or one Daimler-Benz DB 603N, take-off power 2,051kW (2,750hp), with two-stage DB twin-supercharger with integrated heat exchange cooler and with contra-rotating three-blade VDM propellers.

Junkers Jumo 213E with engine-mounted cannon.

Dimensions	DB 603M engine		Jumo 213E engine		DB 603N engine	
Span	11.00m	36ft 1in	11.00m	36ft 1in	–	
Sweep	-8° at 0,25 chord		-8° at 0,25 chord		–	
Wing area	18.0m²	193.7ft²	18.0m²	193.7ft²	26.0m²	279.8ft²
Aspect ratio	6.72 : 1		6.72 : 1		5.91 : 1	
Length overall	9.60m	31ft 6in	9.64m	31ft 7in	9.60m	31ft 6in
Height overall	2.90m	9ft 6in	2.90m	9ft 6in	2.90m	9ft 6in

Weights						
Empty equipped	3,260kg	7,186lb	3,200kg	7,054lb	–	
Loaded	4,380kg	9,656lb	4,480kg	9,876lb	5,230kg	11,529lb
Max wing loading	234kg/m²	49.9lb/ft²	249kg/m²	51.0lb/ft²	201kg/m²	41.1lb/ft²

Performance						
Max speed	860km/h at 11,000m		860km/h at 11,000m		880km/h at 11,000m	
	534mph at 36,000ft		534mph at 36,000ft		546mph at 36,000ft	
Rate of climb	17.2m/sec at 9,000m		17.2m/sec at 9,000m		25.5m/sec at 9,000m	
	56.4ft/sec at 29,500ft		56.4ft/sec at 29,500ft		83.6ft/sec at 29,500ft	
Service ceiling	14,500m	47,500ft	14,500m	47,500ft	–	
Time to 12,000m	12.2 minutes		12.2 minutes		–	
Max range	1,340km	832 miles	1,340km	832 miles	–	
Landing speed	167km/h	103mph	167km/h	103mph	–	

Armament

One 30mm MK 103 engine-mounted cannon firing through the propeller hub, plus two 30mm MK 108 wing-mounted cannon. Detailed plans and drawings for this project, which was probably evolved as a competitor to the Ta 152, were completed by Siegfried Günter and his team for the Americans in Penzing in mid-1945.

Piston-engined high performance fighters

The creation of the Jägerstab (Fighter Staff) on 1st May 1944, and the consequent effective take over of fighter production by the Reich's Ministry of Armaments and War Production, heralded a new organisation and general tightening up of all development activity. But this last attempt to instil some sort of order was doomed to failure as all the old mistakes were still far from being rectified and the omissions of the past were now impossible to make good.

On 21st July 1944, at about the same time as they issued the specification for a single-jet air superiority fighter to be powered by the Heinkel HeS 011, the Fighter Staff – as part of the emergency fighter programme – drew up the requirement for a conventional piston-engined high performance fighter. This was to fill the gap and cover the deficiencies inherent in the jet fighter's performance and was intended as a replacement, in the foreseeable future, for the Ta 152.

It was therefore required that any such 'future Otto fighter' should:
- offer increased endurance
- be capable of combating the expected incursions of American Boeing B-29 Superfortress bombers at heights of 9,000 to 10,000m (29,500-32,800ft), and
- also be able to operate and fight at low altitudes.

The technical requirements of the specifications thus laid down the following:
- a high maximum speed, if possible in excess of 800km/h (497mph)
- the ability to fit various powerplants, some as yet still in the development stage
- single pusher-engine arrangement
- a tricycle undercarriage, and
- an endurance of at least two hours at 10,000m (32,800ft).

When the endurance requirement for the single-jet fighter was upped to two hours on 11th January 1945, the General Staff demanded that of the 'high performance Otto fighter' be increased to three hours. In both instances these fresh requirements led either to new or redesigned proposals, or to abandonment altogether. In the face of such constant changes in specifications over a relatively short period of time, a rational development programme was all but impossible.

BLOHM UND VOSS

As was the case with nearly every fighter specification issued, this new proposal again saw the Blohm und Voss 'development factory' joining Dornier, Focke-Wulf and Henschel in the list of contenders. And if, for production reasons, their Project P.207 represented the aerodynamic state-of-the-art for fast 'Otto' fighters of the early war years, so the subsequent Project P.208 introduced an entirely new and unusual aerodynamic layout which would influence and determine all Dr Richard Vogt's further work right up until the war's end.

The arrangement of the wing and control surfaces of the P.208, although acknowledged as being excellent in terms of flight characteristics and inherent strength, have – despite a recommendation by the USA National Aeronautics and Space Administration (NASA) and several practical experiments (the Rockwell XFV-12A) – failed to find favour with today's aircraft manufacturers. But what has not been, may yet still be.

Blohm und Voss P.207

July/August 1944

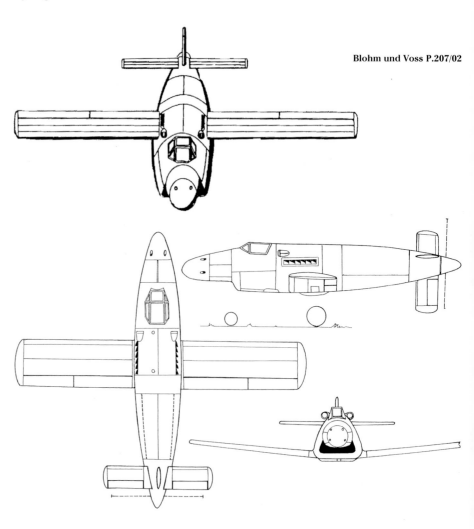

Blohm und Voss P.207/02

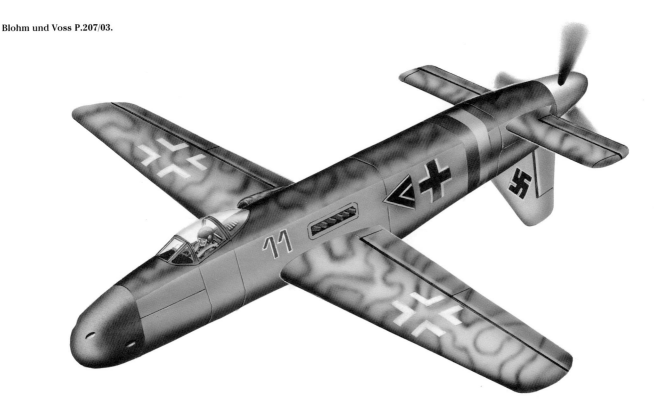

Three versions of this first proposal are known. As a result of the very narrow and concise nature of the specifications issued, all bore a marked resemblance to the Dornier and Focke-Wulf designs. No information is available on the P.207/01 with the Jumo 213J. But it was presumably similar in most respects to the P.207/02, in which Dr Vogt proposed to fit the 2,984kW (4,00hp) Argus As 413. This aircraft was of extremely simple construction, with a rectangular, constant-chord, 12m (39ft 4½in) span wing and cruci-

form tail surfaces. Its armament consisted of four MK 108 cannons grouped in the nose. The somewhat smaller and aerodynamically refined P.207/03 displayed certain parallels with the BV P.193 ground-attack concept, which also featured a ventral fin and rudder arrangement designed to protect the pusher propeller from contact with the ground.

Despite its pusher propeller and tricycle undercarriage, the project gave the impression of being very much an emergency solution, combining as it did the theory of modern

aerodynamics with the quickest and most basic of production methods. Furthermore, the performance figures failed to measure up to expectations. In August 1944 Dr Vogt decided to embark upon an entirely new design. He again opted for a combination of exacting aerodynamics with the simplest of constructions and managed in the process to develop an unusually elegant and futuristic concept which would, however, have required more than a little research and development work before evolving into a combat aircraft.

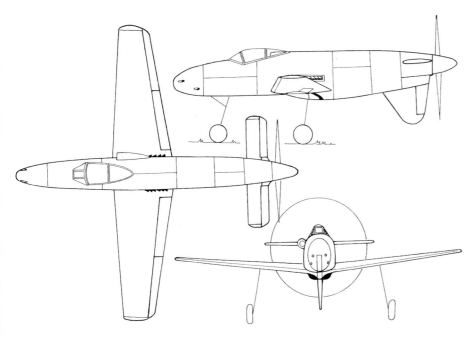

Powerplant

One DB 603G liquid-cooled 12-cylinder inverted-vee engine, take-off power 1,417kW (1,900hp), 3.2m (10ft 6in) diameter propeller driven by extension shaft.

Dimensions (reconstructed)

Span	9.90m	32ft 6in
Wing area	16.35m²	175.9ft²
Aspect ratio	6.0 : 1	

(The wings were very similar to those of the Bf 109E)

Length overall	9.73m	31ft 10in
Height overall	4,60m	15ft 1in

Weights (estimated)

Loaded	4,000kg	8,818lb

Performance

No data available; it seems doubtful whether this project could have reached the specified speed.

Armament

Two 30mm MK 103 cannon and two 20mm MG 151 cannon fixed forward-firing in the nose.

Blohm und Voss P.208

Design work from August to November 1944

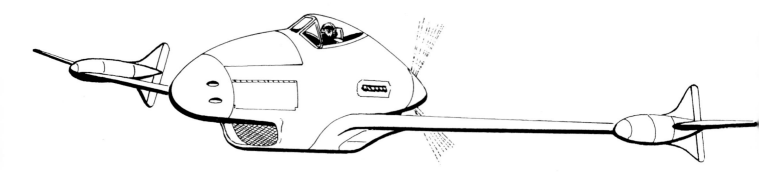

This unusual project was also proposed in three separate main variants, which would have differed only in engines and equipment, and thus in weights and dimensions. The first, designated BV P.208/01, was to be fitted with the Jumo 222E/F. The second, originating at the same time, was the slightly larger P.208/02 which, with a 2,984kW (4,000hp) Argus As 413 engine, would not have been exactly underpowered. Designed somewhat later in the autumn of 1944, the P.208/03 was intended to make use of the less powerful Daimler-Benz DB 603N and DB 603L engines which were then already in series production.

Blohm und Voss saw the following advantages in their chosen design:

- The simplest pusher engine arrangement without the need for an extension shaft, i.e. lightweight, cheap, easy to maintain and reliable.
- Minimum total surface area, combining a short fuselage with small wings and control surfaces, to permit highest possible maximum speed.
- Lowest overall weight, contingent upon a lighter engine installation, small wings and short fuselage.
- Simplest production, due to constant chord wing and deletion of fin and rudder. Load-bearing fuselage structure unbroken by integral engine compartment.
- Limited proportion of Duraluminum to overall weight by extensive use of sheet metal in easily manufactured thicknesses.

These features, plus several others, resulted in a highly original and clever aerodynamic arrangement, of which Dr Vogt wrote:

The outboard elevator surfaces also served simultaneously as ailerons and allowed the landing flaps to extend across a greater part of the wingspan. That in turn improved lift during take-off and landing, and resulted in a higher permissible wing-loading.

The object of the design was plainly to reduce expenditure on tail and control surfaces to the absolute minimum. The overall dimensions which were thus achieved resulted in considerable savings in weight and production costs and, at the same time, offered improved flight performance.

Blohm und Voss invested a considerable amount of research and development work in this aircraft. The chief designer himself returned to it time and again, often changing only the smallest of details, or the co-ordination between tail and control surfaces, or altering the dimensions of various component parts. But at no time did he divert from the basic concept which, in his opinion, was the right one.

There were even practical trials of these unconventional aerodynamics, carried out in low-speed flight by a suitably converted Skoda-Kauba SkV light aircraft. The way ahead, first demonstrated by the P.208, was to be continued with the BV P.209, P.210 and BV 212. Even the layout of the BV 215 night fighter, although jet-powered, revealed its close relationship to its piston-engined forerunner.

Above and below: **Blohm und Voss P.208/02.**

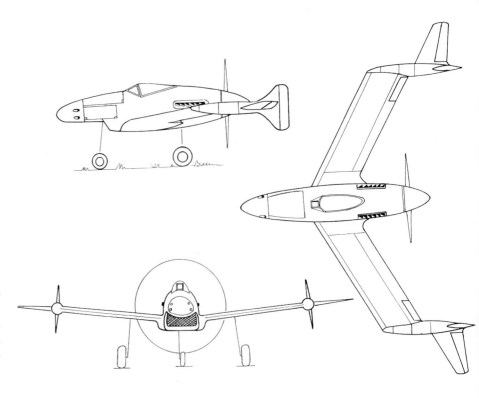

Blohm und Voss P.208/03

15th November 1944

Over 60% of the BV P.208's structure made use of steel. Well over half of the swept wing, for example, consisted of a stiffened steel shell which also served as an integral fuel tank. The short Duraluminum monocoque fuselage housed a welded steel pressure cabin.

The aircraft's performance would perhaps not quite have met the Luftwaffe's requirements. But the DB 603L was at least in series production at Daimler-Benz's No.90 works, and the stage reached in design and development would have permitted detailed construction to have begun immediately.

After the General Staff's upgraded requirements, particularly in terms of endurance, which would have necessitated a change in design at the very least – and with the company becoming ever more deeply involved in jet fighter development – Blohm und Voss decided to cease all further work on their high performance piston-engined fighter.

Powerplant

One Daimler-Benz DB 603L, liquid-cooled 12-cylinder inverted-vee engine with two-stage supercharger and supercharger air cooler with impeller inlet guide vane. Maximum take-off power: 1,361kW (1,825hp); with MW 50 injection: up to 1,566kW (2,100hp) with 3.4m (11ft 2in) diameter four-blade propeller.

Dimensions

Span:	9.50m	31ft 2in
Sweep	30° at 0.25 chord	
Wing area	19.0m²	204.5ft²
Aspect ratio	4.75 : 1	
Length overall	9.20m	30ft 2in
Height overall (ex propeller)	3.46m	11ft 4in

Weights

Empty equipped	4,145kg	9,138lb
Loaded	5,005kg with 600kg fuel	
	11,033lb with 1,322lb of fuel	
Max wing loading	264kg/m²	1,288lb/ft²

Performance

Emergency boost with MW 50

Max speed	790km/h at 9,000m	490mph at 29,500ft
Initial rate of climb	18m/sec	59ft/sec
Time to 11,400m	27 minutes	
Endurance	1.85 hours at 9,000m	
Range	1,230km (764 miles) at 9,000m	

Endurance and range given at maximum permissible constant power.

Armament

Three 30mm MK 108 cannon as weapon-pack in nose.'

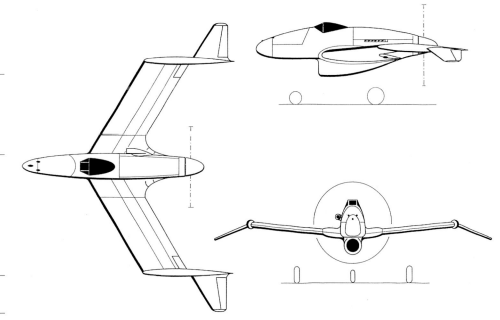

DORNIER

Dornier Do 335 developments

Not unnaturally, the Friedrichshafen firm of Dornier based their proposal to the specification on the Do 335. This machine, the fastest piston-engined aircraft in the world to enter series production, had first flown on 26th October 1943, and had proved its excellence from the very outset. The specification re-quirements of July 1944 seemed to have been made for Dornier – their prior experience with the Do 335 could be utilised to the full.

V1 prototype of the revolutionary piston-engined Do 335 Pfeil fighter.

Do 335 V9, completed to pre-production standards, May 1944. Ken Ellis collection

Dornier P.247/6 high performance fighter
Autumn 1944

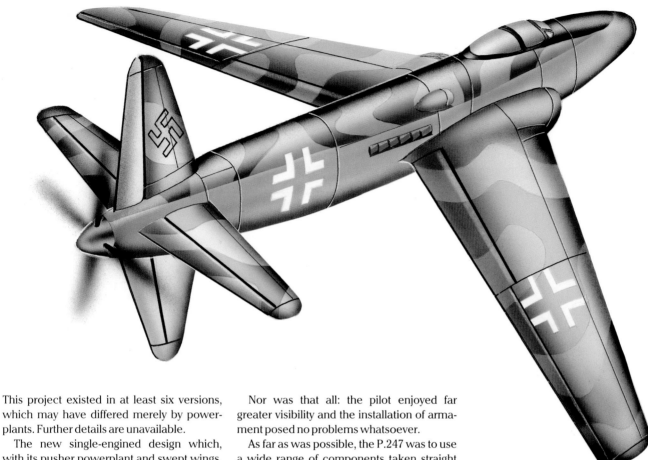

This project existed in at least six versions, which may have differed merely by power-plants. Further details are unavailable.

The new single-engined design which, with its pusher powerplant and swept wings, made full use of modern aerodynamics, promised performance figures appreciably better even than those of the larger and heavier, but twin-engined, Do 335.

Nor was that all: the pilot enjoyed far greater visibility and the installation of armament posed no problems whatsoever.

As far as was possible, the P.247 was to use a wide range of components taken straight from Do 335 production, such as the undercarriage and the tail surfaces, in order to minimise development and production time.

Powerplant
One Junkers Jumo 213J liquid-cooled 12-cylinder inverted-vee engine; special emergency rating with MW 50: 1,671kW (2,240hp); 3.0m (9ft 10in) diameter pusher propeller driven via an extension shaft.

Dimensions
Span	12.0m	39ft 4in
Sweep	28° at 0.25 chord	
Wing area	25m²	269ft²
Aspect ratio	6.0 : 1	
Length overall	12.06m	39ft 7in
Height overall	4.40m	14ft 1in

Weights (estimated)
Loaded	6,000-6,200kg	13,227-13,668lb

Performance
Max speed at ground level	835km/h	518mph

Armament
Three 30mm MK 108 cannon as weapon-pack in nose. The aircraft could also operate as a fighter-bomber.

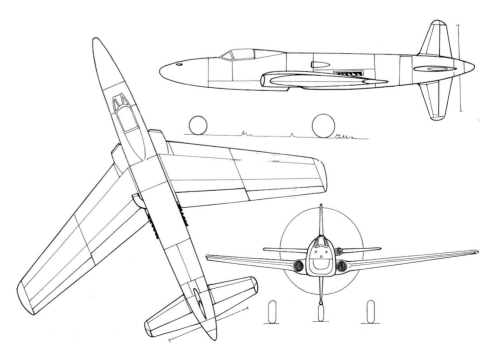

FOCKE-WULF

Focke-Wulf high performance fighter with Jumo 222E/F

3rd October 1944

Powerplant

One Junkers Jumo 222E/F liquid-cooled four-row radial engine with two-stage supercharger; with MW 50 injection for altitudes up to 10,000m (32,800ft) and GM-1 injection for altitudes above 10,000m. Take-off rating: 1,865kW (2,500hp); emergency power with MW 50: 2,163kW (2,900hp). Junkers VS 13 five-bladed pusher propeller of 3.4m (11ft 1⅛in) driven via an extension shaft.

Dimensions

Span	12.80m	41ft 11in
Sweep	28° at 0.25 chord	
Wing area	33.0m²	355.2ft²
Aspect ratio	5.0 : 1	
Length overall	13.70m	44ft 10in
Height overall	4.50m	14ft 9in

Weights

Empty equipped	5,340kg	11,772lb
Loaded	6,730kg with	14,836lb with
	850kg fuel	1,873lb fuel
Max wing loading	204kg/m²	996lb/ft²

Performance

Max speed	805km/h	500mph
	at 11,000m	at 36,000ft
Initial rate of climb	21.5m/sec	70ft/sec
Time to 6,000m	5.4 min10,000m	10.7 min
Range at max permissible	1,100km	683 miles
power	at 11,000m	at 36,000ft
Range at economic cruise	2,590km	1,833 miles
	at 7,000m	at 23,000ft

Endurance at max permissible power 1.9 hours at 11,000m
Endurance at economic cruise 5.5 hours at ground level

Armament

One 30mm MK 103 cannon in nose, plus two 30mm MG 213/30 (MK 213C) cannon to left and right of cockpit. Radio equipment: Standard equipment for single-seat fighters with Funkgerät (FuG – radio or radar set) 16ZY, FuG 25 and FuG 125 VHF R/T.

With the layout of the high performance fighter already dictated to a great extent by the specification requirements, the proposals emanating from Focke-Wulf at Bad Eilsen were very similar in parts to those of Dornier. But Prof Kurt Tank and his team also attempted to fulfil the even more rigorous requirements of January 1945. They continued work on their 'Otto' projects until Göring's cancelled the entire programme order on 22nd February.

Compared to the 'Fighter with Jumo 222C/D' of October 1942, the series of designs commencing in August 1944 clearly illustrated the aerodynamic advances made in the interim, as evidenced by the configuration of the powerplant and the swept wings. General arrangement drawing No.0310 025-501, dated 30th August 1944, showed the wing to possess a sweep of 35° (which would have been more applicable to a jet fighter), whereas detailed drawing No.0310 025-506 of 2nd October 1944 indicated that this had been reduced to 28°.

The large surface radiators of 1942 had given way to a central, relatively well protected fuselage-mounted radiator located ahead of the engine. This arrangement, which included a cooling fan to provide additional airflow when taxying and during take-off, permitted a reduction in the radiator's surface area. Cooling air was delivered via two

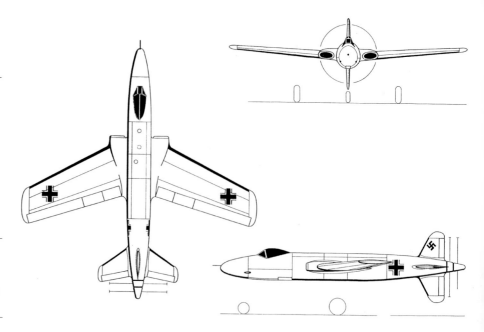

wing root intakes to the radiator which, for aerodynamic reasons, was buried in the fuselage. Warm air was expelled through an annular slot positioned between the radiator and the powerplant.

Pilot, armament, engine installation and all fuel were located within the fuselage, whose cross-section was determined by the size of the powerplant.

The design department worked on this project until about the end of November 1944, in order subsequently to be able to compare it against the work of their competitors. A somewhat smaller version (span 11m/36ft 1in, loaded weight 6,096kg/13,439lb), powered by the DB 603N with a take-off rating of 2,051kW/2,750lb), was also under development. In January/February 1945 Focke-Wulf

modified this concept into the last known designs to result from this specification. Due to their greater range, these latter types were both larger and heavier.

Focke-Wulf high performance fighter with Argus As 413

1st October 1944

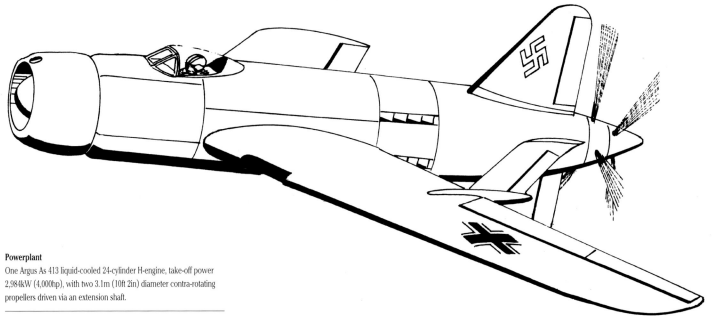

Powerplant
One Argus As 413 liquid-cooled 24-cylinder H-engine, take-off power 2,984kW (4,000hp), with two 3.1m (10ft 2in) diameter contra-rotating propellers driven via an extension shaft.

Dimensions
Span	16.40m	53ft 9in
Sweep	31° at 0.25 chord	
Wing area	55m²	592ft²
Aspect ration	4.9 : 1	
Length overall	14.20m	46ft 6in
Height overall	4.70m	15ft 6in

Weights
Empty equipped	8,000kg	17,636lb
Loaded	9,800kg with	21,604lb with
	1,400kg of fuel	3,086lb of fuel
Max wing loading	178kg/m²	868.9lb/ft²

Performance
Max speed	820km/h	509mph
	at 10,300m	at 33,800ft
Initial rate of climb	21m/sec	69ft/sec
Service ceiling	14,100m	46,250ft
Time to 10,000m	13 min	
Endurance	2 hrs at 10,000m at max constant power	

Armament
Two 30mm MK 103 cannon, plus two 30mm MG 213/30 (MK 213C) cannon in forward fuselage. Radio equipment: Standard fighter equipment.

Work on this design commenced at the same time as that on the high performance fighter with Jumo 222E/F. For in response to Luftwaffe requirements, the intention was for an Argus As 413 engine in the 4,000hp (2,984kW) power range – built around the main components of the Jumo 213 – also to be utilised.

In contrast, for example, to Blohm und Voss, Focke-Wulf came up with an almost entirely new concept for this powerful engine. The prominent annular radiator located in the nose was regarded as one of the best solutions in terms of cooling efficiency and drag characteristics. But there were certain disadvantages, which could not be ignored: here was the ideal space for items as armament, search radar or nosewheel compartment was automatically eliminated.

Other considerations included impairment of forward visibility and the danger of fuselage laminar separation, especially when the

slotted flaps were extended. Placing of cooling water delivery and drainage pipes may also have posed not insignificant problems.

The chosen aerodynamic configuration featured forward-swept horizontal tail surfaces (the 'Victoria tail') connected to wing rib trailing-edge extensions. Quite apart from the extremely stable structural bracing this arrangement provided, it also promised an appreciable reduction in drag.

Focke-Wulf used this same tail surface arrangement, which was also the subject of a NASA study in the 1980s, on another project. This design of November 1944, for which no documentation is available, was apparently to have been powered by a Jumo 222E/F with provision for two additional BMW 003 jet units.

The 'Victoria tail' layout of the Argus As 413-engined Focke-Wulf project of 1st October 1944.

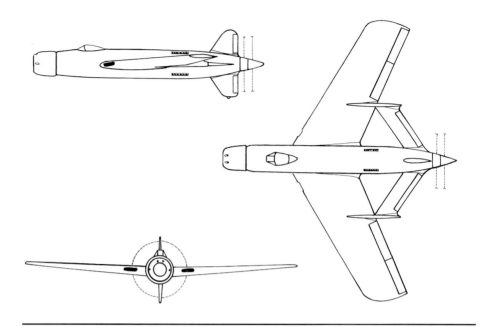

Focke-Wulf high performance fighter with Argus As 413
20th February 1945

Prof Tank's design bureau based its concept for a high performance fighter with extended range on the October 1944 project powered by a Jumo 222E/F described above.

Two proposals were put forward: a high performance fighter with the Jumo 222E/F or with the Argus As 413. Apart from the powerplants, these two proposals differed only marginally in dimensions.

Given a halfway normal development period for the airframe, and assuming that the engines were available, the first examples of this machine could perhaps have been delivered to the Luftwaffe in 1948. In view of the rapid development of the jet fighter, with its lighter and simpler construction, questions as to the sense of pursuing such a course should already have been asked as early as July 1944.

The performance-enhanced Focke-Wulf Ta 152 could quite clearly have assumed the role of the piston-engined high performance fighter during any required period of transition to jet operations. These last 'Otto' fighter projects continue to hold a fascination for the technically-minded even today, as they represent the final chapter of an era which dominated aviation technology for decades.

Powerplant
One Argus As 413, take-off power 2,984kW (4,000hp), with two 3.5m (11ft 6in) diameter contra-rotating propellers.

Dimensions

Span	15.20m	49ft 10in
Sweep	24° at 0.25 chord	
Wing area	42m²	452ft²
Aspect ratio	5.5 : 1	
Length overall	15.35m	50ft 4½in
Height overall	4.70m	15ft 5in

Weights
Although no data are available, a loaded weight in the region of 10,160–10,668kg (10.0-10.5 tons) could be expected.

Performance
No performance figures are available; it may be assumed, however, that – with the exception of endurance (which at maximum permissible constant power would be approximately three hours at 10,000m/32,800ft) – the performance data for this design would show a slight improvement on those quoted for the high performance fighter with As 413 of 1st October 1944.

Armament
One 30mm MK 103 cannon in the nose, plus two 30mm MK 103 cannon to the left and right of the cockpit.

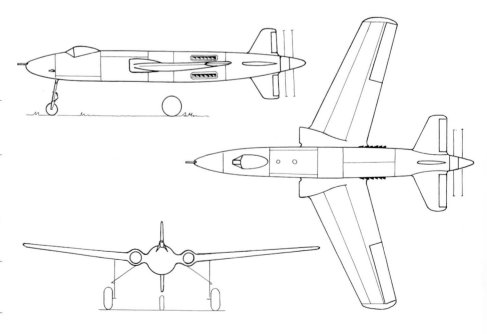

Chapter Two

Single-seat jets

Germany's plans for the production of a pursuit or air superiority fighter, like so many of their armament programmes, followed a characteristically tortuous and uneven course with signs of a cohesive policy apparent only here and there along the way. The responsibility for this state of affairs rested with the political leadership, and particularly with the Reich's Air Ministry (Reichsluftministerium – RLM) under Hermann Göring, whose working methods and nepotism had evoked criticism from both the Luftwaffe and the industry from a relatively early stage onwards.

It all began in 1935 with the rigid insistence on just one standard fighter, and ended in the exact opposite: in utter disarray, which resulted in new and improved types entering service much too late, or too hastily, or even not at all. As well as the constant changes in military requirements dictated by the course of the war, it was the plethora of parallel development programmes which, more than anything else, stood in the way of success. Here, too, a proper concentration of effort and resources was only in evidence at infrequent intervals.

Thus, for example, the Messerschmitt Bf 109 – dating back to 1934-35 – had to carry the main burden of the fighter war right up until the bitter end in 1945.

Until Albert Speer's Reichsministerium für Rüstung und Kriegsproduktion (RfRuK – Reich Ministry of Armament and War Production) belatedly took over control of aerial re-armament at the beginning of 1944, the leadership of the RLM had shown itself all but incapable of translating military and economic requirements into practical measures. In their defence it has to be said that the outbreak of war found the Luftwaffe still in the throes of a period of expansion and thus relatively unprepared, that the leadership's at times totally wrong assessment of situations greatly hampered any rational planning, and that the time span in question was in an era of radical and far-reaching changes for aviation and weapons technology.

But there were also the rivalries, jealousies and intrigues within the industry itself and, not least, the tendency on the part of Ger-

many's scientists and engineers – a tendency which would have been admirable under other circumstances – to examine, explore and develop almost to perfection any and every possible design project or promising scheme that came their way. All of which led to a veritable flood of projects which, even in

the fighter sector, was to provide a springboard for the future development of much of today's military and commercial aviation technology.

Broadly speaking, work on jet fighter projects developed along the following lines: after Ernst Heinkel had successfully tested

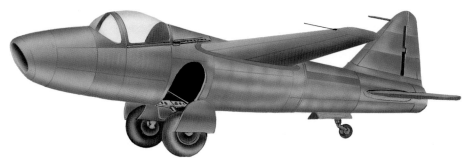

The Heinkel He 178 heralded the era of turbojet supremacy.

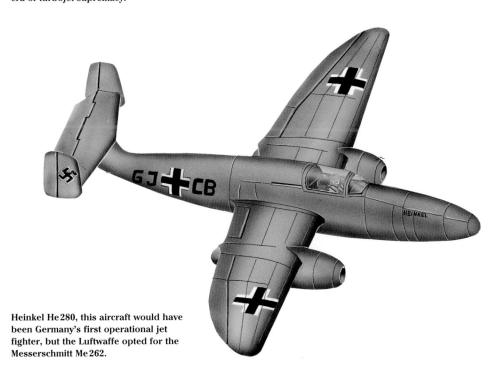

Heinkel He 280, this aircraft would have been Germany's first operational jet fighter, but the Luftwaffe opted for the Messerschmitt Me 262.

Messerschmitt Me 262 Schwalbe.

the jet engine and proved its basic feasibility as a powerplant in the He 178, development work was to continue, albeit with no great sense of urgency; priority at first being given to existing and well-known technology. Towards the end of the 1930s the RLM had stated, with some justification, that for an imminent conflict – which, it was generally held, would be a brief one – proven aircraft types had to be available. Developments for any future hostilities were therefore not at the forefront of current interests.'

Nevertheless, the new jet propulsion offered an unimaginable advantage in performance over any potential enemy. The fighter arm, in particular, would be the first to benefit from the increased speeds which would be achievable.

Even before the outbreak of war, Germany's two leading fighter aircraft designers, and producers of the then fastest aircraft in the world, Ernst Heinkel and Willy Messerschmitt, had each begun work on a jet-powered fighter. Constrained by the unreliability and low power output of the early jet turbines, both opted for a twin-engined layout. Although the effect of wing sweepback was already known of, wind tunnel test results on the exact behaviour of this new wing concept were not yet available. Both designs displayed almost conventional aerodynamics. It was not until mid-1943 that new shapes began to replace previously familiar configurations to any great extent. One exception to this was Alexander Lippisch, whose interceptor, fighter and fast bomber designs displayed from the very outset his inherent genius for combining the new propulsion systems with his own brand of modern, almost timeless, aerodynamic forms.

With the German Reich being pushed more and more on to the defensive, 1943 was to see an increase in new projects activity. On the fighter side, however, which was still

failing to attract the necessary priority, development work was dominated by improvements to existing types and by new single-jet designs; the latter, as a result of the growing shortages in men and materials, being built in the simplest and most economical manner possible. But, as before, the jet engines now under development still constituted an element of uncertainty – and would continue so to do until the war's end.

At the close of 1942 and the beginning of 1943, Bremen-based Focke-Wulf, creators of the successful Fw 190, joined in the programme then being launched to produce an efficient single-jet fighter to meet current requirements.

Other manufacturers and design bureaux threw their hats into the ring:

– Arado: wanted to build upon their good, but somewhat faded, reputation for fighter design and production.
– Heinkel: after seeing no future for the He 280, and despite other major commitments, wanted to remain in the running at all costs.
– Blohm und Voss: had very little experience to date in the fighter sector.

During the first half of 1944, with the results of high speed and swept wing research becoming widely available, a number of advanced – mostly single-jet – designs began to appear, whose superior technology, it was hoped, would make up for the Allies' overwhelming weight of numbers. That year also saw an increase in the number of manufacturers and designers keen to produce a jet-powered air superiority fighter in response to the huge and ever growing threat of the Allied bombing campaign; companies such as:

– Junkers: whose capacity was already fully stretched with an extensive research programme and with work on a jet bomber.

– Henschel: who were working on a very interesting project and, last but not least
– the Horten brothers: whose small but highly efficient team were involved in developing a concept not unlike that of Alexander Lippisch.

As the war dragged on, especially into its fifth and six years, there were shortages everywhere: in the workforce, in airfields, in powerplants, in materials and – above all – in pilots with even a modicum of training. The planners in Berlin tried to adapt to the situation. But what has been lost cannot be regained – and too much time and capacity had already been frittered away.

In the second half of 1944, German aircraft manufacturers were issued with two specifications, amongst others, for a single-jet fighter. One laid down exacting technical and military requirements as the basis for a single-jet fighter, powered by the Heinkel HeS 011, intended as a future replacement for the Me 262 Schwalbe (Swallow), and

The second, an invitation to tender for a quick and simple to build, Volksjäger or (People's Fighter), which was, however, soon 'overtaken' by demands for even simpler and more basic machines.

While the latter resulted in the technological dead end that was the He 162 (known as Spatz – Sparrow by Heinkel and with the unofficial name Salamander), the work begun on a successor to the Me 262 formed the basis for post-war fighter development as typified by such aircraft as the North American F-86 Sabre and the Mikoyan-Gurevich MiG-15 'Fagot'.

ARADO

With the Arado Ar 65 and Ar 68 biplanes this well-known company produced the first fighter aircraft for the Third Reich's fledgling Luftwaffe. But although the firm's design department worked on a whole series of, at times, highly unusual fighter proposals right up until the war's end – initially at Brandenburg on the Havel and later, from 1944, at Landeshut in Silesia – the early biplanes were to remain the sole examples out of all its fighter designs to enter series production. Much better known, and to be seen in various forms in the post-war years, was Arado's other work on fast bombers, on unusual and heavily-armed general purpose aircraft, on very modern battle zone tactical transports and, not least, on the development of new wing shapes such as those adopted, in particular, by Great Britain.

Arado Ar 234 developments

At the end of December 1941 Arado attempted for the first time to make use of a turbojet engine in one of its fighter designs. Project E.480 originated at the turn of the year 1941-42. This envisaged the use of a jet turbine in conjunction with the Daimler-Benz DB 614 piston engine.

A second, pure jet variant was planned at the same time. Unfortunately, all that remains as evidence of this work are performance diagrams and weight tables.

In May 1943, Arado tried to promote interest in a fighter version of their Ar 234 Blitz (Lightning, Project E.370) then under construction for reconnaissance. But the RLM rejected these overtures, pointing to the Me 262 which was already flying and which had, moreover, been designed as a fighter from the outset.

The company had to rethink their strategy for producing a viable fighter aircraft.

In August 1943 the design department completed an extensive study entitled, 'Proposals for the further development of a fast two-seater'. This analysed and described in detail the future development of a two-seat multi-purpose aircraft (fast bomber, heavy fighter, reconnaissance aircraft, night fighter and all-weather fighter).

Running to almost 100 pages, this study – signed by Dipl-Ing Walter Blume, but primarily the work of Dipl-Ing Wilhelm van Nes – dealt with the fighter question in an appendix. Van Nes argued in this context that what was required effectively to combat bombers was a long range fighter with a good rate of climb at all altitudes. He put forward three fighter proposals: one a pure twin-jet, one solely rocket powered, and one – the most favoured of the three – a 'combination fighter' with a mixed powerplant consisting of jet engine and rocket motor combined.

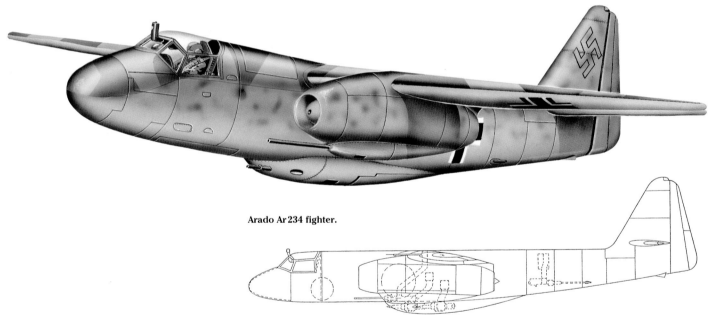

Arado Ar 234 fighter.

Starting point for the development series: the Arado Ar 234 V17 with two BMW 003s (and underwing rocket assistance take-off pods).

Arado target concept:
TEW 16/43-15 'combination fighter'
20th March 1943

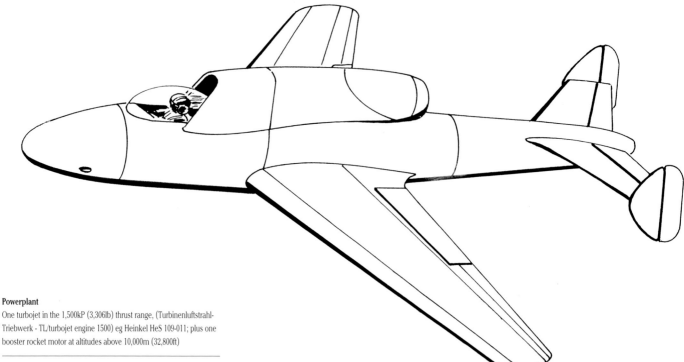

Powerplant

One turbojet in the 1,500kP (3,306lb) thrust range, (Turbinenluftstrahl-Triebwerk - TL/turbojet engine 1500) eg Heinkel HeS 109-011; plus one booster rocket motor at altitudes above 10,000m (32,800ft).

Dimensions

Span	10.30m	33ft 9½in
Sweep	25° at 0.25 chord	
Wing area	19.0m²	204.5ft²
Aspect ratio	5.6 : 1	
Length overall	11.75m	38ft 6in
Height overall	2.80m	9ft 2in

Weights

Empty equipped	4,150kg	9,149lb
Take-off weight	6,670kg	14,704lb
Max wing loading	350kg/m²	71.6lb/ft²

Performance

Max speed	856km/h	531mph
	at 8,000m	at 26,250ft
with rocket motor	approx 920km/h	approx 571mph
	at over 10,000m	at over 32,800ft
Rate of climb	33.4m/sec	109ft/sec
with rocket motor	250m/sec (!)	820ft/sec (!)
Time to 8,000m	32 secs with rocket motor	
Service ceiling	13,300m	43,600ft
with rocket motor	18,800m	61,600ft
Range	1,200km	745 miles
	at 12,000m	at 39,000ft
with rocket motor	115km	71 miles
	at 8,000m	at 26,250ft

Armament

Two 15mm MG 151/15 cannon, plus one 30mm MK 103 cannon.

Equipment

Standard fighter R/T equipment. Special features: Undercarriage fitted with special spherical tyres, primarily for reasons of space (housing mainwheels in wing section).

This proposal almost anticipates the E.580, Arado's later response to the Volksjäger requirement. As with an earlier Focke-Wulf study, the similarities to the Heinkel He 162 are clearly apparent.

This advanced proposal stood very little chance of being realised, due primarily to the near insuperable problems which the intended powerplant would have posed at that time.

After the war the victorious Allies built a number of 'combination fighters' (mostly in prototype form only) for the interceptor role. These included the American Republic XF-91 Thunderceptor, the French Dassault MD.550 Mirage I and Sud-Est SE.212 Durandal and the British Saunders-Roe SR.53, all of which were abandoned in the development stage in favour of fast climbing fighters with more powerful afterburning turbojet engines.

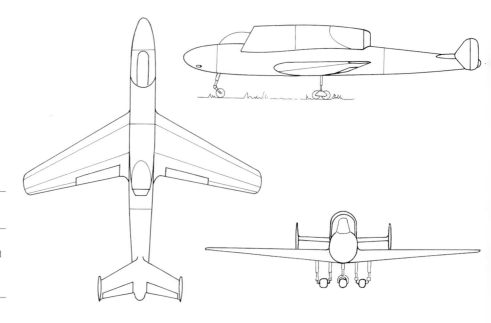

Arado TEW 16/43-23 jet fighter

3rd June 1943

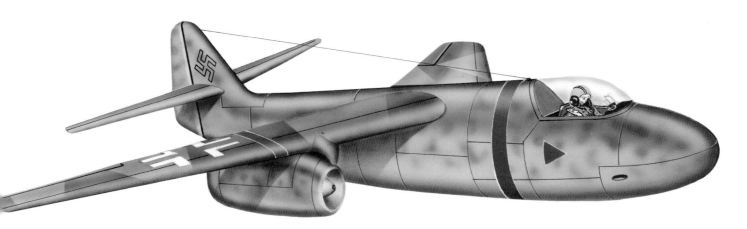

In May 1943 Arado had put forward to the RLM a proposal for an extremely heavily armoured fighter developed from the Ar 234. But its projected performance obviously failed to satisfy, offering no appreciable advantages over the Me 262 which was already undergoing flight tests. Van Nes hoped, however, that by employing a swept wing, by reducing the overall dimensions and, above all, by fitting more powerful engines, he would achieve a higher rate of climb and an endurance sufficient to be able to offer an effective counter to Allied bombers. In terms of dimensions and weights the design was thus roughly comparable to the Me 262. The design was intended to permit speeds in the region of 1,000km/h (621mph), Arado anticipated speeds in excess of that figure. As a pure jet interceptor fighter, range and endurance figures would not have been particularly high; Arado offered no data in these areas.

Arado's design bureau subsequently concentrated on two-seat, fast general purpose or bomber aircraft. It was not until the closing months of the Third Reich that the company again put forward proposals for jet-powered fighters. In addition to their E.580 design (Volksjäger specification) and the E.581 proposal for a successor to the Me 262, these consisted in the main of heavy fighters to be developed out of the Ar 234, none of which, however, progressed beyond the drawing board stage. These latter proposals differed from the Ar 234B and 'C reconnaissance-bombers only in terms of military equipment fitted and a new cockpit arrangement.

Powerplant
Two Heinkel HeS 109-011 each rated at 1,300kP (2,865lb) thrust.

Dimensions
Span	10.60m	34ft 9in
Sweep	25° at 0.25 chord	
Wing area	20.0m²	215.2ft²
Aspect ratio	5.6 : 1	
Length overall	9.40m	30ft 9¼in
Height overall	2.69m	8ft 9½in

Weights
Empty equipped	4,480kg	9,876lb
	with 2,520kg fuel	with 5,555lb fuel
Take-off	7,000kg	15,432lb
Wing loading	350kg/m²	71.6lb/ft²

Performance
Max speed	920km/h	571mph
	at 10,000m	at 32,800ft
Initial rate of climb	48m/sec	157ft/sec
	12,000m *	39,000ft *
	* to be reached in six minutes	
Service ceiling	12,000m	39,000ft

Armament
One 15mm MG 151/15 cannon, plus two additional cannon (eg MK 213C).

Special features
Nosewheel equipped with space-saving spherical tyres.

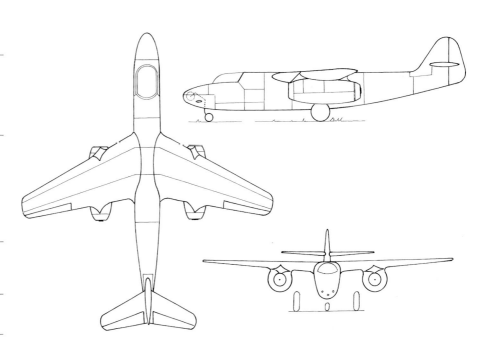

BLOHM UND VOSS

The smaller companies involved themselves in the development of almost every kind and type of aircraft just as much as did the larger German manufacturers. The resulting rivalries, with all their inherent drawbacks and the consequent dissipation of capacities, were a direct result of the RLM's wasteful armament policy. It was a situation which did not improve until the advent of Speer's Ministry towards the closing stages of the war.

The long-established Hamburg shipbuilding firm of Blohm und Voss set up an aircraft manufacturing division in 1933. In the 12 years until 1945 this division was responsible for no less than 215 projects, few of which, however, progressed to the factory floor, let alone into series production.

Alongside their well-known large flying-boat designs, which were produced in some numbers, Blohm und Voss drawing boards gave rise to a whole range of highly unusual general purpose aircraft, reconnaissance types, dive-bombers, fighter-bombers, heavy bombers and – not least – fighters.

The reasons for this exceptionally high degree of new project activity were twofold: arising from the fact that the works rarely had many of their own designs in full series production and, in the person of Dr Richard Vogt, Blohm und Voss's unusually gifted and highly creative chief designer, who liked nothing better than to turn his back on the tried and tested and, with all the confidence of a master of his craft, to strike out along paths unknown. The work of Dr Vogt and his team represents an important contribution to aviation technology. Presumably at the instigation of the RLM, Dr Vogt began work on jet fighter development towards the end of 1942 and the beginning of 1943.

Of the BV 175 shipboard fighter and the single-seat, Jumo-powered P.190 (P – projekt, project) little more than the project numbers is known. With the strikingly modern looking BV 197 and the BV 198 high altitude fighter, Dr Vogt followed fairly conventional lines. But in the twin-jet P.202 fighter design he came up with a highly unusual solution to remedy the swept wing's shortcomings in low-speed flight: the one-piece swivel wing, which had both positive and negative sweep at high speed.

With the highly individual P.209, P.210 and P.212 designs Blohm und Voss attempted to produce a single-jet successor to the Me 262. Immediately prior to this the firm had been working on their Project 211 which, in the opinion of some experts, was the best proposal to come out of the Volksjäger contest of September 1944.

For his fighter projects, unlike all his other designs, Dr Vogt chose to use a symmetrical layout. Nevertheless, he introduced a profusion of new ideas with nearly every new drawing; ideas which would have required careful, and sometimes protracted, testing. Despite his work often departing from the accepted norm, Dr Vogt never lost his sense of the practicable. He demonstrated this with, among others, his own unconventional BV 141 reconnaissance aircraft. In the 1970s, it was NASA who proved the feasibility of his swivel wing concept in flight tests.

The powers-that-be in the RLM and Technische Luftrüstung (TLR – Technical Air Armament Board) often found it impossible to go along with his ideas. In the light of the then current situation, the expenditure required for the necessary research and development was simply too high.

Blohm und Voss are most associated with marine aircraft, for example, the prototype BV 238 during trials on Lake Schaal, April 1944.
Ken Ellis collection

Blohm und Voss P.197

August 1944

In terms of shape and aerodynamics a very clean twin-jet fighter design with powerplant, dimensions and weights comparable to that of the Me 262. The Hamburg firm moreover demonstrated – at least by mathematical calculation – that the performance of the Me 262, especially its maximum speed, could be improved still further by the use of modern aerodynamics.

What is not clear, quite apart from the possible difficulties arising from the arrangement of the intake, is just how the problematical low speed properties of the swept wing were to be improved, as there are no aids such as slots or flaps indicated on the surviving original drawing.

The general layout is reminiscent of many successful post-war designs.

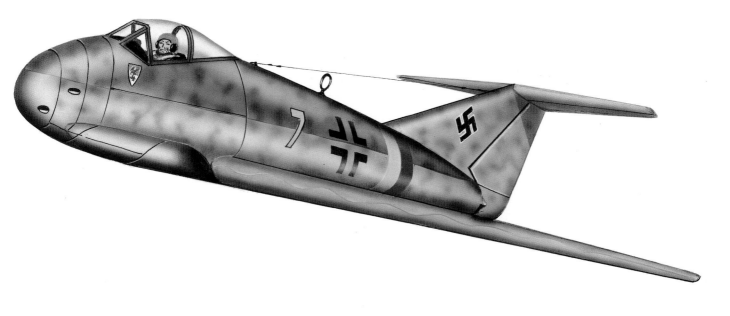

Powerplant
Two Jumo 109-004 each rated at 890kP (1,962lb) static thrust, alternatively two BMW 109-003 each rated at 800kP thrust (1,763lb).

Dimensions

Span	11.10m	36ft 4½in
Sweep	35° at 0.25 chord	
Wing area	20.5m²	220.6ft²
Length overall	9.00m	29ft 6in
Height overall	3.64m	11ft 10½in

Weights

Take-off weight (Jumo 004)	7,100kg	15,652lb
Max wing loading	364kg/m²	70.8lb/ft²

Performance Data for two Jumo 004 at 100% thrust.

Max speed	1,060km/h	658mph
	at 8,000m	at 25,250ft
Initial rate of climb	21m/sec	69ft/sec
Height to be reached in 10.1 minutes		
	10,000m	32,800ft
Service ceiling	12,500m	41,000ft

Armament
Two 30mm Mk 103 cannon, plus two 15mm MG 151/15 cannon.

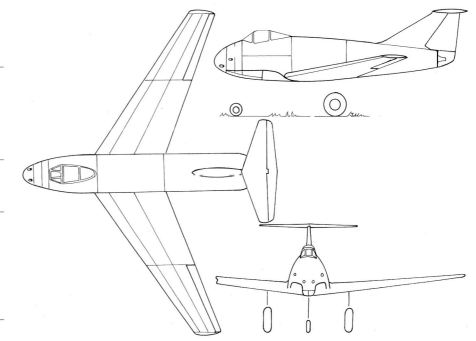

Blohm und Voss P.198

1944

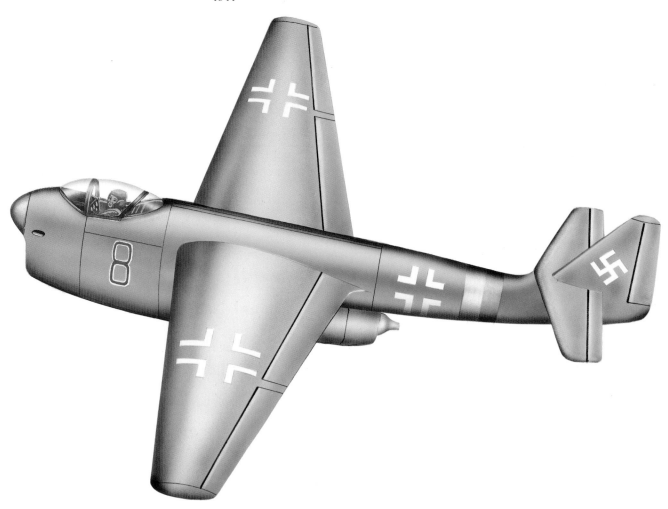

Powerplant

One BMW 109-018 turbojet rated 3,400kP (7,495kg) static thrust.

Dimensions

Span (zero angle of sweep)	15.00m	49ft 2in
Wing area	33.5m²	360ft²
Aspect ratio	6.7 : 1	
Length overall	12.80m	41ft 10½in
Height overall	4.60m	15ft 1in

Weights

Take-off weight	7,250kg	15,983lb
Max wing loading	216kg/m²	44.2lb/ft²
Ta 152H:	205kg/m²	41.9lb/ft²

Performance

Max speed (approx)	1,000km/h	621mph
Initial rate of climb	45m/sec	147ft/sec
Service ceiling	15,800m	51,837ft
Max range	1,500km	932 miles

Armament

One 55mm MK 412 cannon (further development of MK 112), plus two 20mm MG 150 cannon. Armour-plating, pressure cabin, search radar.

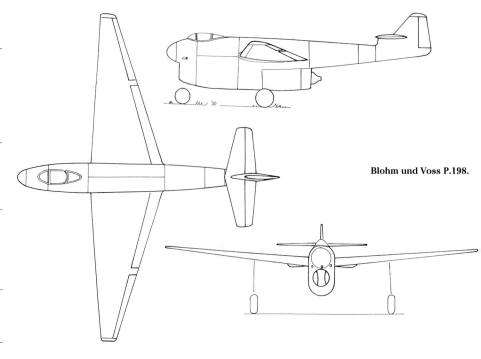

Blohm und Voss P.198.

In order to combat Allied bomber streams, and particularly the fast, high flying reconnaissance aircraft, the Luftwaffe had long been requesting a 'Mosquito-capable' high altitude interceptor fighter.

Messerschmitt (latterly together with Blohm und Voss) and Focke-Wulf had been attempting for some time to develop a special aircraft for this purpose out of their standard Bf 109 and Fw 190 fighters respectively. But to upgrade a piston-engined aircraft for the role required a substantial investment in development costs to cover the complicated internal arrangements of engine, supercharger, intercooler etc. In addition, there was always the danger that a higher operational weight would nullify, at least in part, any improvement in high altitude performance gained from the increased power.

Although the high altitude behaviour of the turbojet engine had not yet been fully investigated, this type of powerplant appeared to offer the possibility of producing a superior aircraft of simple construction. Consequently Dr Vogt combined a simple and aerodynamically straightforward airframe with the most powerful turbojet engine then under development, the BMW 109-018, and hoped by so doing to achieve a more than sufficient advantage in terms of performance. The P.198 proposal was obviously also used for purposes of comparison.

There is no documentation available for a second high altitude fighter design which was given the project number P.199. But this proposal, to be fitted with the far less powerful Jumo 004, was presumably intended as an 'intermediate solution' fighter.

Blohm und Voss P.202

1944

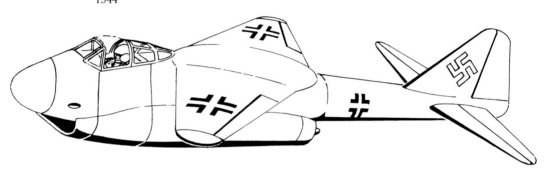

The intensive research into the swept wing, which had been going on since 1939, had confirmed the expected advantages to be gained at high speeds. But it had also brought to light a number of problems, among them low speed flight behaviour and difficulty of construction. Dr Vogt attempted to overcome these disadvantages by employing a one-piece swivel wing.

In July 1944 Messerschmitt also investigated this unusual method of producing variable sweep, tasking his Oberammergau project bureau with examining its feasibility, before finally deciding on a 'standard' variable-sweep wing, which he intended to use, among others, on his P.1101 fighter, and which after the war was successfully flown on the American Bell X-5. Some 25 years later NASA 're-invented' the one-piece swivel wing, successfully testing it on the Ames AD-1 'oblique wing' research aircraft which first flew on 21st December 1979. The projected follow-up, a practical demonstration of this unusual concept on a large passenger-carrying airliner, is however still awaited.

Powerplant
Two BMW 109-003 each rated at 800kP (1,763lb) thrust.

Dimensions
Wing may be slewed up to 35°, roll and slip moments controlled automatically.

Span (zero angle of sweep)	11.98m	39ft 3½in
(at 35° sweep)	10.06m	33ft 0in
Wing area	20.0m²	215ft²
Length overall	10.45m	34ft 3½in
Height overall	3.70m	12ft 1in

Weights
Take-off weight	5,400kg	11,904lb
Max wing loading	270kg/m²	55.3lb/ft²

Performance
No data available.

Armament
Two x 30mm MK 103 cannon to left and right in forward fuselage, plus one 20mm MG 15¼₀ cannon centrally mounted in nose.

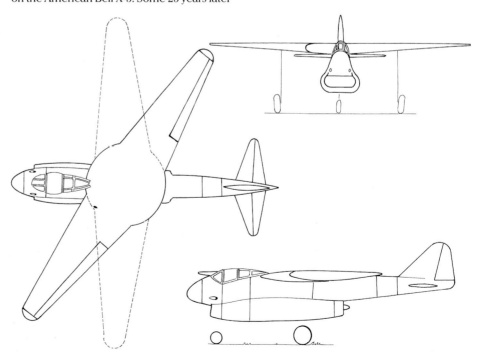

FOCKE-WULF

Compared to Heinkel or Messerschmitt the Bremen firm of Focke-Wulf was a relative latecomer to the field of jet fighter development. The reasons for this were no doubt the precedence given to, and the time and energy expended in, preparing the Focke-Wulf Fw 190 for series production; this aircraft making its operational Luftwaffe debut in the late summer of 1941.

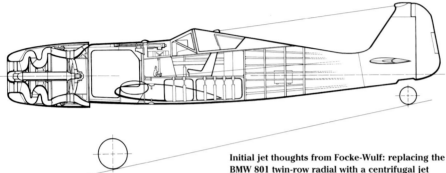

Initial jet thoughts from Focke-Wulf: replacing the BMW 801 twin-row radial with a centrifugal jet engine. John Weal

Focke-Wulf were finally to embark on the new propulsion technology at the end of 1942 when they modified a Fw 190 by replacing its bulky BMW 801 twin-row radial with a simple centrifugal jet engine of their own design. Similar conversions immediately after the end of the war would, incidentally, result in the Soviet Union's first jet fighters (eg the Yakovlev design bureau basing its Yak-15 on the piston-engined Yak-3U fighter). Due to a number of technical inadequacies, plus other more basic considerations, this first proposal was quickly shelved.

Professor Kurt Tank's design department then immediately began work on a fundamentally new study, incorporating the latest state-of-the-art technology, which was submitted to the RLM at the beginning of 1943. The core of this study centred around two single-engined, heavily armed jet fighter proposals utilising the smallest possible dimensions commensurate with their intended role. A design team had thus, at this early stage, already formulated the thoughts and concepts which would later result in the production of the Heinkel He 162.

Following on from this, the project engineers began work on a whole series of jet fighters culminating in 1945 with the Tank Ta 183, a design which – to anticipate events somewhat – had a great influence on, above all, Soviet post-war jet fighter development. The first design of this series, that of March 1943, clearly revealed its direct descent from

a piston-engined fighter; not least by the retention of a tailwheel undercarriage layout. As this would undoubtedly have led to unsatisfactory taxying and ground-handling characteristics, this first proposal quickly gave way to a second design, which featured a nosewheel tricycle undercarriage. In June 1943 the project engineers worked on this second proposal to a detailed design stage, only then to realise that such a layout, with the nosewheel positioned immediately in front of the engine intake – the latter itself enjoying only minimal ground clearance – would inevitably pose unavoidable dangers, such as stone ingestion if operated from unsurfaced forward landing strips, for example. In addition, it was feared that the powerplant would suffer serious damage in the event of a belly landing. Consequently the third design, of November 1943, was provided with a powerplant faired into the contours of the fuselage. While this eliminated the weaknesses of the second design, the proposed hooded engine intakes produced increased drag which would, in turn, lead to a marked deterioration in estimated performance.

Immediately thereafter, in December 1943, Focke-Wulf struck out in a new direction; Tank's project engineers opting for a twin

rudder arrangement supported by tailbooms attached to a reduced-span mainplane. Engine air for the jet powerplant was to be delivered via more aerodynamically efficient side intakes. To improve rate of climb, provision was made for two additional, jettisonable rocket engines.

This proposal provided the basis for the series of Flitzer (Whizzer or Dasher) designs which would occupy the bureau's energies until finally superseded by the Ta 183 in December 1944.

In Great Britain, in the meantime, the de Havilland DH.100 Vampire (nicknamed initially 'Spider Crab') had appeared. Very similar in layout to the proposed Flitzer, this had already successfully made its maiden flight on 20th September 1943. Although it did not see service in the Second World War, the Vampire was built in large numbers and is still flying today in the hands of 'warbird' enthusiasts. After design number four also promised to be anything but satisfactory in terms of horizontal speed, Tank dared all, making the one big technological leap which, at that time, was available only to German aircraft manufacturers: with design number five of January 1944 he forsook the path of conventional aerodynamics and designed a machine with sharply swept, thin profile wings and a so-called 'T' tail consisting of swept horizontal tail surfaces sitting atop an equally swept narrow chord fin and rudder. Now equipped with the more powerful Heinkel HeS 011 engine, this aircraft also boasted much smaller overall dimensions, the result of the skilful layout and arrangement of its major components. The basic design for the Ta 183 was on the boards.

Following on its heels, and for purposes of comparison, a greatly improved Flitzer model was designed in February 1944. This jet fighter, design number six, featured a moderately to those of the Vampire, now being located in the wing roots.

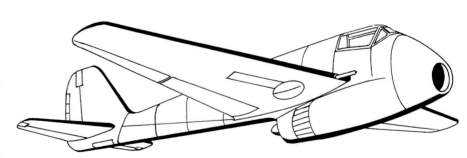

First design for the Focke-Wulf air superiority fighter.

It was also powered by the Heinkel HeS 011, plus an integral auxiliary rocket motor manufactured by Messrs Hellmuth Walter of Kiel.

How next to proceed? While continuing with the theoretical work, Tank also ordered the construction of free-flying 1:10 scale models of both the fifth design (known in-house as Huckebein after a well-known cartoon character) and the sixth (Flitzer) in order to carry out practical tests. These free-flight trials gave rise to some misgivings as to the flying characteristics to be expected from design number five. Doubts were also expressed regarding tail flutter of the extremely narrow, sharply swept fin and rudder and, not least, the installation of the undercarriage was also posing problems.

Kurt Tank decided to defer further work on the fifth design and to concentrate instead on developing the Flitzer project, with which he initially participated in the tender for a single-jet fighter replacement for the Me 262. It was not until later in 1944, when Focke-Wulf saw no further possibility of increasing the still inadequate top speed of the Flitzer, that Tank returned to the fifth design of the previous January. Under his leadership the design bureau recommenced work on this project, now designated Ta 183, which, by the war's end, was showing signs of great promise.

A somewhat unusual development of the basic Flitzer programme was the seventh design of July 1944 which was a proposal for a strike fighter version to be powered by an HeS 021 turboprop engine. As there was a requirement for such an aircraft, and as a basically similar powerplant was already in existence, this proposal was given serious consideration. Despite further development, this project was also to fall victim to the decision, taken at the end of 1944, to concentrate on the Ta 183. In the light of the desperate situation in which the German Reich found itself, the demise of design number seven was inevitable; the expenditure involved in developing and maintaining such a fighter aircraft with its specialised engine, shaft, gearing and propeller was simply too great.

One minor idiosyncrasy of the Focke-Wulf design department should also be mentioned. Unlike other manufacturers, the firm did not use its own internal project numbering system. Their work was either allocated a number by the RLM, or the designs and project descriptions were simply numbered sequentially. Some sources identify Focke-Wulf projects by their drawing numbers. This is incorrect and can lead to confusion. It must be realised that a single project could well consist of several or more drawings, each differing at the very least in the final digit, and thus displaying apparently different numbering.

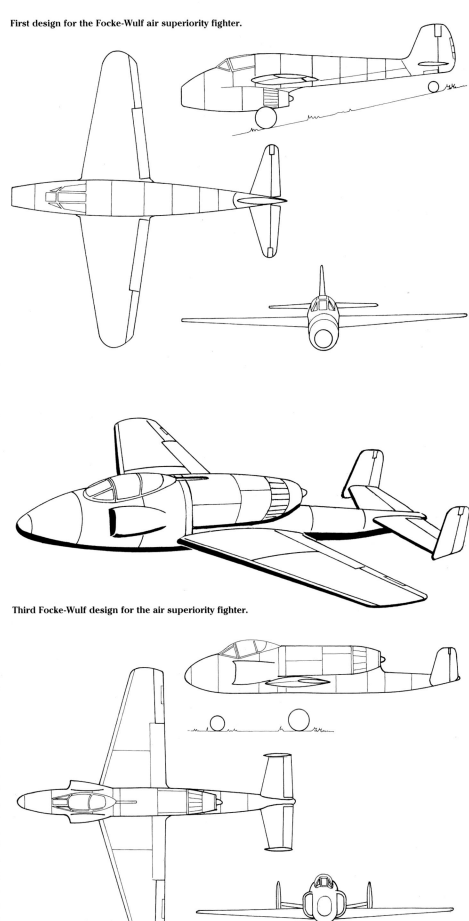

First design for the Focke-Wulf air superiority fighter.

Third Focke-Wulf design for the air superiority fighter.

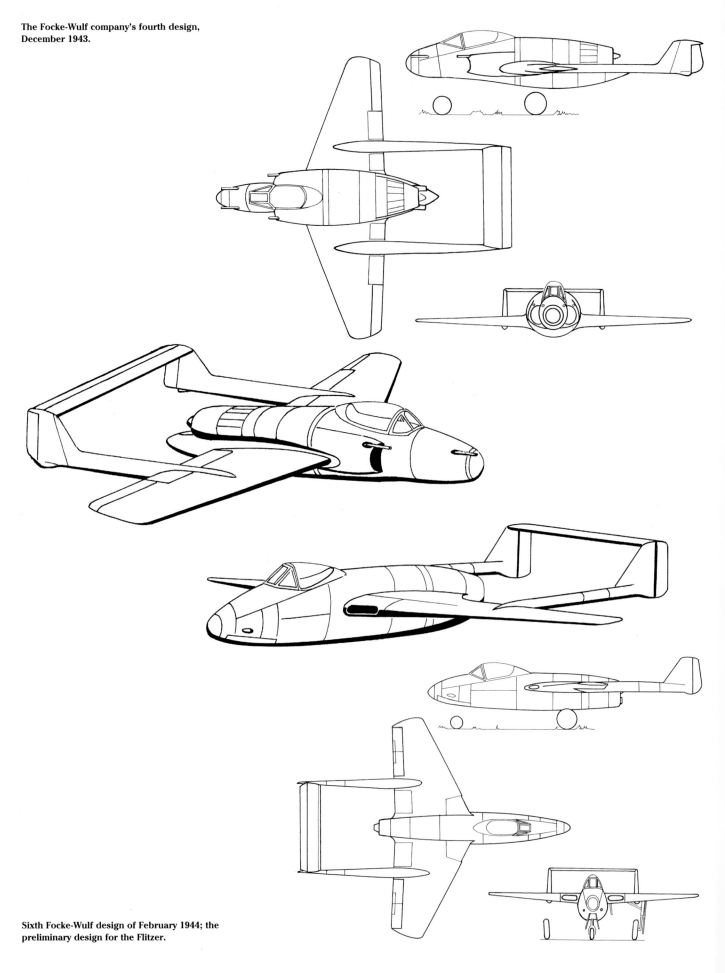

The Focke-Wulf company's fourth design,
December 1943.

Sixth Focke-Wulf design of February 1944; the
preliminary design for the Flitzer.

De Havilland DH.100 Vampire prototype during roll-out at Hatfield on 16th August 1943. Britain's Flitzer, it undertook its maiden flight four days later. Ken Ellis collection

Flight tests with a model of the fifth Focke-Wulf design at Bad Eilsen.

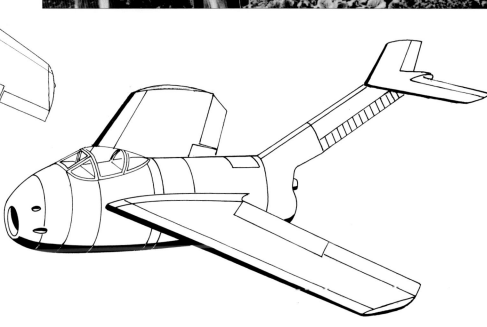

The fifth Focke-Wulf air superiority design.

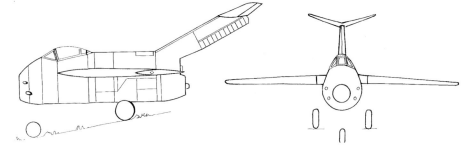

Focke-Wulf Proposal 1

7th December 1942

Taken from the study 'Basic Principles for the Design of a Turbojet-Powered Fighter'.

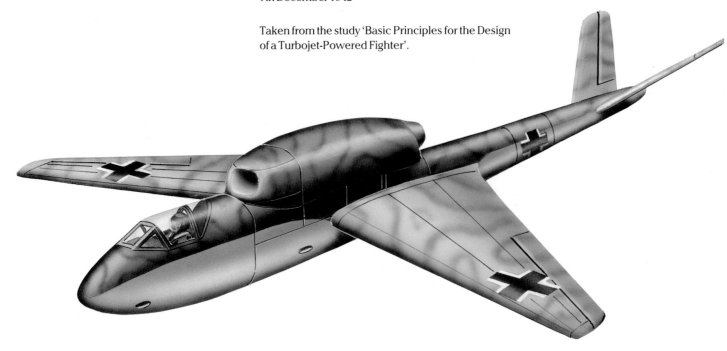

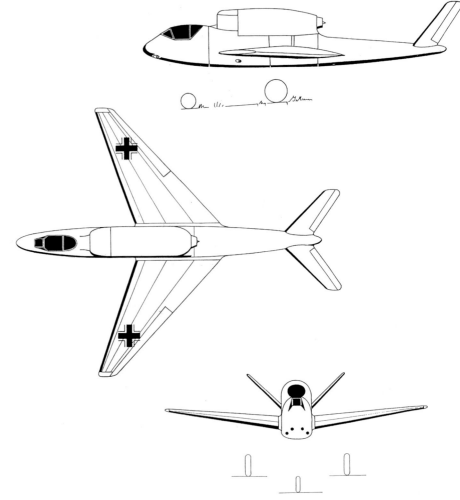

Powerplant

BMW P.3302 turbojet (predecessor of the BMW 109-003) rated at 600kP (1,322lb) static thrust, or one Junkers Jumo 004 rated at 635kP (1,399lb) static thrust (1942 specification).

Dimensions

Span	8.20m	26ft	10⅛in
Sweep	30° negative		
Wing area	14m²	150.6ft²	
Aspect ratio	4.8 : 1		
Profile	NACA 000012-1.130, symmetrical profile with 12% thickness ratio.		
Length	10.50m	34ft 4⅛in	

Weights

Empty equipped			
with BMW P.3302	1,900kg	4,188lb	
Take-off weight			
with BMW P.3302	3,000kg	6,613lb	
with Jumo 004	3,350kg	7,385lb	
Max wing loading	239kg/m²	48.9lb/ft²	

Performance

Max speed, approx,			
100% thrust	800km/h	497mph	
	at 8,000m	at 26,250ft	
150% boost with Jumo 004	930km/h	577mph	
	at 4,500m	at 14,750ft	
Initial rate of climb			
at 100% thrust	11m/sec	36ft/sec	
at 150% boost	21.7m/s	71ft/sec	
Service ceiling	10,800m	35,500ft	
at 150% boost	13,600m	44,600ft	
Endurance	45 mins	at 6,000m	19,750ft
	90 mins	at 12,000m	39,250ft

Armament

Two 30mm MK 108 cannon plus two 15mm MG 151/15 cannon.

Focke-Wulf Proposal 2
22nd December 1942

An alternative to Proposal 1 with conventional aerodynamics, likewise taken from the study 'Basic Principles for the Design of a Turbojet-Powered Fighter'. In effect, Focke-Wulf was anticipating the design of the Heinkel He 162 Volksjäger. It must be presumed that the Technisches Amt (the RLM's technical office responsible for the design, development and maintenance of equipment) used these proposals as a basis for their September 1944 specification calling for a 'Single-engined jet fighter of the simplest and cheapest construction powered by the BMW 003'. Such concepts were certainly known and were not 'developed within a few days'.

Together with those of Alexander Lippisch, these designs constituted the first steps taken in Germany towards production of a single-seat, single jet engine air superiority fighter.

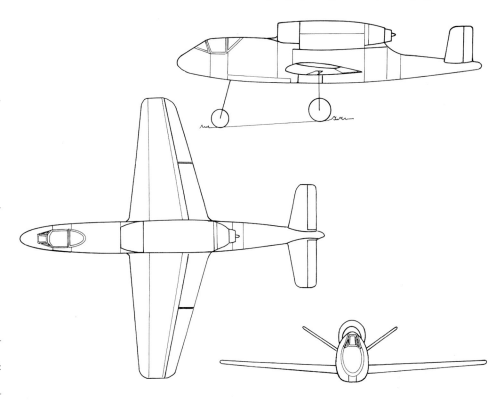

Powerplant

Data for the Heinkel He 162 is given for purposes of comparison.
One BMW P.3302 rated at 600kP (1,322lb) static thrust, provisional data.
(He 162: one BMW 109-003A rated at 800kP – 1,763lb – static thrust)

Dimensions

Span		8.20m	26ft 10½in
	He162	7.20m	23ft 7in
Wing area		14.00m²	150.6ft²
	He162	11.16m²	120ft²
Aspect ratio		4.8 : 1	
	He162	4.65 : 1	
Length overall		9.25m	30ft 3⅛in
	He162	9.05m	29ft 8in

Weights

Empty equipped		1,900kg	4,188lb
	He162	1,610kg	3,549lb
Take-off		3,000kg	6,613lb
	He162	2,541kg	5,601lb
Max wing loading		214kg/m²	43.8lb/ft²
	He162	228kg/m²	46.7lb/ft²

Performance

Max speed (approx)		800km/h	497mph
(approx)	He162	840km/h	521mph
Initial rate of climb		11m/sec	36ft/sec
	He162	21.5m/sec	70ft 6in/sec
Service ceiling		10,800m	35,400ft
	He162	12,000m	39,250ft
Endurance 45 mins		at 6,000m	20,000ft
48 mins	He162	at 6,000m	20,000ft

Armament

Two 30mm MK 108 cannon plus two 15mm MG 151/15 cannon (He 162: two 20mm MG 151/20 cannon).

Focke-Wulf second design

9th June 1943

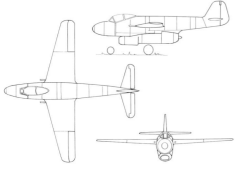

From the series of seven designs, described above, with which Focke-Wulf laid the foundation for their further fighter development. This design, the subject of extensive research, displayed a layout also examined in 1943 by Messerschmitt and, somewhat later, by Blohm und Voss. Calculations showed that the use of modern aerodynamics did not promise any appreciable speed advantage. In addition, further investigation and wind tunnel tests indicated the distinct disadvantages inherent in a swept (leading edge) wing in terms of construction and, above all, in low speed flight performance. The main reasons for the adoption of a ventral engine arrangement were accessibility – ie ease of maintenance for the then still highly unreliable powerplants – and reduction of duct losses.

The disadvantages of this concept were, as already described, the positioning of the nosewheel immediately ahead of the jet intake, the increased drag offered by the externally mounted powerplant and the attendant dangers involved in a belly landing. The all-metal aircraft was to be constructed of Duraluminum and steel.

The second Focke-Wulf proposal, with underslung turbojet; initial layout.

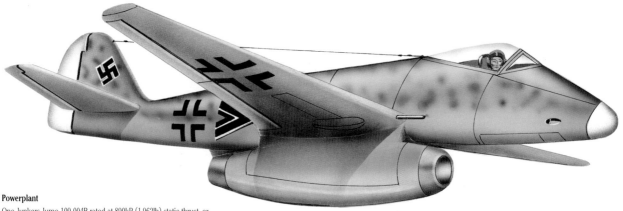

Powerplant

One Junkers Jumo 109-004B rated at 890kP (1,962lb) static thrust, or one Junkers Jumo 109-004C rated at 1,015kP (2,237lb) static thrust with 120% boost: 1,200kP (2,645lb) static thrust, approx.

Main design for the second Focke-Wulf fighter proposal.

Dimensions

Span	9.70m	31ft 9½in
Wing area	15.0m²	161.4ft²
Aspect ratio	6.2 : 1	
Length overall	9.85m	32ft 3½in

Weights

Empty equipped	2,410kg	5,313lb
Take-off	3,350kg	7,385lb
	with 700kg fuel	with 1,543lb fuel
Max wing loading	223kg/m²	45.6lb/ft²

Performance

Max speed		
Jumo 004B, 100% thrust	825km/h	515mph
	at 4,000m	at 13,000ft
Jumo 004C at 120% boost	870km/h	540mph
	at 4,000m	at 13,000ft
Initial rate of climb	20m/sec	65ft/sec
Service ceiling	12,400m	40,600ft
Max range	640km	397 miles

Armament

Two fuselage-mounted 30mm MK 108 or MK 103 cannon, plus two 20mm MG 151/20 cannon in wing roots.

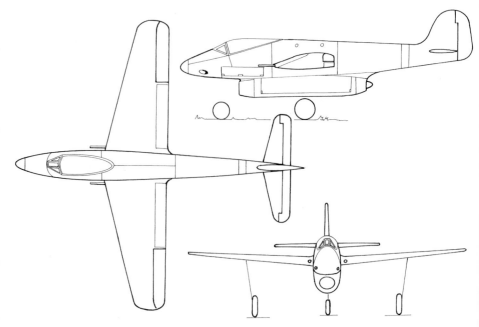

Focke-Wulf turboprop strike fighter

July-December 1944

Focke-Wulf foresaw a number of advantages in this projected turboprop-powered strike fighter developed out of, and in parallel to, the Flitzer. The DB 109-021 turboprop, developed by Daimler-Benz AG from the Heinkel HeS 011, promised high thrust, especially at or near ground level. This would have permitted the turboprop strike fighter to take-off from even the smallest forward landing strips without rocket assistance. It would have been particularly suitable for low level operation, eg as a fighter-bomber.

In the fighter role it was superior to every piston-engined machine. It would have outclassed the pure jet fighters (of that period) in take-off, climb and acceleration. It also possessed appreciably greater endurance and longer range.

In layout this first turboprop fighter design (Focke-Wulf design number seven, 7th July 1944) replicated almost exactly the Flitzer proposal of February 1944 (the sixth design) with its twin-boom arrangement already familiar from the Fw 189 Uhu (Owl).

In its final form, as projected at the end of November 1944, the turboprop strike fighter had been almost completely redesigned. More reminiscent of the Ta 183, it now possessed a

Post-war American equivalent of the turboprop fighter, the Republic XF-84H.

sharply swept wing and orthodox (central) tail unit. The powerplant, however, remained the same.

After the war the Americans produced the Republic XF-84H (originally XF-106), an experimental turboprop fighter which had also originated out of a pure jet fighter design – the F-84F Thunderstreak. After the construction

of two prototypes, and despite promising performance figures, the Pentagon cancelled further development. Like the earlier Focke-Wulf projects before it, it too had obviously fallen victim to the overcomplicated powerplant arrangement and high development costs.

Focke-Wulf turboprop strike fighter seventh design

Fighter and fighter-bomber project developed from the Flitzer design; work initiated in July 1944, data as of 18th August 1944.

Powerplant

One Daimler-Benz DB 109-021 turboprop (based upon HeS 011) of mixed construction with countershaft, gearing and 2.8m (9ft 2in) diameter three-bladed variable pitch propeller. Take-off rating: 1,492kW (2,000hp) with 770kP (1,697lb) residual thrust.

Dimensions

Span	8.00m	26ft 2in
Sweep	30° at 0.25 chord	
Wing area	17.0m²	182.9ft²
Aspect ratio	3.76 : 1	
Length overall	9.00m	29ft 6in
Height overall	2.65m	8ft 8in

Weights

Empty equipped	3,585kg	7,903lb
Fuel load	1,128kg	2,486lb
Loaded	5,000kg	11,022lb
Max wing loading	294kg/m²	60.2lb/ft²

Performance

Max speed at ground level	845km/h	525mph
at 10,000m (32,800ft)	910km/h	565mph
Initial rate of climb	40m/sec	131ft/sec
Max range	1,460km	907 miles
	at 10,000m	at 32,800ft
Endurance (at ground level)	40 min (fully loaded)	
	70 min (economic cruise)	

Armament

Standard armament: two fuselage-mounted 20mm MG 213 cannon firing through propeller disc plus two wing-mounted 20mm cannon.
Projected variants:
two fuselage-mounted 30mm MK 103 cannon, or
two fuselage-mounted 30mm MK 103 plus two wing-mounted 15mm MG 151/15 cannon, or
two fuselage-mounted 20mm MG 151/15 plus two wing-mounted 30mm MK 108 cannon.

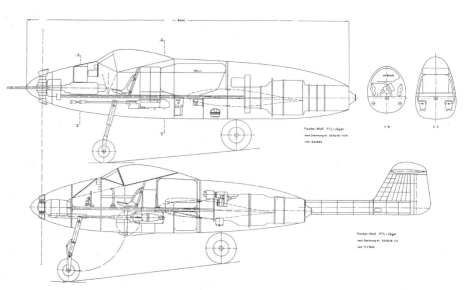

Focke-Wulf's turboprop strike fighter; the seventh design.

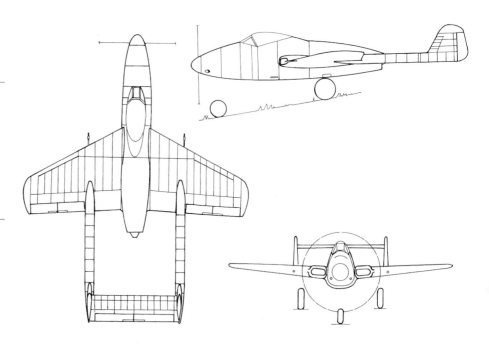

Focke-Wulf turboprop strike fighter
November 1944

Powerplant

Daimler-Benz DB 109-021 turboprop (based upon He S 011) of mixed construction with countershaft, gearing and 2.8m (9ft 2in) diameter three-bladed variable pitch propeller. Take-off rating: 2,984kW (2,000hp) with 770kP (1,697lb) residual thrust.

Dimensions

Span	8.20m	26ft 10½in
Sweep	31° at 0.25 chord	
Thickness ratio	10%	
Wing area	17.5m²	188.3ft²
Aspect ratio	3.84 : 1	
Length overall	10.80m	35ft 4½in
Height overall	3.10m	10ft 1in

Weights

Empty equipped	3,396kg	7,486lb
Fuel load	1,200kg	2,645lb
Loaded	4,900kg	10,802lb
Max wing loading	280kg/m²	57.3lb/ft²

Performance

Max speed	900km/h at 9,000m	559mph at 30,000ft
Initial rate of climb	39m/sec	128ft/sec
Max range, fully loaded	1,020km at 7,000m	633 miles at 23,000ft
Endurance, fully loaded at 7,000m		1.17 hours

Armament

One engine-mounted 30mm MK 103 cannon firing through propeller hub, plus two fuselage-mounted 20mm MG 213 cannon.

Having now recognised the inherent deficiencies of the basic Flitzer concept, Focke-Wulf completely redesigned the turboprop strike fighter in a new, aerodynamically improved form.

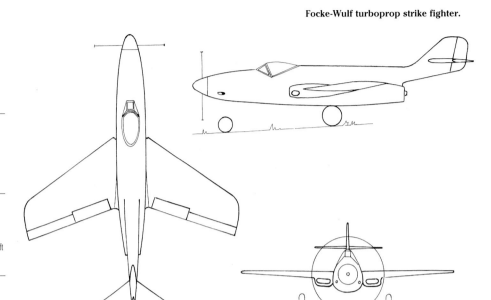

Focke-Wulf turboprop strike fighter.

Focke-Wulf twin-engined jet fighter

November 1944

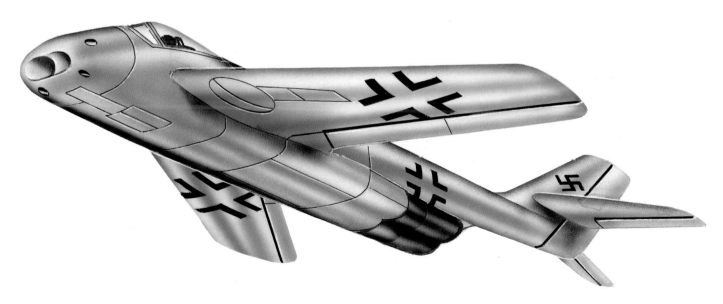

Based upon the work carried out on the single-jet Me 262 successor and the turboprop strike fighter, Prof Tank submitted a proposal for a relatively heavy twin-jet fighter which could also be employed as a fighter-bomber and in the role of long range patrol fighter.

Powerplant

Two Heinkel HeS 011 each rated at 1,300kP (2,865lb) static thrust.

Dimensions

Span	12.50m	41ft 0in
Sweep	40° at 0.25 chord	
Wing area	39.0m²	419ft²
Aspect ratio	4.0 : 1	
Length overall	12.75m	41ft 9½in
Height overall	4.06m	13ft 3½in

Above dimensions same for all three intended roles: fighter (F), fighter-bomber (FB) and long range fighter (LR)

Weights

Loaded	F	7,400kg	16,313lb
	FB	9,000kg	19,841lb
	LR	8,850kg	19,510lb
Max wing loading	F	190kg/m²	38.9lb/ft²
	FB	231kg/m²	47.3lb/ft²
	LR	227kg/m²	46.4lb/ft²

Performance

Max speed at	F	1,078km/h	669mph
8,000m (26,250ft)	FB	1,074km/h	667mph
	LR	1,068km/h	663mph
Initial rate of climb	F	25.4m/sec	83ft/sec
	FB	20.6m/sec	67ft/sec
	LR	20.2m/sec	66ft/sec
Max range at 11,000m (36,000ft) at max economic cruise			
	F	1,370km	851 miles
	FB	1,640km	1,019 miles
	LR	2,440km	1,516 miles
Max endurance at 11,000m (36,000ft) at max economic cruise			
	F	2.17 hours	
	FB	2.48 hours	
	LR	3.78 hours	
Service ceiling	F	15,000m	49,000ft
	FB	14,500m	47,500ft
	LR	14,000m	46,000ft

Armament

Four 30mm MK 108 cannon or four 20mm MG 213 cannon in nose (all variants) plus: 1,000kg (2,200lb) jettisonable load (LR).

In terms of dimensions, weights and engine power, these figures are an excellent example of the realistic nature of Focke-Wulf's projected figures. The Focke-Wulf rate of climb for the fighter-bomber and the long range variant was about 15 minutes to 10,700m.

An interesting comparison study is provided by the data for the American McDonnell XF-88, prototype for the well known F-101 Voodoo which saw service in large numbers.

Compared to the swept-wing Me 262 development project (HG III), the Focke-Wulf proposal would certainly have been slower but, due to its lower wing loading, it would have proved superior to the former in both the climb and turn and, not least, in its weapon and load carrying capacity.

Further work on the design was deferred in favour of the single-jet fighter project, but it subsequently served as the basis for Focke-Wulf's jet-powered night and all-weather fighter designs.

McDonnell XF-88 comparison data

Powerplant

Two Westinghouse XJ34-WE-13 turbojets each rated at (1,361kg) static thrust.

Dimensions

Span	39ft 8in	12.09m
Sweep	35° at 0.25 chord	
Wing area	350ft²	32.5m²
Aspect ratio	4.5 : 1	
Length overall	54ft 1½in	16.50m
Height overall	17ft 3in	5.26m

Weights

Empty equipped	12,140lb	5,507kg
Take-off	18,496lb	8,390kg
Max wing loading	52.8lb/ft²	258kg/m²

Performance

Max speed at ground level	641mph	1,032km/h
Rate of climb to 35,000ft (10,700m)	14.5 minutes	
Range	1,736 miles	2,795km

Armament

Six 20mm cannon

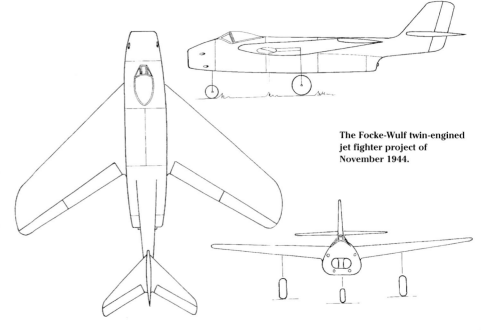

The Focke-Wulf twin-engined jet fighter project of November 1944.

McDonnell XF-88; predecessor of the F-101 Voodoo long range fighter.

Had detailed discussions about this design taken place, strong criticism would no doubt have been voiced about the length of the intake duct required for the two jets, the amount of additional space this occupied and the increased drag thus generated. Possible solutions, such as wing root leading edge or fuselage side intakes, could then have been implemented by Focke-Wulf; as was successfully demonstrated some years later in the USA by, among others, McDonnell with their XF-88 (which was then developed into the F-101 Voodoo) and F3H Demon.

HEINKEL

The name Ernst Heinkel will forever be linked to two outstanding and pioneering events in aviation history: the creation of the first aircraft to be powered by a liquid-fuel rocket motor, the He176; and the development and construction of the world's first jet aircraft, the He178. The powerplant of this latter epoch making machine, which first flew on 27th August 1939, was likewise a product wholly of the Heinkel factory. Behind both it was Heinkel himself who was the decisive driving force. Like Messerschmitt, he too had set himself the task of building the fastest aircraft in the world. Consequently he regarded the creation of extremely fast, superior fighter aircraft as his own particular forte.

When the RLM discontinued tests and further development of the rocket-powered He 176, Heinkel attempted to build upon the success of the purely experimental He178 by seeking a contract for the series production of its immediate successor, the twin-jet He 280. But for a variety of reasons major success eluded him. It was his rival Messerschmitt who came out on top with contracts for a piston-engined pursuit fighter (Bf109), for a rocket-powered interceptor (Me163) and for a twin-jet fighter (Me262).

Despite these setbacks the Heinkel works remained involved in jet fighter development until the end of the war, making their mark time and again with a number of highly individual proposals and projects. In 1943, following an RLM directive, they produced their first designs for a Jumo 004-powered fighter. Designated the P.1069, this was very similar in layout to Focke-Wulf's Design number two of June 1943.

When it became apparent that the performance of the unswept, mid-wing P.1069 would not come up to expectations, two further fighter projects appeared before the end of that same year. Under the guiding hand of Heinkel's head of projects Siegfried Günter, these explored new territory; the P.1070 pro-

posal being a twin-jet, tail-less aircraft, while the P.1071, similarly powered by two Junkers Jumo 004 turbojets, featured an asymmetrical fuselage arrangement. Unfortunately, there is no documentation available relating to this work.

Project P.1073 of July 1944 represented a most interesting venture. Here, probably for the first time in the history of aviation technology, Günter submitted a proposal for a fighter based upon the concept of 'area rule' as patented by Junkers in March 1944. Heinkel returned to this project at the beginning of September to provide the basis for their first proposals to meet the requirement for the single-jet successor to the Me 262.

Günter even used the P.1073 as a starting point when submitting his first designs in response to the so-called crash programme to design and build a 'Single-seat fighter of the simplest construction to be powered by the BMW 003'. Consequently, the first documents relating to this project, also of September 1944, bore this designation. Heinkel was awarded the contract and the aircraft was built in record time under the RLM designation 8-162 (or He162).

Günter was less successful with his proposals for a successor to the Me262. At the beginning of 1945 he therefore decided to embark upon a completely new design designated the P.1078. But this bold venture, too, failed to win favour with the Deutsches Forschungsinstitut für Luftfahrt (DVL - German Aviation Experimental Establishment) who had been brought in to act as consultants. They objected above all to the, in their perception, insufficient maximum speed and to the 'risk-associated' layout. This judgement decided the official bodies against awarding a development contract. In the summer of 1945 Siegfried Günter and part of his team continued work on this project under American supervision at Penzing near Landsberg and even went on to develop several alternatives.

Heinkel capitalised on the head start given by the pioneering He178 to produce the twin-jet He280. Production success went instead to Messerschmitt.

Heinkel P.1073 fast jet fighter

July 1944

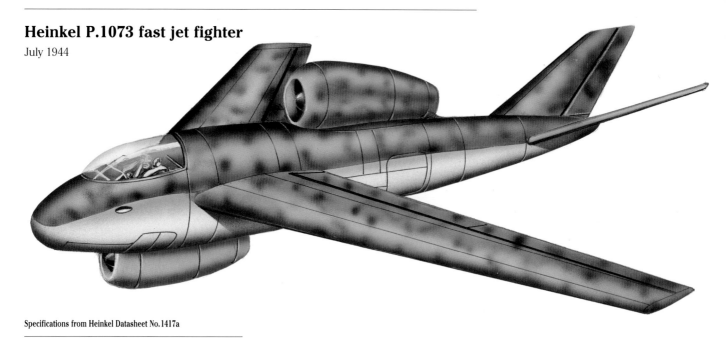

Specifications from Heinkel Datasheet No.1417a

Powerplant

Two Heinkel HeS 011 each rated at 1,500kP (3,306lb) static thrust or two Junkers Jumo 004 each rated at 1,015kP (2,237lb) static thrust.

Dimensions

Span	12.00m	39ft 3in
Sweep	30° at 0.25 chord	
Wing area	22.0m²	236ft²
Aspect ration	6.5 : 1	
Profile thickness	10%	
Length overall	10.32m	33ft 10in
Height overall	3.40m	11ft 1in

Weights

Empty equipped	HeS	4,410kg	9,722lb
	Jumo	4,110kg	9,060lb
Take-off	HeS	6,100kg	13,447lb*
	Jumo	5,800kg	12,786lb*
Initial wing loading	HeS	277kg/m²	56.7lb/ft²
	Jumo	264kg/m²	54.0lb/ft²

* each with 1,500kg (3,306lb) of fuel in protected fuselage tanks

Performance

Max speed,	HeS	1,010kmh/h	627mph
	Jumo	940km/h	584mph
Initial rate of climb,	HeS	35m/sec	114ft/sec
	Jumo	31m/sec	101ft/sec
Time to 11,000m	HeS	10 minutes	(36,000ft)
	Jumo	14.5 minutes	
Service ceiling	HeS	14,000m (approx)	46,000ft
	Jumo	12,000m	39,250ft
Max range		1,000km	621 miles
Max endurance	HeS	59 minutes	
	Jumo	76 minutes	

With 1,000kg (2,204lb) additional fuel in two underwing tanks:

Max range	HeS	1,500km	932 miles
	Jumo	1,600km	994 miles
Max endurance	HeS	100 minutes	
	Jumo	128 minutes	

Armament

Three 20mm MG 151/2a cannon below pilot's seat to left and right of the cockpit.

In a similar manner to Blohm und Voss with their P.197, Heinkel also attempted, under commission from the RLM, to improve the flight performance of the Me 262 by use of the most modern aerodynamics. The expected entry into service of enemy jet fighters meant that, most important of all, a higher maximum speed was required. In addition, the project engineers were also considering the use of more powerful engines.

Part of the specification stated 'If enemy single-seat jets enter service, the superiority of the Me 262 can no longer be counted upon because its conventional unswept wing, with the underslung engine nacelles, creates too much drag.' This was a reference to area rule; it went on to say: 'A new design can only be justified if it offers a substantial increase in critical speed over the Me 262. Such an increase presupposes the thinnest possible, sharply swept wing but also, above all, a material improvement in the design and arrangement of the engine nacelles.' In closing, it read: 'The P.1073 jet fighter has been designed for the HeS 011 powerplant. Until this reaches series production the Jumo 004 will be fitted. The latter offers a more limited, but nonetheless considerable increase in maximum speed compared to that of the Me 262.'

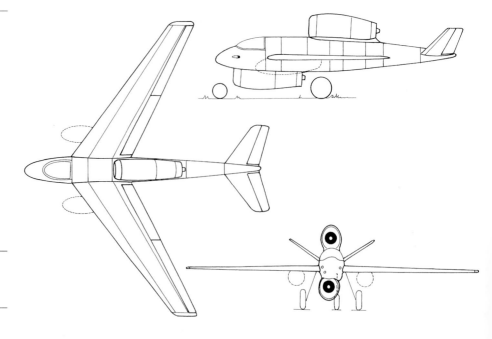

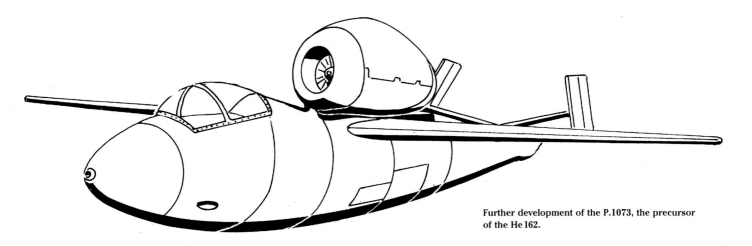

Further development of the P.1073, the precursor of the He 162.

In the single-jet further developments of the P.1073 it was the under-fuselage engine which was deleted. With its limited ground clearance and the positioning of the nose-wheel immediately ahead of the intake, this would undoubtedly have given rise to much criticism in Luftwaffe circles. On the other hand, Heinkel's designers were convinced that a jet engine mounted beneath the fuse-lage improved both visibility for the pilot and his chances of survival if forced to bail out. Another unresolved factor was the influence which Mach disturbances around the cockpit canopy would have on the airflow in front of a dorsal turbojet intake.

The RLM refused to listen to these argu-ments, and so the proposals derived from the P.1073 for a Volksjäger (People's Fighter) and for a 'High Performance Fighter' to be pow-ered by the HeS 011 were fitted with a dorsal-mounted 'piggy-back' engine.

HORTEN

Walter and Reimar Horten

The Horten brothers foresaw the advantages of their flying-wing designs being applied pri-marily to relatively large, long or ultra long range aircraft. So, strictly speaking, they pro-duced only one single-seat fighter design dur-ing the war years; albeit one which would reach supersonic speeds. The philosophy be-hind the two brothers' research reflected that of Dr Alexander Lippisch, who was working on similar projects in Vienna.

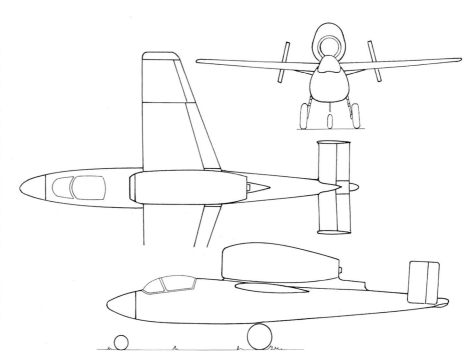

Horten Ho X (Ho XIIIb) underside view reconstructed from available data by Ingolf Meyer.

Horten Ho X (Ho XIIIb)
1944/45

Work on this scheme began with the construction of free-flying models, each weighing 8-10kg (17-22lb) and featuring a sharply swept wing of some 3m (9ft 9⅓in) span. These were then used to carry out the first practical flight tests in Göttingen.

In 1943, in order to gain quick results from a manned aircraft, the small company used their Ho IIIb flying-wing glider as the basis to build an experimental glider incorporating

Crew
Pilot in prone position in cockpit with slightly curved Plexiglas canopy faired into wing contour.

Powerplant
One Heinkel HeS 011A-0 rated at 1,300kP (2,865lb) static thrust; later a more powerful version with 1,500kP (3,306lb) static thrust; provision for additional rocket booster.

Dimensions
Span	7.20m	23ft 7in
Sweep	Delta with 70° leading edge	
Wing area	37.8m²	406ft²
Aspect ratio	1.37 : 1	
Profile thickness	7%	
Length overall	10.0m	32ft 9½in
Height overall (approx)	4.20m	13ft 8in

Weights
Take-off	6,000-7,000kg	13,227-15,432lb
Max wing loading	160-185kg/m²	32.7-37.8lb/ft²

Performance
Max speed	1,200km/h at 6,000m (M= 1.07)	745mph at 19,750ft
Service ceiling	15,000m	49,000ft
Range	2,000km	1,242 miles

Armament
Three or four 30mm MK 108, or three or four 30mm MK 213C cannon.

60° leading edge sweep. For camouflage purposes, and to disguise any connection to work on the Ho X fighter, this 12.4m (40ft) wingspan aircraft was given the designation Ho XIIIa. Further work on the supersonic delta continued under the designation of Ho XIIIb. Flight tests with the Ho XIIIa commenced with the first flight on 27th November 1944 and were only terminated by the ending of the war. During that time 20 flights, totalling some ten hours, provided valuable information on the slow speed flight characteristics of the sharply swept flying-wing planform.

Details as to the final layout of the supersonic delta are contradictory. The British Royal Aircraft Establishment Report FA.259/1 of October 1945, for example, states that:

In appearance the Horten X resembles the Lippisch designs for high speed and supersonic aircraft, especially the P.13. Horten declared that he had not known anything of Lippisch's work until arriving in London.

The major difference in the design lies in the fact that Horten regarded a special vertical surface as unnecessary, whereas Lippisch favoured a very large vertical rudder assembly.

It is possible that this last sentence does not refer specifically to the Horten Ho X, but rather to the design philosophy as a whole. In the 1982 book *Flying-Wing, the Story of Horten Aircraft 1933-1960* Reimar Horten himself remarks:

With a half span of only 3.6m and a length of 10m, aerodynamic rudders were no longer sufficient. The Ho X (XIIIb) was therefore equipped with a keelfin from the start. Furthermore, in the trans-sonic flight range an aerodynamic rudder would generate shock waves on the wing's upper surface.

In further work on supersonic aircraft carried out in Argentina in 1953, Reimar Horten and his then colleague, Dr Karl Nickel, also made provision for a relatively large rudder assembly from the outset.

Illustrations of the Ho X and Ho XIIIb often appear in literature. But these do not resemble the descriptions given by Reimar Horten in the above-mentioned book. Using this source, and with the aid of the British report already quoted, which also includes an illustration, an attempt has been made to reconstruct the aircraft. All drawings, calculations and other documentation were presumably lost in the final days of the war.

In 1945 a wooden glider version was under construction, parts of which were found by the British after the capitulation. In a second phase of the development this glider was to have been motorised by fitting an Argus As 10c engine. Only after thorough tests at up to 500km/h (310mph) was the proposed HeS 011-powered supersonic fighter to have been built. This step-by-step procedure adopted by the Horten works was similar to that followed during their development of the earlier Ho IX. From this it is clear that the gestation period of the Ho X would certainly have required several years.

Together with the work of Dr Lippisch, this aircraft represents the first steps on the road to the modern high speed, jet-powered delta-winged aircraft of today. Many years after the war the British tested an aerodynamic concept closely resembling the Horten design with their Handley Page HP.115. The data gathered in subsonic flight by this short span delta with a leading edge sweep of almost 70° was incorporated in the Anglo-French Concorde supersonic transport programme.

The Ho XIIIb as represented in post-war literature.

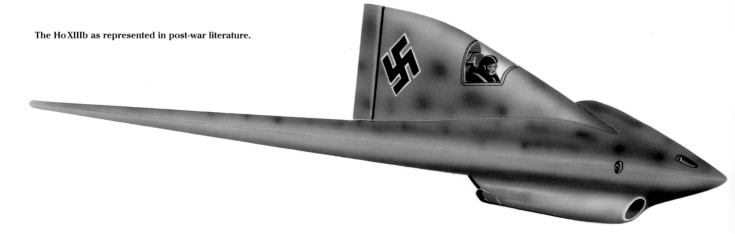

LIPPISCH

Dr Alexander Lippisch was an eminent man of science and extraordinarily gifted designer, and like the Horten brothers, occupies a special place in this survey of German aviation projects. He had at his disposal what was, in effect, his own large aircraft works where his revolutionary ideas, studies and designs – all far ahead of their time – could be realised. Touched by a genius which could at times be decidedly impetuous, he was always dependent on collaboration with established aircraft manufacturers, an arrangement which was not without its complications and which did not always run smoothly. After all, each of these manufacturers had their own ideas, development programmes and chief designers who did not, indeed should not, want to be made to feel inferior to Lippisch and his work.

It was not until he moved to Vienna that he was given his own works with a staff of 110. This factory had previously produced water heaters, and the only knowledge of aircraft manufacturing it possessed was purely from hearsay. The conversion to the building of wooden aircraft was particularly difficult, as almost all of the necessary machinery was lacking. By the end of the war, apart from a few models, they had succeeded in producing just the centre fuselage section of the Delta VI V1.

After more than four years of collaboration with the Messerschmitt company at Augsburg

– years marked with successes, but also with jealousies and petty intrigues – Dr Lippisch became head of the Luftfahrtforschungsanstalt (LFA – Aviation Research Institute) in Vienna, which was part of the LFA Munich-Ottobrunn organisation.

During his time with Messerschmitt, apart from the Me 163, Lippisch had been responsible for a wide range of designs intended for the most diverse of purposes and roles. The studies into jet fighters which he carried out there during the early war years are covered in some detail as these clearly document the very beginnings, the first tentative steps, towards today's modern single-jet fighters. While so doing, Lippisch had anticipated much which would not become common knowledge and practice in aviation technology until many years later. Even at the end of the war, his was still a progressive influence at Messerschmitt; as witness the Enzian surface-to-air missile, the P.1111 and P.1112 tailless fighter designs and the projected P.1108 long range bomber.

In Vienna he concentrated more and more on new wing forms and new methods of propulsion. He broke new ground with his work, begun in the 1920s, on the delta wing and with his studies in the field of ram jet engines, in particular of new types of combustion chambers and the use of solid fuels.

In addition to this pioneering research

work, which he backed up with wind tunnel tests and flight trials using models, there was also a whole range of projects which could be realised fairly quickly and which Lippisch wanted to build in experimental and operational form in collaboration with other manufacturers such as Henschel. Examples of the latter were the ram jet-powered P.13a and 'b, and the twin-jet Delta VI fighter, whose performance was superior to that of the Me 262 but which was constructed of 'non-essential' tubular steel and plywood.

One last observation regarding the designations used by Lippisch. At Messerschmitt he began with Project (P).01 and ended with P.20. He retained most of these designations after the move to LFA in Vienna, but renumbered a few and altered the original design or role of others several times. In Augsburg, for example, his design in competition to the Do 335 was designated P.13. Later, in Vienna, he used P.13 to identify the ram jet-powered fighter mentioned above. Work on the P.11 fast jet bomber was also begun at Messerschmitt, was initially continued as such at LFA in Vienna, but then formed the basis for a fighter which, referring back to even earlier work, was finally designated 'Delta VI'. This represented an almost completely new aircraft when compared to the original. Examples such as these can, and have, led to a certain amount of understandable confusion.

Lippisch Project P.01

In January 1939 Alexander Lippisch and his team had left the Deutsches Forschungsinstitut für Segelflug (DFS – German Research Institute for Sailplanes) at Darmstadt to go to Messerschmitt at Augsburg. There, backed by the industrial giant and on behalf of the RLM, he was to work on a project for a tail-less experimental aircraft to be powered by the new-style rocket engine. Upon the outbreak of war, however, the Ministry withdrew the bulk of its support for the futuristic 'Projekt X' aircraft which, for reasons of secrecy, was given the RLM number 8-163; a number which had already been allocated to another Messerschmitt design intended as a competitor to the Fieseler Fi 156 Storch liaison aircraft.

Lippisch, who had foreseen this development, therefore turned his mind, in keeping with the times, towards a military application for his project. From the designs of April 1939 there thus emerged an interceptor fighter which, after the successful flights of the DFS 194 experimental aircraft and the considerably more advanced Me 163A, again found wide support from the RLM. The end result of all these endeavours was the emergence of the now familiar operational Me 163B Komet. (Pure rocket-propelled fighters are a study in their own right and are dealt with in this book only when they relate to turbojet or mixed-powerplant developments.)

Back in 1939, and with some justification,

Lippisch did not entirely trust the new rocket engine, which was then still under development and suffering all sorts of problems. He therefore kept all his options open with regards to the powerplant of his proposed operational fighter, not wishing to see the whole project brought to a halt should – as seemed quite likely – the rocket engine prove a complete failure. So, in addition to the rocket-powered P.01 proposals, he produced a number of designs to be powered by the equally new turbojet engine, of which no operational examples – it must be admitted – existed either. Nonetheless, Lippisch's work was distinguished, above all, by its combination of a new form of propulsion allied to new aerodynamic principles. Taken together, these should have given the aircraft excellent flight characteristics, which unfortunately it is now impossible to substantiate due to a complete lack of performance data.

These projects represent the first tail-less aircraft to be powered by jet propulsion. The tests on wing sweep carried out at this time in the wind tunnel of the Aerodynamische Versuchsanstalt (AVA – Aerodynamic Research Institute) in Göttingen were almost certainly used as a basis for the design.

Initially, as a military variant of the Me 163 experimental aircraft, the P.01 was given the RLM designation 8-263. Then in 1941 it received the designation Me 327. But when the experimental aircraft was finally designated the Me 163A, and the direct operational derivative became the Me 163B, the RLM number 263 was allocated to the further development of the latter. In the autumn of 1944 project Me 327 was cancelled in favour of the Me 163B.

Armed Me 163A within project P.01

The origins of the Me 163A experimental aircraft, which made its first unpowered flight on 13th February 1941, lay in the DFS 39. Construction of the Me 163A was carried out by Lippisch and his team in the spring and summer of 1939. When Lippisch received the first, still vague, details of the turbojet engine, he produced an initial study in April 1939 for a small experimental aircraft featuring a nose intake and an unusual – for him – short span wing layout somewhat reminiscent of the Lockheed F-104 Starfighter.

Dimensions

Span	7.50m	24ft 7in
Sweep*	approx 24°	
Wing area	19m²	204ft²
Aspect ratio	2.96 : 1	
Length overall	6.60m	21ft 7in
Height overall	3.20m	10ft 6in
*reduced sweep in region of the ailerons		

Weights

Empty equipped	2,200kg	4,850lb
Loaded weight	4,270kg with	9,413lb with
	2,100 litres of fuel	461 gallons of fuel
Me 163A	2,400kg	5,291lb
Initial wing loading	225kg/m²	46lb/ft²
Me 163B	203kg/m²	41.5lb/ft²

Performance   No data available.

Armament
Two 15mm MG 151 cannon in wing roots.

Lippisch P.01-111
20th October 1939

In a speech delivered in July 1965, Dr Lippisch explained that this design was, in effect, an armed version of the Me 163A. The powerplant was to be an early Junkers turbojet as conceived by Max Adolf Müller. The wing displayed the usual Department 'L' (the Lippisch design bureau) form and sweep, albeit with a smaller aspect ratio when compared to the Me 163A. See specification table to left.

LUFTWAFFE SECRET PROJECTS: FIGHTERS 1939-1945

Lippisch P.01-112

12th February 1940

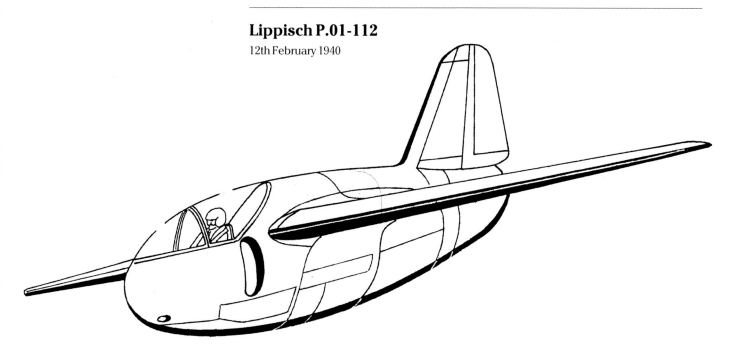

This drawing number was at first assigned in January 1940 to an Me 163A with an enlarged fuselage which was to be used as an unarmed experimental aircraft to study the new boundary layer effect technology. By blowing air across the upper surface of the outer wing in the area of the ailerons, the designers hoped to be able significantly to improve maximum lift and low speed stability while, at the same time, ensuring aileron efficiency under all flight conditions. The necessary air for the system was to be tapped from both engine side air intakes.

In February 1940 this study resulted in a four-gun fighter powered by two BMW P.3304 turbojets buried side-by-side in the fuselage; an arrangement much favoured in later years. On this aircraft, too, Lippisch employed the almost obligatory extendable landing skid and retractable tailskid. He also envisaged the use of a small retractable auxiliary undercarriage. The compact nature of the design did not allow for anything larger. With the exception of these somewhat primitive take-off and landing devices, the whole concept of the fighter had a very modern feel to it.

Powerplant

Two BMW 109-002 (P.3304) turbojets (with Weinrich contra-rotating compressors) each rated at 600kP (1,322lb) static thrust.

Dimensions

Span	8.00m	26ft 3in
Sweep	32°	
Wing area, approx	16m²	172ft²
Aspect ratio	4.0 : 1	
Length overall	7.50m	24ft 7in
Height overall	3.20m	10ft 5in

Weights

Although no weight figures are available, it may be assumed that the loaded weight would have been between 4,000kg and 4,500kg (8,818 and 9,920lb).

Armament

Two 7.92mm MG 17 machine guns in engine air intakes, plus two 15mm MG 151 cannon in forward fuselage below cockpit.

Although no performance data are available, it may be assumed on the basis of the aircraft's layout and engine power that the maximum speed would have been in the region of 1,000km/h (621mph). Like Messerschmitt, Lippisch was also attempting to obtain maximum performance from the smallest possible airframe commensurate with the intended powerplant.

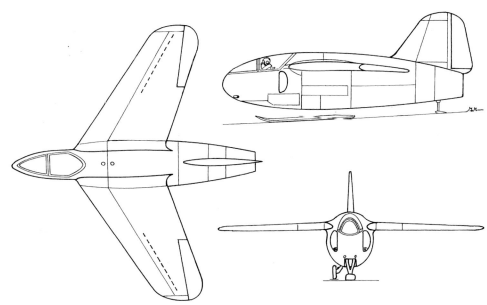

Lippisch P.01-113

17th July 1940

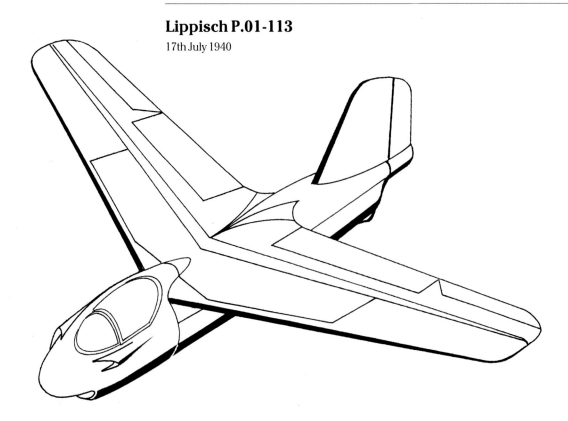

Beginning in July 1940 there appeared a number of fighter proposals which, after the war, Alexander Lippisch was to describe as being work based upon the 'real' P.01 concept. The improved, almost laminar-like, high speed wing profile with its altered shape bore very little relationship to the wing of the Me 163A.

For the first time Department 'L' was examining a mixed-powerplant interceptor fighter designed for high speed climb. This powerplant concept was to reach its culmination - at the same time finale – in 1957 in the British Saunders-Roe SR.53.

The shoulder-mounted swept wing featured particularly large, Flettner-balanced landing flaps.

Powerplant

One BMW turbojet rated in the 600kP (1,322lb) class, either the P.3302 (predecessor of the BMW 003) or the P.3304 (Weinrich/BMW 002), plus one HWK RII-203 liquid fuel rocket motor providing 150-750kP (330-1,653lb) controllable thrust.

Dimensions

Span	9.00m	29ft 6in
Sweep	32°	
Wing area, approx	18m²	192ft²
Aspect ratio	4.5 : 1	
Length overall	6.75m	22ft 2in
Height overall	3.00m	9ft 9⅞in

Armament

Two 15mm MG 151 cannon to left and right of the cockpit.

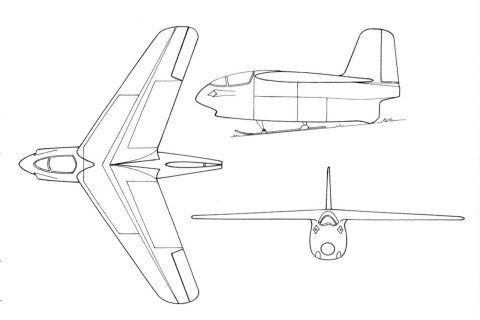

Lippisch P.01-116

12th June 1941

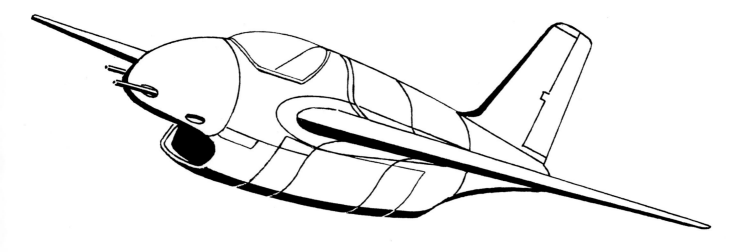

After a break of almost a year, occupied by work on the DFS 194 and testing the Me 163A, Lippisch returned to the P.01.

In the interim, precise data on forthcoming turbojet powerplants had been issued and results from the AVA were also being made ever more widely available to industry.

The shape of the P.01-116 design had begun to display a certain similarity to the Me 163B; the change-over from shoulder to mid-wing arrangement being the result of the most recent wind tunnel tests.

The study made no mention of either a landing skid or undercarriage installation.

Powerplant

One BMW 109-002 (P.3304) rated at 600kP (1,322lb) static thrust.

Dimensions

Span	9.00m	29ft 6in
Sweep	27°	
Wing area, approx	18m²	192ft²
Aspect ratio	4.5 : 1	
Length overall	7.06m	23ft 2in

Armament

Two 7.92mm MG 17 machine guns in the nose, plus two 15mm MG 151 cannon in the lower fuselage section to left and right of the engine air intake.

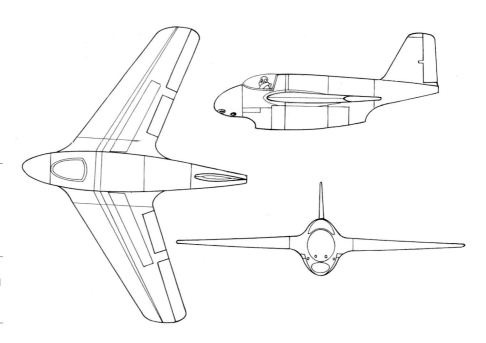

Lippisch P.01-115 interceptor

2nd July 1941

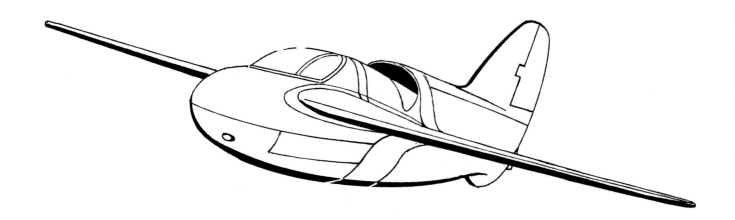

In contrast to the P.01-113, on the P.01-115 the turbojet and the rocket engine had now exchanged places. This resulted in a dorsal air intake situated behind the cockpit, a somewhat unusual arrangement but one which was to be found on a number of post-war designs (eg the North American F-107A, Avro 707B and Sud-Est SE.2410 Grognard). And with the wing, which he had already used on the previous design, Lippisch appears to have found the ultimate form he had been seeking.

This obviously unfinished drawing represented the last study in the P.01 design series in which Lippisch intended to use a turbojet engine. From now on, until the project was discontinued altogether, Department 'L' concentrated solely on liquid fuel rocket motors. When construction of the Me 163B commenced in the autumn of that same year, Lippisch was able to make full use of this extensive preliminary work. In 1943, with the P.20, he resumed his attempts to develop a jet-powered Me 163.

Powerplant

One BMW 109-002 (P/3304) rated at 600kP (1,322lb) static thrust, plus one liquid fuel rocket motor manufactured by Hellmuth Walter, Kiel.

Dimensions

Span	9.00m	29ft 6in
Sweep	27°	
Wing area, approx	18m²	192ft²
Aspect ratio	4.5 : 1	
Length overall	6.75m	22ft 2in

Armament

Two 15mm MG 151 cannon easily accessible in underside of forward fuselage.

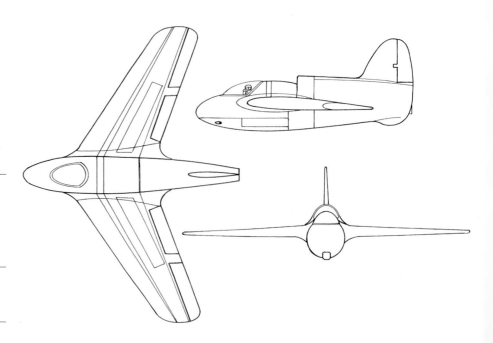

Lippisch P.09

28th October 1941

On 6th August 1941 the Junkers T1 'special engine' achieved a thrust of 765kg (1,686lb) on the test stand, thereby easily exceeding the design requirement of 600kg (1,322lb). And on 25th October 1941 Dr Anselm Franz of the Junkers Otto-Marder-Works (OMV) at Dessau successfully completed a first extended test run of the new powerplant with highly satisfying results. It was clear from this that the engine had great potential.

While Professor Messerschmitt was working closely alongside Department 'L' on his Me 262 and its somewhat problematical BMW powerplant, Lippisch put forward a design for a twin-jet fighter in which he envisaged using the highly promising Dessau engine from the outset. In designing this project Lippisch's colleague Rentel used experiences gained from the P.01 and the Me 163.

As far as is known, project P.09 was the first to propose a powerplant situated in the wing root. Messerschmitt was later to use this arrangement in many fast jet fighter designs.

The advantages of the P.09 were the relatively short development period which would be required, the limited risk inherent in that development, the simple construction and the aircraft's low wing loading.

Against that had to be placed the RLM's un-derstandable reluctance to support yet a third parallel development alongside the already well advanced Me 262 and He 280 projects.

Together with his work on the Me 163B, Lippisch turned his attention increasingly to the development of a fast bomber. There still exists a description of a fast bomber, dated May 1942, which had also been given the number P.09. But this design bears hardly any resemblance at all to the aircraft described above.

Powerplant

Two Junkers T1 'special engines', each rated at approx. 600kP (1,322lb) static thrust, located in fuselage/wing junction.

Dimensions

Span	11.60m	38ft 0in
Sweep	30°	
Wing area, approx	29.5m²	317ft²
Aspect ratio	4.56 : 1	
Length overall	7.10m	23ft 3in
Height overall	3.20m	10ft 5in

Weights

Take off	6,000 to 6,500kg	13,227 to 14,329lb

Armament

Four 15mm MG 151 cannon in easily accessible weapons tray.

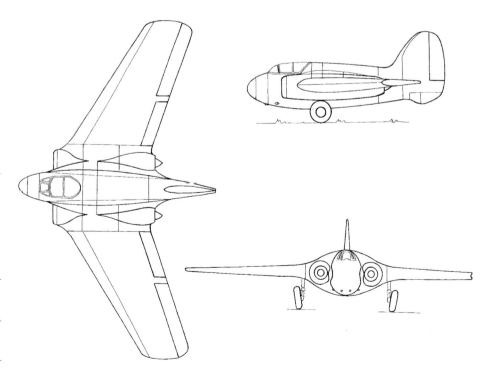

Lippisch P.12 fighter and fast bomber

30th September 1942

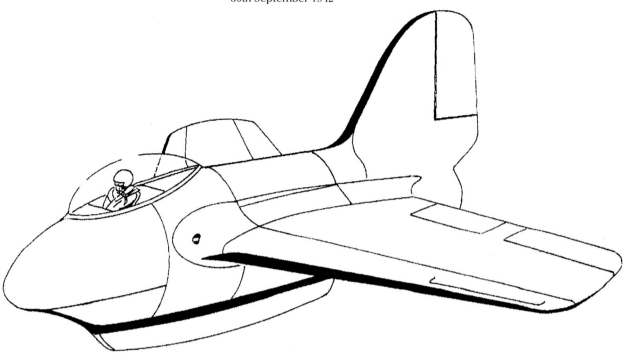

The first details of a new turbojet engine in the 3,000kg (6,613lb) rating range had already reached Augsburg by 1942. The BMW company were planning to produce a jet derivative to this specification from their BMW 028 turboprop engine, which was already under development.

Department 'L' lost no time. Their drawing boards were soon occupied by plans combining this big, 5m (16ft 5in) long powerplant with a suitably enlarged and modified Me 163B airframe. The project engineers studied the installation for use in the fighter and fast bomber roles.

The blown canopy, would have offered the pilot outstanding all-round vision.

Powerplant

One BMW P.3303 (predecessor of BMW 018) rated at 3,000kP (6,613lb) static thrust (projected).

Dimensions (fighter)

Span	11.00m	36ft 0in
Sweep	26°	
Wing area, approx	29m²	312ft²
Aspect ratio	4.17 : 1	
Length overall	7.00m	22ft 10in
Height overall	3.90m	12ft 9½in

Armament

Two 15mm MG 151 cannon in wing roots.

A weak point of the concept was, without doubt, the central fixed skid. In Vienna Lippisch was later to use the project number 12 for a small ramjet-powered experimental delta.

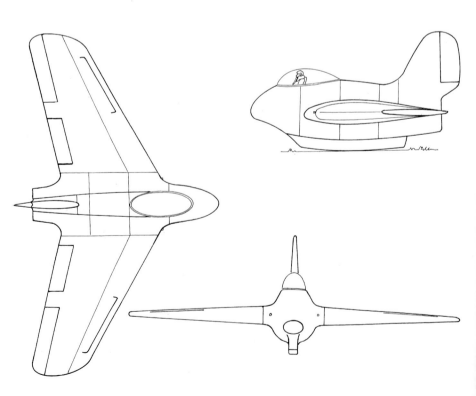

Continuing problems with the rocket motor led Lippisch to consider alternative powerplants for the Me 163B whose airframe and aerodynamics were, by this time, already successfully proven. The DB 605-powered Me 334 and the extensive studies undertaken on the P.20 jet fighter are just two examples. The one time chief test pilot and world's record flyer Dr Ing Hermann Wurster was responsible for the latter.

This fighter study also represented the final project carried out under the leadership of Alexander Lippisch for the Messerschmitt company. On 28th April 1943 Department 'L' disbanded. Lippisch moved to Vienna, taking most of his team with him.

Had work on the P.20 continued, and had the RLM seen fit to put the pressure on, it would have resulted in a desperately needed, superior fighter of simple construction being available in very short order. By the beginning of 1943, moreover, series production of the Me 163B was already under way, several components of which could have been utilised. With the aerodynamic properties already tried and tested, development risks would not have been very great.

Could have, would have ... but the stark reality of the situation was that it was not until the end of 1944, when crisis was already at hand, that an attempt was made to recover lost ground by a futile 'crash action' programme involving the Heinkel He 162. Despite the fact that the growing threat posed by the Allied bombing offensive had already been recognised in 1942, much of 1943 was spent simply upgrading piston-engined fighters to the detriment of the – admittedly more costly – twin-jet Me 262.

Lippisch P.20

16th April 1943

The deep, aerodynamically somewhat less than perfect fuselage permitted a certain freedom in the choice of powerplant. In May 1943, for the purely interceptor role, Dr Wurster investigated the possibility of installing a Walter rocket engine.

In July 1943 Messerschmitt used the P.20, together with a P.1092 proposal, as the subject for a comparison study with the Me 262. The arbitrator, Dipl-Ing Hornung, conceded the benefits of the single-jet fighter in respect of material and labour costs, but considered the Me 262 superior, particularly in terms of load carrying and range. But conditions and operational requirements were changing constantly, and priorities too.

The practicability of the P.20 concept was demonstrated after the war, not just by the British with their Boulton Paul P.111 and Fairey FD.1 experimentals, both of which owed a lot to Lippisch's work, but also, more importantly, by the number of tail-less single-jet interceptors still being built today.

Powerplant
One Junkers Jumo 004C rated at approx 1,000kP (2,204lb) static thrust.

Dimensions		
Span	9.30m	30ft 6in
Sweep	22°	
Wing area	17.3m²	186ft²
Aspect ratio	5.0 : 1	
Length overall	5.73m	18ft 9½in
Height overall	3.02m	9ft 10in

Weights	Source: Technical Specification 90/43	
Empty equipped	2,589kg	5,707lb
Take-off	3,627kg with	7,996lb with
	750kg of fuel	1,653lb of fuel
Max wing loading	205kg/m²	41.9lb/ft²

Performance	Source: Technical Specification 90/43	
Max speed	905km/h	562mph
	at 6,000m	at 19,750ft
Initial rate of climb	18.5m/sec	60ft/sec
Service ceiling	11,600m	38,000ft
Max endurance 1.53 hrs	at 11,000m	36,000ft
Max range	940km	584 miles
	at 11,000m	(36.000ft)

Armament
(Original concept) Two 30mm MK 103 cannon in wing roots, plus two 30mm MK 108 cannon to left and right of the cockpit.

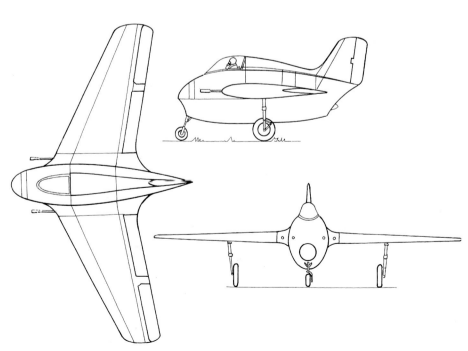

At Augsburg in the late summer of 1942 Alexander Lippisch was working on the P.11 twin-jet fast bomber, designed to carry a weapon load of 1,000kg (2,204lb). A number of variants were proposed, both with and without horizontal tail surfaces, before the P.11 Schnellbomber (Fast Bomber) emerged in its final form in May 1943. But when the Technische Amt in Berlin decided in favour of the Horten brothers' Proposal IX, Lippisch ceased work on the P.11.

In August 1943 he then received an official contract from the RLM to develop a 'Very Fast Bomber' to be based on his earlier research. Lippisch designed a pure delta-winged aircraft with a straight trailing edge. This initially continued to run under the designation P.11. As before, the powerplant was to be a pair of Junkers Jumo 004 turbojets. With the completion of design work on an unpowered glider which was to serve as the initial prototype (V1) for the operational model, the project was renamed 'Delta VI'. At the same time the RLM began to re-exert pressure, bestowing the highest 'DE' priority on the delta which was now to be produced in a fighter version

Lippisch Delta VI twin-jet single-seat fighter
February 1944

as well. The LFA constructed models and mock-ups, carried out wind tunnel tests and slowly made ready for production.

By February 1944 design work on the Delta VI V2, the prototype for the proposed fighter, fighter-bomber and Zerstörer (heavy fighter) models, was nearly complete. It was intended that the actual construction of the four contracted prototypes was to be undertaken by the Henschel works in Berlin. But this remained an intention only. After a lot of to-ing and fro-ing, Lippisch seized the initiative and began building the glider in Vienna at the beginning of 1945. The centre section of the Delta VI V1, the only part of the aircraft to have been completed by the capitulation, fell into the hands of the Americans at Salzburg.

The design and construction of the airframe proved of considerable interest: In contrast to the Delta VI glider, which was built entirely of high grade plywood, the remaining three prototypes were to be of rigid monocoque construction, as were the operational

models when series production commenced. Neither variant made use of a load bearing frame. The stressed skin, formed in simple fashion around a mould, consisted of a filler layer between two outer load bearing layers. The layers were made of Dynal and Tronal, two synthetics developed by Dynamit Nobel of Troisdorf. The synthetics content of the airframe was between 50 and 60%. The aerodynamic shape, the method of construction and the materials used gave the aircraft what would become known as good 'Stealth' characteristics.

The low wing loading promised not only a good climb capability, but also excellent manoeuvrability. From his previous experience with delta-winged aircraft, Lippisch ruled out any danger of a propensity to spin.

On 31st January 1944 Lippisch expressed the hope of being able to commence flight tests with the unpowered glider in April/May; the Delta VI V2, powered by two Jumo 004B turbojets, then being ready to fly in July 1944. By the end of 1944 Henschel had still not begun construction of the prototypes and disagreements between the Berlin firm and Vienna grew increasingly bitter. Nothing is known of the reasons for the delay.

Powerplant

Two Junkers Jumo 004B each rated at 900kP (1,984lb) static thrust, plus four RI-503 solid fuel booster rockets, each of 2,000kP (4,409lb) rated thrust, to assist take-off. The installation of the powerplant was such that, as with the Horten Ho IX, it could not be exchanged for other units without costly modification.

Dimensions

Span	10.80m	35ft 5in
Sweep	37°, leading edge	
Wing area	50.0m²	538ft²
Aspect ratio	2.33 : 1	
Wing profile	relative thickness of 17% at the wing root and 9% at the wing tip.	
Length overall	7.49m	24ft 6in
Height overall	2.76m	9ft 0in

Weights

	(F=fighter, FB=fighter-bomber, Z=Zerstörer)		
Airframe	F	2,000kg (approx)	4,409lb
Loaded	F	7,260kg	16,005lb
		with 3,600 litres	with 951 gallons
		of fuel in wing	of fuel in wing
Max loaded wt	FB & Z	8,000kg	17,636lb
Max wing loading	FB	145kg/m²	29.7lb/ft²
	Z	160kg/m²	32.7lb/ft²

Performance

Max speed	1,040km/h	646mph at
	at 6,000 to 8,000m	19,750 to 26,250ft
Time to height	15min to 10,000m	32,800ft
Range at 8,000-10,000m	approx 3,000km	1,864 miles

Armament

Two 30mm MK 103 wing-mounted cannon; plus provision for additional two 30mm MK 103 cannon or one 75mm BK 7.5 or Düka 75 heavy cannon in external pack(s). Weapon load: max 1,000kg (2,200lb).

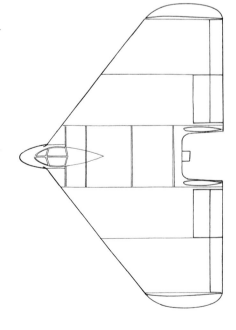

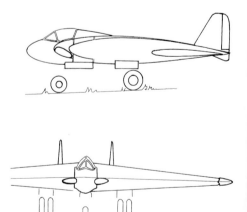

Lippisch P.15 Diana
4th March 1945

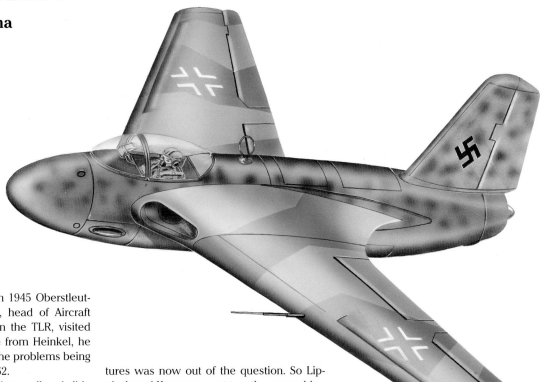

At the beginning of March 1945 Oberstleutnant Siegfried Knemeyer, head of Aircraft Development (Fl-E) within the TLR, visited Vienna. Having just come from Heinkel, he described to Dr Lippisch the problems being experienced with the He 162.

The latter reached for his pencil and slide rule and quickly sketched out his own idea for a comparable aircraft, but one with an even better performance and which, moreover, should be easy to fly.

But Knemeyer knew exactly what he wanted. The situation demanded a fighter which could be assembled quickly, using as far as possible existing parts and components. Time consuming construction of jigs and fix-

tures was now out of the question. So Lippisch and Knemeyer put together a machine made up of parts from the Me 163B and 'C, the He 162 and the Ju 248. Powered by the HeS 011, it was estimated that the aircraft should achieve a maximum speed of 1,000km/h 621mph). The LFA in Vienna constructed a 1:25 scale model, after which it was planned for the Wiener Neustadt Aircraft Works (WNF) to commence series production as quickly as possible.

Within a matter of days, however, the end of the war had brought a halt to this last 'emergency solution' too. The uncompleted project was handed over to the Americans.

Powerplant
One Heinkel HeS 011 rated at 1,300kP (2,865lb) static thrust or, as an alternative or back-up solution, one BMW 109-003 rated at 800kP (1,763lb) static thrust.

Dimensions
Span	10.08m	33ft 1in
Sweep	23°	
Wing area, approx	20m²	215ft²
Aspect ratio	5 : 1	
Length overall	6.40m	20ft 10½in

Weights
Loaded (requirement)	3,600kg	7,936lb
Max wing loading	180kg/m²	36.8lb/ft²

Performance
	(Requirements)	
Max speed	1,000km/h	621mph
Endurance	45 minutes	

In view of the relatively low wing loading, it may be assumed that the aircraft would have possessed a good rate of climb, a service ceiling in excess of those of the Me 262 and He 162, and satisfactory take-off and landing characteristics.

Armament
Two 30mm MK 108 cannon in wing roots, or two 20 mm MG 151 cannon.

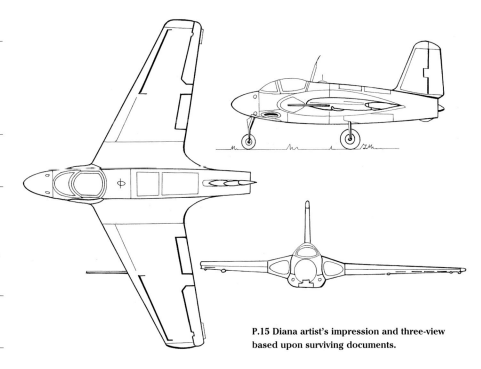

P.15 Diana artist's impression and three-view based upon surviving documents.

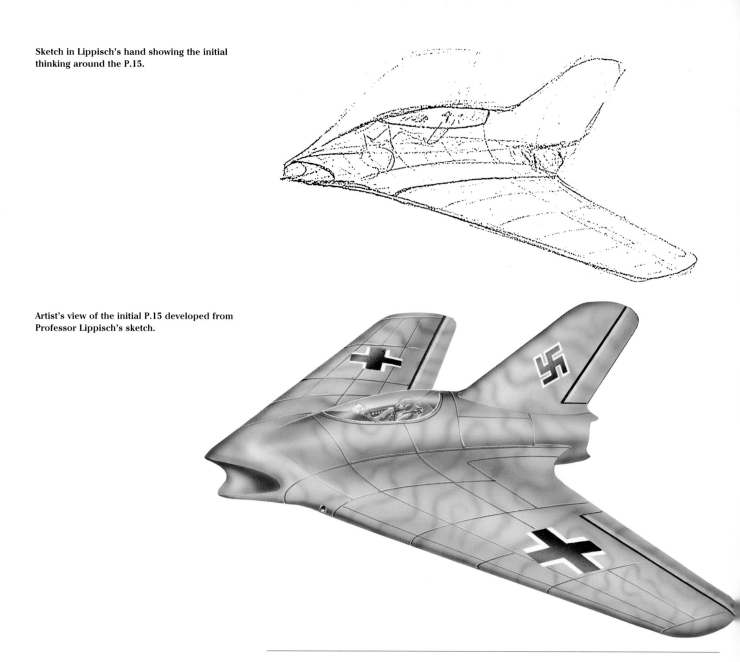

Sketch in Lippisch's hand showing the initial thinking around the P.15.

Artist's view of the initial P.15 developed from Professor Lippisch's sketch.

MESSERSCHMITT

The aviation industrialist and designer Willy Messerschmitt played an outstanding role in the creation of the jet fighter from the very beginning. As early as 1940 the RLM had directed him to develop his P.1065 project, which would eventually result in the Me 262. At the same time his project bureau put forward plans for the P.1070. Compared to the P.1065, this was a somewhat smaller, but appreciably lighter and aerodynamically more sophisticated design, parts of which (eg wing structure and nosewheel) would also later be incorporated into the definitive Me 262.

After these initial projects not a lot happened. Urgent war work, together with Göring's ban on development, were having their effect. It was not until some years later that further fighter proposals would be made.

At the beginning of 1943, despite nearly all its resources being occupied in the series production of such types as the Me 262 and Me 163, in research work on the Me 328 pulse-jet fighter and Me 264 long range bomber, and in the continuing development and upgrading of the Bf109, the company was to launch a new phase in jet aircraft development. Messerschmitt firmly believed that Germany could get by with, and should concentrate on, just one tenth of the number of aircraft types currently in series production. With his P.1090 and P.1092 projects, and his plans for possible other roles for the Me 262, he was, in fact, proposing the adoption of pure multi-purpose aircraft programmes. It was out of further design work on the P.1092 multi-purpose weapons system that a whole range of pro-

posals for single-jet air superiority fighters was to originate.

In mid-1944, a good 12 months later, the chief of the project bureau, Dipl-Ing Woldemar Voigt, and the head of feasibility studies, Dipl-Ing Hans Hornung, used these proposals as a basis to start work on a single-jet successor to the Me 262.

Via projects P.1101 – of which an experimental prototype was built at Oberammergau – and P.1106, the way finally led to the advanced P.1110, P.1111 and P.1112 designs. These represented a wide spectrum of ideas and solutions which anticipated much of what was to become state-of-the-art technology for decades after the war. The victorious powers saved themselves colossal sums in research and development costs.

Messerschmitt P.1070

Early 1940

During initial construction work on the Me 262 (P.1065) jet fighter, another project was launched which clearly surpassed Messerschmitt's own vision of a single-seat 'pursuit fighter'. Project P.1070 represented Dipl-Ing Hans Hornung's attempt to decrease the weight of a twin-jet fighter by reducing its overall dimensions. At the same time, the consequent reduction of surface area and the use of the most up-to-date aerodynamics greatly improved the performance.

The P.1070 served as a comparison to the jet fighter already under construction. But because of its equally high production costs, and the advanced stage of the work on the P.1065, further development was discontinued. The next attempt to reduce the cost of work on the Me 262 would be aimed in a completely different direction.

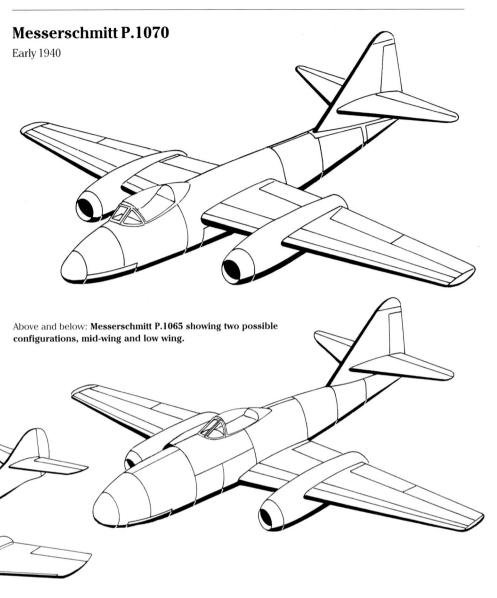

Above and below: **Messerschmitt P.1065 showing two possible configurations, mid-wing and low wing.**

Above left and below: **Messerschmitt P.1070.**

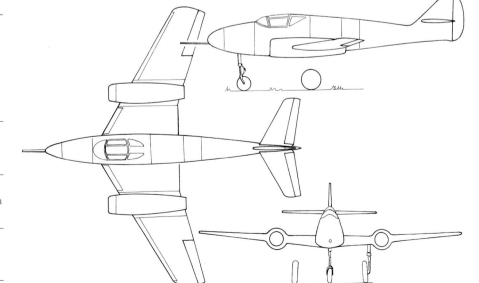

Powerplant
Two BMW turbojets each rated in the 600kP (1,322lb) thrust range.

Dimensions
Span	8.30m	27ft 3in
Sweep	32° at leading edge	
Wing area	13.0m²	139.9ft²
Aspect ratio	5.3 : 1	
Length overall	8.10m	26ft 6in
Height overall	2.90m	9ft 6in

Weights
Loaded	2,800-3,200kg	6,172-7,054lb
Max wing loading	246kg/m²	50lb/ft²

Performance
The only available data is the calculated maximum speed of 1,100km/h (683mph).

Armament
Two 15mm MG 151 cannon in the nose, plus one 13mm MG 131 machine gun alongside the nosewheel well.

Messerschmitt jet-powered Bf 109

20th January 1943

Within the context of Messerschmitt's wide-ranging proposals for standardisation on far fewer basic types, and in the light of the RLM's tight delivery schedules for the Me 262, the project bureau examined the possibility of producing a quick and easy to assemble jet fighter based upon types either already available or at least fully engineered (in this case, primarily the Me 155). The Augsburg team were thus looking along similar lines to Kurt Tank with his jet-powered Fw 190. But Messerschmitt, too, were to abandon the idea fairly quickly; it being discovered upon closer examination that the expenditure involved would, in fact, be not much less than that required for the Me 262. The number of compo-

nents which could be taken over from types already in production was extremely limited. The resulting aircraft would give every impression of being very much a makeshift solution and, in any case, by this time flight tests of the Me 262 were already at an advanced stage.

The basic design of the jet-powered Bf 109 was similar in principle to that of the Me 155B high altitude fighter, which had also been developed out of the familiar standard Bf 109.

The nosewheel was taken from the Me 309. But the wing, the nose section including the armament, the main undercarriage and the fuel tank installation all had to be built completely from scratch.

The jet-powered Bf 109 was not the final attempt to produce a jet fighter in short order out of existing components, as witness the Messerschmitt P.1095 and Lippisch P.15 Diana projects.

Powerplant

Two Junkers Jumo 004B-1 each rated at 900kP (1,984lb) static thrust.

Dimensions

Some data reconstructed

Span	13.00m	42ft 7in
Wing area	19.5m²	209.9ft²
Aspect ratio	8.6 : 1	
Length overall	9.20m	30ft 2in
Height overall	2.60m	8ft 6in

Weights

Loaded, including approx 750 litres (164 gallons) of fuel, but excluding

the pressure cabin	4,750kg	10,471lb
Max wing loading	243kg/m²	49.7lb/ft²

Performance

No data calculated; these should have been comparable to those of the Me 262.

Armament

One 20mm MG 151 cannon and two 30mm MK 103 cannon as a weapon pack in nose.

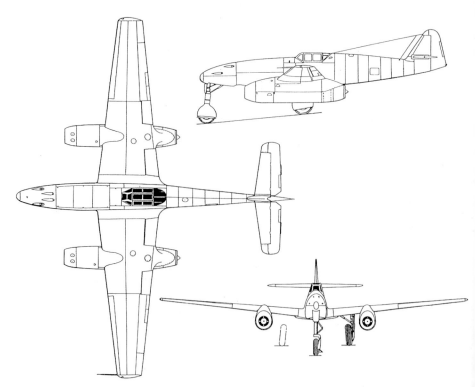

Messerschmitt P.1092

At the beginning of 1943, with the military and economic circumstances of the Reich having taken an irrevocable turn for the worse, with the Allied bombing offensive growing daily and with German ground forces retreating on all fronts, Professor Messerschmitt submitted a written report demanding that the multiplicity of types currently in series production for the Luftwaffe, which had by now grown to a staggering 51, should be drastically reduced. Messerschmitt was convinced that every operational requirement could be met by just five basic types. The validity of his argument was underlined by the increasing frequency of the damaging bottlenecks occurring in both the labour force and the supply of materials.

In 1943 he tried to turn the Me 262 into a true multi-purpose weapons system by expanding the number of its intended roles (initially

The Junkers Jumo 004 turbojet used throughout the P.1092 project; illustrated is the series production 004B variant.

trainer, interceptor, fast bomber and reconnaissance; then heavy fighter and night-fighter). With the same objective in mind his new jet project, the P.1092 which, in comparison to the Me 262 was both smaller and simpler, was designed from the outset to be a multi-purpose aircraft.

The first design proposals for the P.1092 of May 1943 consisted of the following:

– P.1092A fighter with one Jumo 004 turbojet engine.
– P.1092B interceptor with one HKW 109-509A rocket motor.
– P.1092C fast bomber with two Argus pulse-jets.
– P.1092D single-seater with two Jumo 004s for the Zerstörer, long range fighter, high altitude fighter, very fast bomber, dive-bomber and torpedo-bomber roles.
– P.1092E – two-seater with two Jumo 004s, as a night fighter and heavy fighter.

The above series, which to simplify matters used the outer wing section of the Me 262, was intended to perform the combined roles

of such diverse types as the Me 163B, the Me 328B, and even the Me 262, and eventually to replace them altogether.

But at the RLM Messerschmitt was able to push through only those plans regarding the expansion of the Me 262's roles. By this stage the powers-that-be in Berlin were no longer inclined to agree to the development of an (almost) entirely new weapons system. They were much more interested in seeing a simplified, single-jet air superiority fighter offering a better performance than the Me 262.

So in June/July 1943 a second set of design proposals for the P.1092 concentrated solely on just such an aircraft, which could fulfil, at most, one secondary role as a fighter-bomber. The design team was led by Dipl-Ing Hans Hornung in close collaboration with Professor Messerschmitt and Dipl-Ing Woldemar Voigt. The drawings were done either by Hornung himself, or by Project Group 1 under his close supervision. They number among some of the most advanced plans to be produced in 1943.

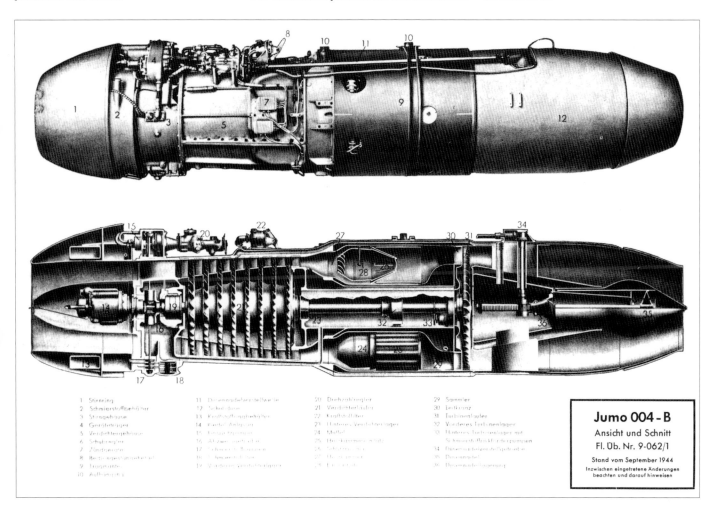

Jumo 004 - B
Ansicht und Schnitt
Fl. Üb. Nr. 9-062/1

Stand vom September 1944
Inzwischen eingetretene Änderungen
beachten und darauf hinweisen

This design showed certain similarities to Focke-Wulf's jet fighter design number 2 (PII) which originated at the same time.

The powerplant is admittedly a little more accessible for purposes of maintenance, but here too the nosewheel was located immediately ahead of the jet intake in a distinctly 'engine-imperilling fashion'. Just like the competition in Bremen, Messerschmitt was still opting to forego any high speed performance advantages to be gained by the use of a sharply swept wing.

Messerschmitt P.1092A

Fighter variant of the multi-purpose aircraft of 25th May 1943.

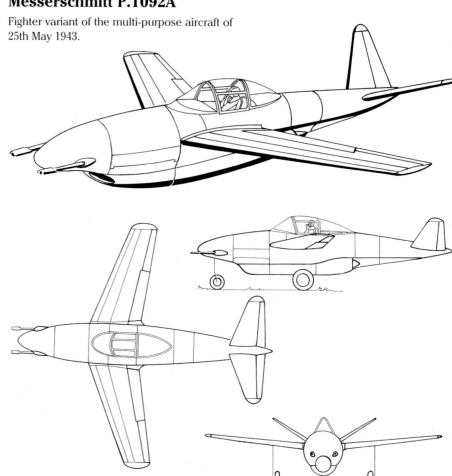

Powerplant

One Junkers Jumo 004C rated at 1,015kP (2,237lb) static thrust.

Dimensions		
Span	8.40m	27ft 6in
Wing area	12.0m²	129ft²
Aspect ratio	5.9 : 1	
Length overall	9.00m	29ft 6in
Height overall	2.50m	8ft 3in

Weights		
Loaded, approx	4,000kg with	8,818lb with
	1,200 litres fuel	263 gallons of fuel
Max wing loading, approx	330kg/m²	67.5lb/ft²

Performance

No performance calculations are available.

Armament

Two 30mm MK 103 cannon in the nose.

Powerplant

One Junkers Jumo 004C rated at 1,015kP (2,237lb) static thrust.

Dimensions		
Span	8.50m	27ft 9½in
Sweep	31° / 18° at 0.25 chord	
Wing area	13.5m²	145ft²
Length overall	8.23m	27ft 0in
Height overall	3.26m	10ft 7in

Weights		
Loaded	3,850kg with	8,487lb with
	1,200 litres fuel	263 gallons of fuel
Max wing loading	285kg/m²	58.3lb/ft²

Performance		
Max speed	910km/h at 6,000m	565mph at 19,750ft
Initial rate of climb	18.3m/sec	60ft/sec
Service ceiling	11,600m	38,000ft
Time to 3,000m (9,800ft)	3.1 minutes	
Time to 9,000m (29,500ft)	14.25 minutes	
Time to 11,000m (36,000ft)	24.65 minutes	
Max endurance at 9,000m	2 hours	
Max range at 9,000m	1,025km	636 miles
Take-off run	700m	2,300ft

Armament

Two 15mm MG 151/15, plus two 30mm MK 103 cannon in forward fuselage to left and right of the engine intake.

Messerschmitt P.1092/1 fighter

8th June 1943

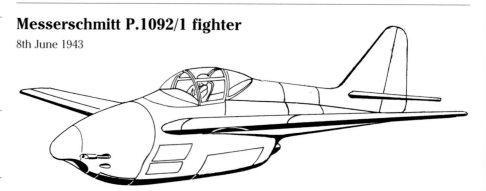

This was the first proposal to come out of the P.1092A fighter series. To counteract shortcomings of the swept wing at low speeds, Hornung chose, for the first time, to employ a wing featuring variable sweep. The increased chord at the wing root also made the accommodation of the main undercarriage that much easier. The nosewheel, for which there was very little space, was now located more advantageously aft of the engine air intake. Taken overall, the fighter's undercarriage offered extremely limited ground clearance.

Based on this design further studies were carried out in an attempt to improve the aircraft, particularly in terms of the fuselage and wing contours. As a result, at the beginning of July 1943, Hornung was able to put forward a new proposal featuring much cleaner lines than the original model, and one which again bore a marked resemblance in some areas to the Me 262.

Messerschmitt P.1902/2 single-jet fighter

3rd July 1943

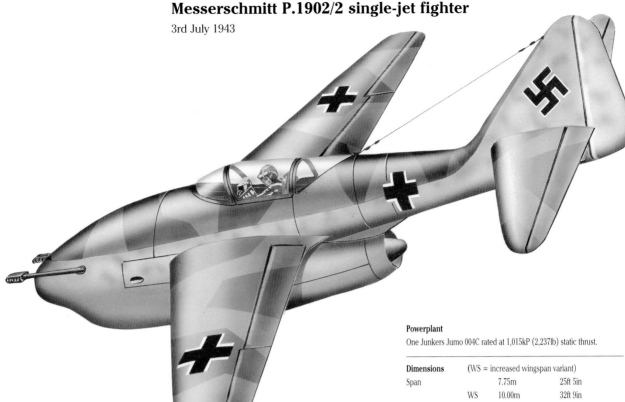

The alternative variant of the above with the increased wing span (WS in the data table), was also used for preliminary investigations into a lighter weight high altitude fighter, but the results did not meet expectations.

Together with the Lippisch P.20 and the Me 262, the P.1092/2 project was used in-house as a subject for comparative performance calculations. As the arbitrator, Hornung rated the P.1092 higher than the P.20, but assessed the Me 262 as being the superior overall.

As a result he now attempted to re-arrange the fuselage components to achieve more space. This increased the fuel capacity to 1,250 litres (274 gallons). At the end of 1944, in other words months later, the Messerschmitt project bureau found themselves repeating this procedure with design P.1106.

Powerplant

One Junkers Jumo 004C rated at 1,015kP (2,237lb) static thrust.

Dimensions	(WS = increased wingspan variant)		
Span		7.75m	25ft 5in
	WS	10.00m	32ft 9in
Sweep		21.5° at 0.25 chord	
Wing area		12.7m²	136ft²
	WS	14.45m²	155ft²
Aspect ratio		4.73 : 1	
	WS	6.92 : 1	
Length overall		8.10m	26ft 6in
Height overall		3.65m	11ft 10in

Weights			
Empty equipped		2,626kg	5,789lb
	WS	2,692kg	5,934lb
Loaded*		3,664kg	8,077lb
	WS	3,730kg	8,223lb
Max wing loading		288.5kg/m²	59lb/ft²

* With 750kg (1,652lb) fuel, which in 1943 still amounted to 1,000 litres (219.9 gallons). At the end of 1944, due to the then heavier diesel fuel, it would have been approx. 900 litres (197.9 gallons).

Performance			
Max speed at 6,000m		931km/h	578mph
(19,700ft)	WS	914km/h	567mph
Initial rate of climb		18.4m/sec	60ft 4in/sec
	WS	18.3m/sec	60ft/sec
Service ceiling		11,200m	36,750ft
	WS	12,100m	39,700ft
Max endurance	at 10,000m (32,800ft)		1.26 hours
	WS		1.59 hours
Max range		870km	540 miles
		at 11,000m	at 36,000ft
	WS	970km	602 miles
		at 11,800m	at 38,700ft
Take-off run		690m	2,263ft
	WS	635m	2,083ft

Armament

Two 30mm MK 103 cannon, plus two 15mm MG 151/15 cannon in fuselage to left and right of the powerplant.

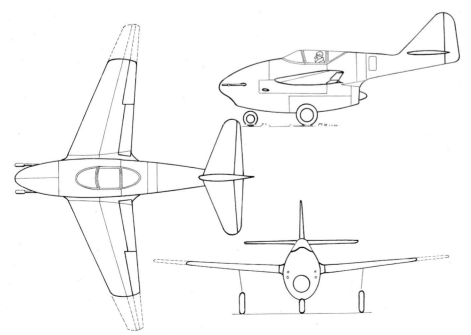

Messerschmitt P.1092/3

16th July 1943

Powerplant

One Junkers Jumo 004C rated at 1,015kP (2,237lb) static thrust.

Dimensions

Span	9.40m	30ft 9in
Sweep	18°	
Wing area	12.7m²	136ft²
Aspect ratio	7.0 : 1	
Length overall	8.10m	26ft 6½in
Height overall	3.60m	11ft 9in

Apart from the increased range, the performance and weight data should have been roughly comparable to those of the P.1092/2 .

Armament

Four 30mm MK 108 cannon in the nose.

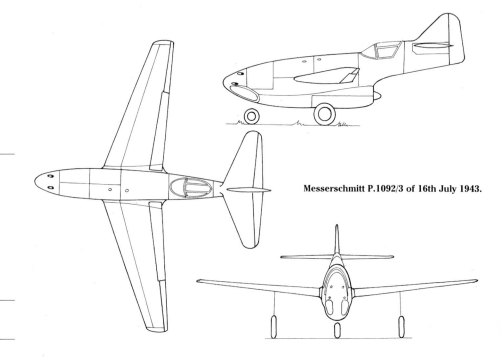

Messerschmitt P.1092/3 of 16th July 1943.

In a further proposal the project engineers examined yet another alternative. With the P.1092/4 they moved the cockpit much further forward into the nose. This meant that the weapons bay was now occupied by the pilot's position, but the latter was afforded a much greater field of visibility.

The final design of the series, the P.1092/5 of 20th July 1943, represented something of a compromise between the two and resulted in a cross sectional build-up which, it must be said, did nothing to improve the aerodynamics. The unslotted wing with its large area of flap was taken largely from the Me 262, as were the tail surfaces and the control system.

The technical data for the P.1092/4 and /5 proposals correspond to those for the preceding P1092/3 given above.

The extensive work on the P.1092 series served as a foundation for the design of the successful and highly promising P.1101 in the autumn of 1944.

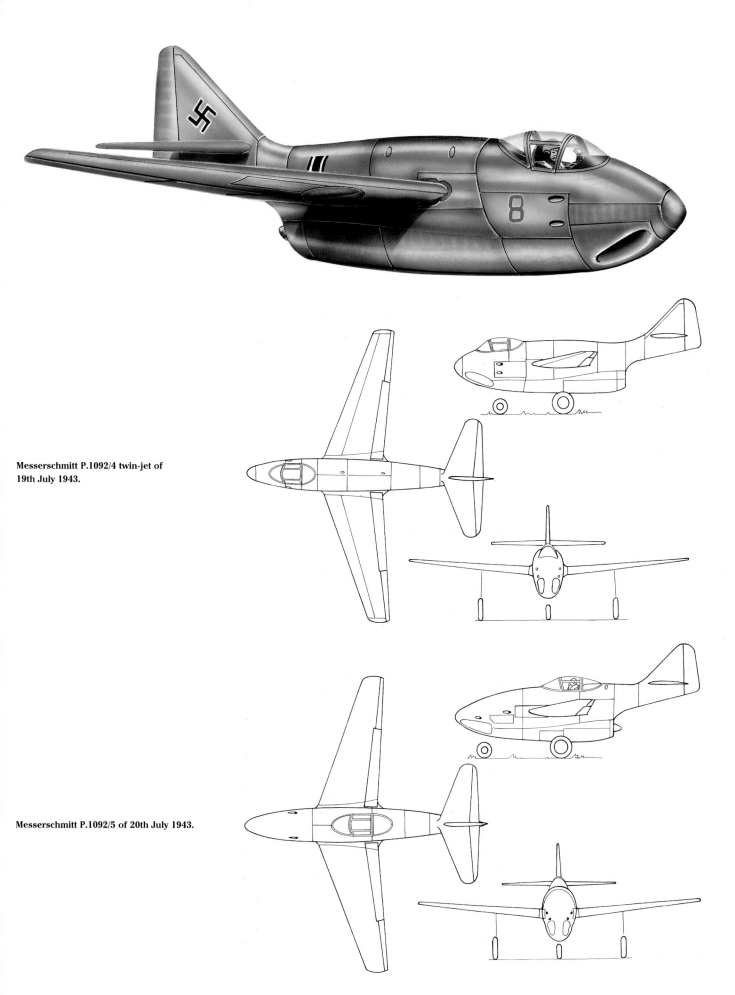

Messerschmitt P.1092/4 twin-jet of 19th July 1943.

Messerschmitt P.1092/5 of 20th July 1943.

Messerschmitt P.1095

Autumn 1943

Along with the group working around Hans Hornung, other Messerschmitt designers were also occupied, at least from time to time, with the development of the single-seat jet-powered fighter.

These included Dipl-Ing Rudolf Seitz who, with several other colleagues (Dipl-Ing Prager, Dipl-Ing Mende, Ing Kaiser) had been occupied since May 1943 at the firm of Jacobs-Schweyer GmbH at Darmstadt in preparing the Me 328B model for series production.

When the Me 328 was provisionally put on hold on 3rd September 1943, Seitz attempted to re-equip this fully developed (pulse-jet powered) aircraft with a turbojet powerplant. But the resulting fighter had a number of severe drawbacks:
- too high a wing loading
- too short an endurance
- of necessity, a fixed undercarriage.

Attempts to increase the wingspan to 9m (29ft 6in), and to make at least the nosewheel retractable, did not make the proposal any more viable. Seitz therefore decided to embark on an almost complete re-design. On closer examination, however, this proved to be an aircraft made up in the most part of major structural components taken from existing models.

The P.1095 is known to have been projected in two different versions. In the first study, which consisted of a modified and enlarged Me 328 with underslung engine, Seitz investigated its possibilities as a pure fighter design. A subsequent, extensively reworked P.1095 resulted in a fighter which could also be employed in the secondary roles of ground-attack, fast bomber or reconnaissance. Being underpowered, technologically already obsolescent, and with a nosewheel located in front of the ventral engine air intake, the aircraft – which incorporated substantial elements of both the Me 309 (tail and main undercarriage) and the Me 262 (wing, cockpit and controls) in its structure – simply had no future.

From a manufacturing standpoint, however, the fighter version, with its acceptable weight figures, could have proved a very interesting proposition indeed.

Flight testing the unpowered Me 328A.

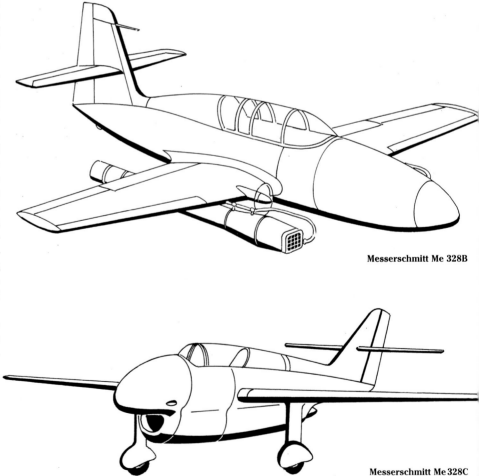

Messerschmitt Me 328B

Messerschmitt Me 328C

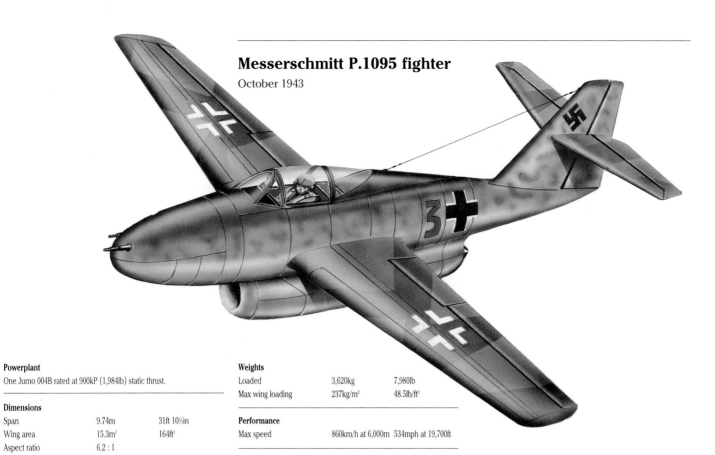

Messerschmitt P.1095 fighter
October 1943

Powerplant
One Jumo 004B rated at 900kP (1,984lb) static thrust.

Dimensions

Span	9.74m	31ft 10½in
Wing area	15.3m²	164ft²
Aspect ratio	6.2 : 1	
Length overall	9.71m	31ft 9in
Height overall	3.38m	11ft 1in

Weights

Loaded	3,620kg	7,980lb
Max wing loading	237kg/m²	48.5lb/ft²

Performance

Max speed	860km/h at 6,000m 534mph at 19,700ft

Armament
Two 30mm MK 103 cannon in the nose.

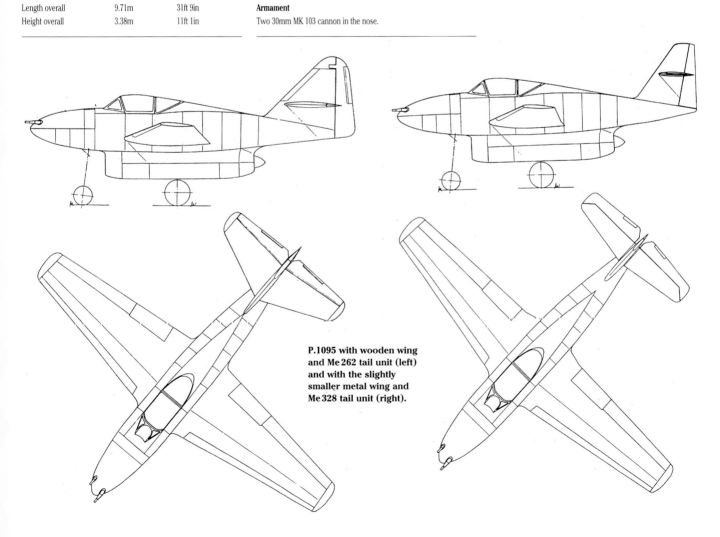

P.1095 with wooden wing
and Me 262 tail unit (left)
and with the slightly
smaller metal wing and
Me 328 tail unit (right).

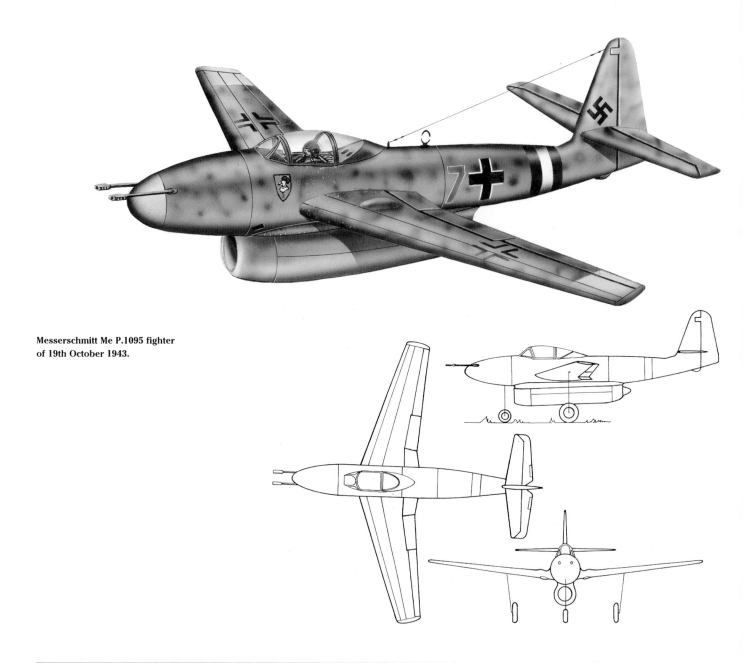

Messerschmitt Me P.1095 fighter of 19th October 1943.

Messerschmitt Me 262 HG III fighter and trials aircraft

For Professor Messerschmitt the perfectionist, the final version of the Me 262 did not live up to all his hopes and aspirations. In some areas he still regarded the design, which was to a certain extent the result of necessary compromise, as capable of improvement. His main aim was to increase the maximum speed of his revolutionary jet fighter.

From the very first studies carried out in 1939 for what was to become the Me 262, Messerschmitt had intended to house the jet powerplant within the wing, not only to save weight but also to reduce drag. These plans foundered on the continually changing projected dimensions of the first 'special (ie jet) powerplants'.

Another possible way to achieve a reduction in drag at high speeds was to make use of the swept wing effect discovered by Professor Adolph Busemann in 1935. When, at the beginning of the 1940, the first concrete results of swept wing research were made available to the German aviation industry, Messerschmitt planned for the first time in April 1941 to fit the Me 262 – which, incidentally, had successfully completed its maiden flight that same month powered by a piston engine – with a 35° swept wing. But the pressure of urgent war work did not permit such a radical change to be made at that time.

In July 1943, when problems with the Mach effect ('compressibility') began to show that

the Me 262 was reaching the limit of its performance, things started moving again.

The first serious plans for a high speed programme with the Me 262 were drawn up early in 1944. Dipl-Ing Seitz, having returned in the meantime from Darmstadt, was to take charge of the work with his project group.

Together with the research nature of the project, a document dated 16th February 1944 laid down a specific requirement for an aerodynamically refined, improved performance Me 262 for operational service.

Shortly thereafter, in March 1944, a plan was submitted showing how this 'new' Me 262 was to be achieved in three stages –

The Me 262A-1a (V167) initial design, undergoing tests at Lager Lechfeld near Augsburg.

Messerschmitt Me 262 HG III stage I (HG I)

Features to be included at this stage:

– Widening the chord of the inner wing section by inserting a fillet to increase the angle of sweep between the engine nacelle and the fuselage.
– New design low drag cockpit canopy.
– Swept horizontal tail surfaces.

In January 1945 Messerschmitt's chief test pilot, Karl Baur, commenced flight tests with the Me 262 V9 ('VI+AD'; werk nummer 130 004) which had been partially modified to the above standard. Contrary to the satisfactory wind tunnel test results, the swept horizontal tail surfaces gave rise to problems with the aircraft's stability. The last known version of the Me 262 HG III, which was tested by the British in the LFA wind tunnel at Volkenröde in November 1945, had been refitted with a standard tail unit.

The low drag cockpit canopy, however, fulfilled all expectations, although test pilots Baur and Lindner were not enamoured of the restricted freedom of movement.

Messerschmitt Me 262 HG III stage II (HG II)

– New wing incorporating 35° sweep.
– Improved engine nacelles.
– Low drag cockpit canopy.
– Swept horizontal tail surfaces.

Messerschmitt later also investigated a 'V'-tail version. The construction of a trials aircraft was preceded by extensive wind tunnel tests.

Before the Me 262 HG II (werk nummer 111 538) could commence flight trials it was seriously damaged in a ground accident. Repairs were not completed at war's end.

Messerschmitt Me 262 HG III stage III

– New wing incorporating 45° sweep.
– More centralised engine installation in wing roots. The definitive form of the air intakes is uncertain. During tests both a slightly elliptical and an 'extremely flattened' intake shape were to have been investigated.
– Low drag cockpit canopy.
– Swept horizontal tail surfaces.

This almost completely new aircraft was the subject of much discussion, investigation and wind tunnel testing. Capitulation brought all construction work to a complete halt. At the end of 1944, the possibility of using more powerful engines arose, these had, of course, been incorporated in the plans.

Messerschmitt Me 262 HG III

22nd December 1944

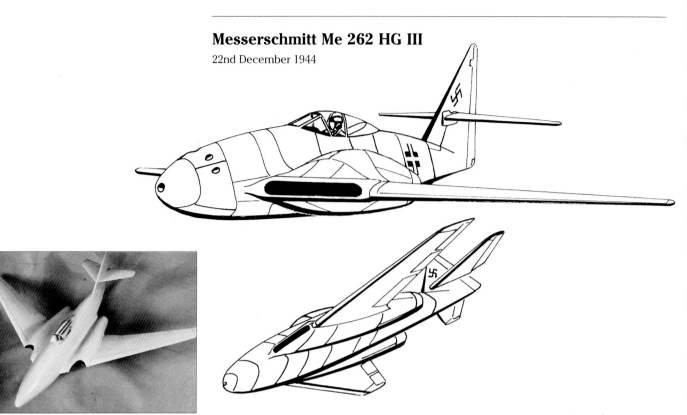

Original scale model of the Messerschmitt
Me 262 HG III.

Powerplant
Two Junkers Jumo 004D (improved Jumo 004B) each rated at 930kP
(2,050lb) static thrust. Installation of either the Heinkel HeS 011 or
BMW 003 also possible.

Dimensions
Span	11.08m	36ft 4½in
Sweep	46.5° at 0.25 chord	
Wing area	28.5m²	306ft²
Length overall	10.60m	34ft 8½in
Height overall	3.78m	12ft 5in

Weights
Empty equipped		4,325kg	9,530lb
Loaded	(benzine fuel)	6,451kg	14,221lb
		with 2,400 litres	with 527 gallons
	(diesel fuel)	6,697kg	14,764lb
		with 2,400 litres	with 527 gallons
Max wing loading		235kg/m²	48lb/ft²

Performance
Max speed (M = 0.96) 1,100km/h 683mph
Messerschmitt was obviously preparing to mount an assault on the
sound barrier with this aircraft. No further performance data available.

Armament
The same as Me 262A-1a four 30mm MK 108 cannon in the nose.
Radio Equipment: FuG 16ZY (VHF/RT), FuG 25a (ground-to-air IFF)

Together with the work on the single-jet high
performance fighter powered by the HeS 011,
the improved performance HG III variant of
the Me 262 represented the most modern and
furthest advanced German fighter project in
existence at the end of the war. Its only disadvantage when compared to the single-jet
fighter would have been the relatively high
expenditure in material and production costs.

With this project, and with the P.1101,
P.1110, P.1111 and P.1112 designs, the south German
company of Messerschmitt stood at the very
pinnacle of world aircraft manufacturing in
1945. Its influence on post-war aviation technology has reflected this position.

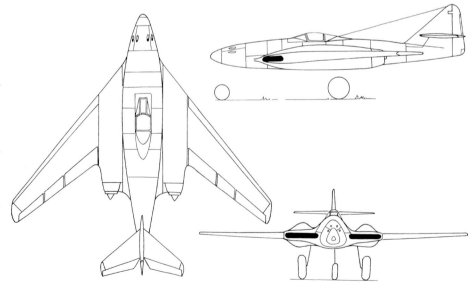

Chapter Three

Jet Heavyweights

The initial role of the heavy fighter, or Zerstörer, in the early years of the war was to combat enemy fighters over hostile territory. Its primary task of defending its own bombers required it to fly close escort to the slower bomber formations and perforce denied it the tactical manoeuvrability and flexibility of a typical fighter. A heavy fighter therefore needed two things: a superior performance allied to a long range.

In the light of the near total failure of the Messerschmitt Bf 110 to fulfil this intended role, provision of a replacement became a matter of the utmost priority. Together with a sufficient supply of fuel, a second crew member – to act as navigator and radio-operator, and to man the defensive armament if any – was all but indispensible.

The designers thus found themselves in the somewhat unenviable position of having to produce a relatively large aircraft possessing a performance superior to that of enemy fighters. Jet propulsion could ensure such a superiority, but high fuel consumption and consequently a limited range at first mitigated against its use.

By the closing years of the war conditions had changed. New requirements had arisen and traditional roles had to be redefined and sometimes reassigned. In defence of the Reich duties the heavy fighter was to become, in effect, the counterpart to the 'interceptor'. As the fighting fronts retreated ever closer to the Homeland, prior warning of aerial attack grew progressively shorter. For defending fighters, rate of climb became as important as maximum speed in terms of performance criteria. But even taken to its extreme, for point defence in the style of the Me 163B for example, this could not guarantee total success and defensive cover would inevitably remain patchy.

It would make much more sense for 'patrolling' heavy fighters to be able to attack the fighter escorted, heavily armed bomber streams several times; ideally during the approach to – or otherwise when departing – the target area. There was also the possibility of employing such aircraft in a secondary role as fighter-bombers to attack enemy targets.

The new heavy fighter would thus bear a close relationship to the original Zerstörer,

which were now being deployed almost exclusively against Allied bombers: either by day as heavy weapons carriers, or by night equipped with the latest in electronics and radar.

A relatively large aircraft would also lend itself quite easily to a variety of roles simply by change of equipment fit. Heavy fighter proposals were therefore usually to be found within the context of multi-purpose aircraft projects. The groundwork for the weapons systems of the post-war years had thus been laid. Proposals specifying a 'jet-powered heavy fighter' as being the primary role or function were fairly rare.

The German concept of a heavily, multiarmed all-weather fighter aroused great interest among the victorious Allies. France was later to produce the Sud-Ouest SO.4050 Vautour, which was very similar to the Messerschmitt P.1099, Britain the de Havilland DH.110 (later the Sea Vixen), Sweden the SAAB J32 Lansen, the Soviet Union the Yakovlev Yak-25 'family' and, finally, the United States the Northrop F-89 Scorpion and the McDonnell F-101 Voodoo.

Pre-production model of the French Sud-Ouest SO.4050 Vautour.

Gotha P.60A heavy fighter
January 1945

Crew
One pilot and one radio operator/navigator in prone position.

Powerplant
Two BMW 003 each rated at 800kP (1,763lb) static thrust.

Dimensions

Span	12.40m	40ft 8in
Sweep	46° at 0.25 chord	
Wing area	46.8m²	503ft²
Length overall	9.50m	31ft 2in
Height overall	3.15m	10ft 4in

Weights

Empty equipped	4,190kg	9,237lb
Loaded	7,450kg with	16,424lb with
	approx 2,500 litres	approx 550 gallons
	of fuel	of fuel

Performance

Max speed	915km/h	568mph
	at 7,000m	at 20,000ft
Initial rate of climb	14m/sec	46ft/sec
Service ceiling	12,500m	41,000ft
Time to 8,000m	14.1 minutes	26,250ft
Time to 10,000m	21.5 minutes	32,800ft
Endurance at 100% thrust	approx 2 hours	
	at 12,000m	39,000ft
Range at 100% thrust	approx 1,600km	994 miles
	at 12,000m	39,000ft

Armament
As heavy fighter: Four 30mm MK 108 or two 30mm MK 103 cannon in wing centre section to left and right of crew cabin.
As reconnaissance aircraft (secondary role): two Rb 50/18 cameras.

The Gotha P.60 heavy fighter the project resulted from the development work carried out by the Gotha company on the Horten Ho IX. This was initially intended to culminate in series production as a structurally improved Go 229.

Gotha was requested by the Oberkommando der Luftwaffe (OKL – Luftwaffe High Command) to incorporate the experience gained from the Horten Ho IX/Go 229 into a new design.

OKL requirements included:
 – A crew of two.
 – A pressure sealed high altitude cabin.
 – A standard tricycle undercarriage.
 – A greater range than the Go 229.
 – The option of installing more powerful engines.

Gotha's head of design, Ing Hünerjäger, and his chief aerodynamicist, Dr Göthert, also incorporated the latest high speed research into their design, a move which was not accepted without a certain amount of reservation by Walter and Reimar Horten. They also evaluated the most recent developments in alternative construction and the running and operation of turbojet engines.

Structurally, the P.60A and P.60B were identical. The crew was accommodated in a prone position in a pressure sealed cabin fully faired into the nose contours. The airframe consisted of a plywood-skinned tubular steel centre section structure with all-wooden, lattice work outer wings.

Elevators and ailerons were combined in the one control surface (elevon) on the trailing edge of each outermost wing section. Rudder control was provided in a highly unusual manner; two telescopic control surfaces being simultaneously extended above and below each wingtip. Fuel was carried in the outer wings and in a centre-section tank.

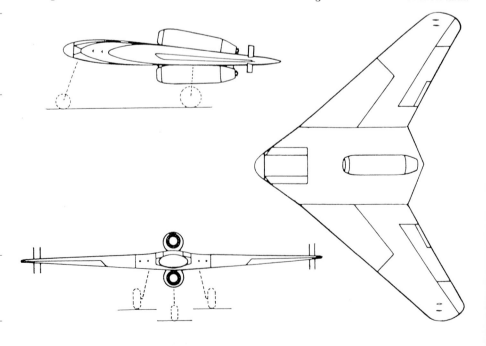

Gotha P.60B heavy fighter

March 1945

On 28th February 1945 the General der Jagd-flieger (Air Officer Commanding Fighters) laid down new requirements for both single- and twin-jet fighter projects.

His demands included, among other things, a more comprehensive equipment fit and, above all, a greater endurance. Take-off on grass should not exceed 1,000m (3,250ft). Ing Hünerjäger and Dr Göthert therefore decided to enlarge their original P.60 design into the P.60B, while still continuing development of the former as an 'immediate solution' under the designation P.60A as described above.

The company proposed a third variant, designated the P.60C, as their tender to the night fighter specification issued on 27th January 1945. But the capitulation of Germany in May perforce denied the designers and aerodynamicists of the Gothaer Waggonfabrik any practical demonstration of their ideas and proposals. It is only today, after decades of being a mere pipe dream, that the aerodynamic planform championed back in 1945 has re-emerged centre stage in the shape of America's so-called 'stealth' bomber, the Northrop B-2A Spirit.

Crew
Pilot and radio operator in pressure sealed cabin.

Powerplant
Two Heinkel HeS 011 turbojets each rated at 1,300kP (2,865lb) static thrust. Provision for additional 2,000kP (4,409lb) thrust rocket motor.

Data below for the heavy fighter variant unless given with an 'R' for the reconnaissance (secondary) role.

Dimensions

Span		13.50m	44ft 3½in
Sweep		46° at 0.25 chord	
Wing area		54.7m²	589ft²
Aspect ratio		3.3 : 1	
Length overall		9.90m	32ft 6in
Height overall		3.50m	11ft 6in

Weights

Empty equipped		5,161kg	11,377lb
Loaded		9,953kg with	21,942lb with
		3,500kg of jet fuel	7,716lb of jet fuel
Loaded (max)	R	11,000kg with	24,250lb with
		2,600kg of jet fuel	5,731lb of jet fuel
		plus 1,700kg	plus 3,747lb
		of rocket fuel	of rocket fuel
Max wing loading		182kg/m²	37.2lb/ft²
	R	201kg/m²	41lb/ft²

Performance

Max speed		980km/h at 6,000m	608mph at 20,000ft
Initial rate of climb		19m/sec	62ft/sec
R		60m/sec	196ft/sec
Time to height	30.5 min	to 14,000m	46,000ft
R	2.6 min	to 9,000m	29,500ft
Max Endurance	2.4 hrs	at 14,000m	46,000ft
R	3.7 hrs	at 14,000m	46,000ft
Max Range		approx 2,800km+	1,739 miles+
		at 14,000m	46,000ft
R		2,100km	1,304 miles
		at 14,000m	46,000ft

Armament
As Heavy Fighter:
Four 30mm MK 108 or four 30mm MK 213C cannon in wing centre section to left and right of crew cabin. Weapon load: provision for weapons racks. As reconnaissance aircraft (secondary role): one Rb 50/18 and One Rb 30/18 cameras.

Radio equipment
FuG 15 R/T, FuG 25a IFF and FuG 125 radio beacon receiver.

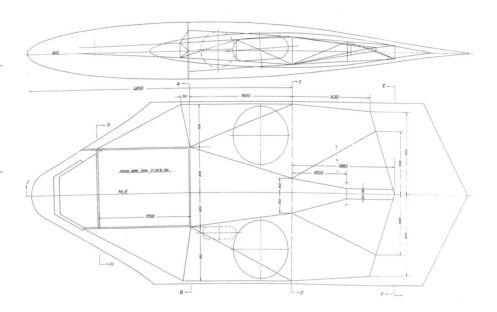

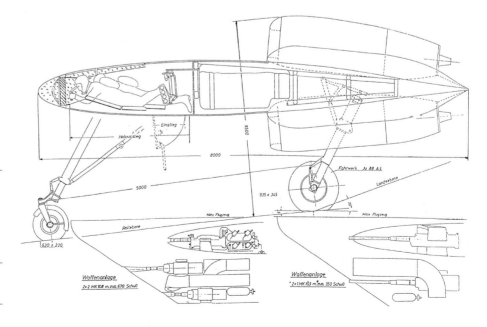

Messerschmitt P.1099

March 1944

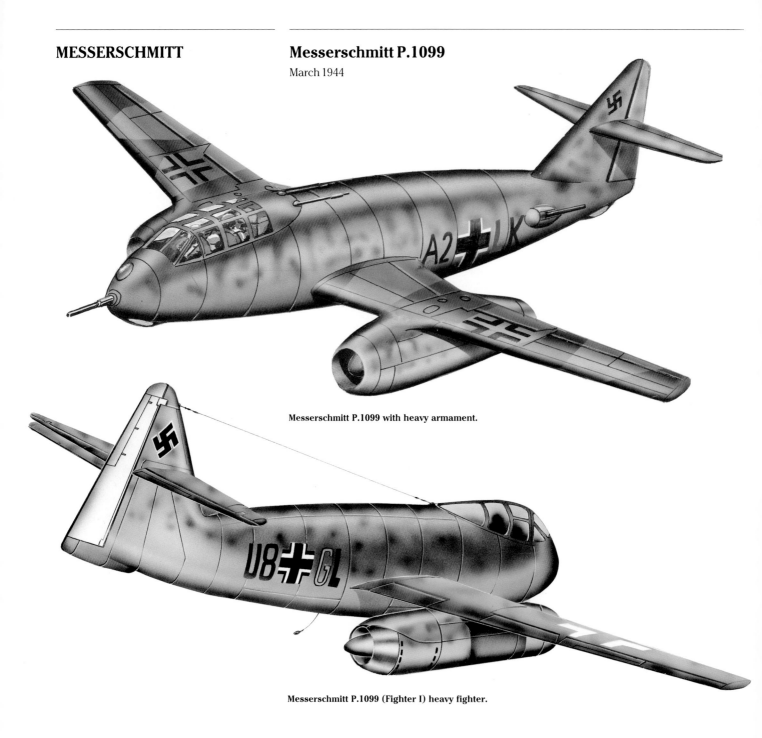

Messerschmitt P.1099 with heavy armament.

Messerschmitt P.1099 (Fighter I) heavy fighter.

In the summer of 1943 proposals for 'possible alternative roles' for the Me 262 jet fighter included interceptor, fast bomber, reconnaissance aircraft and trainer. Its employment as a night or all-weather fighter had not yet then been envisaged. This was to change at the beginning of 1944 when, in February, proposals were first put forward under the project designation P.1099 for an enlarged-fuselage Me 262 intended to combat the heavily-armed Allied four-engined bombers in the heavy fighter, Zerstörer and night fighter roles.

In the course of further work on the project these proposals crystallised into just the one:

for a all-weather heavy fighter whose sub-variants would differ only in armament detail. It was at this stage that the planned rearward-firing gun barbettes, characteristic of the Me 210 and the Me 410 Hornisse (Hornet), were deleted.

Project 1099's wing and tail surfaces were largely taken over straight from the Me 262. For centre of gravity reasons the engine nacelles were moved slightly further aft. The fuselage was of completely new design. The undercarriage, too, was redesigned for projected all up weights of up to 10 tonnes or more.

Crew
Pilot and radio operator/navigator in two-man cabin.

Powerplant
Two Junkers Jumo 004C each rated at 1,015kP (2,237lb) static thrust.

Dimensions
Span	12.61m	41ft 4⅛in
Wing area	22.0m²	237ft²
Aspect ratio	7.2 : 1	
Length overall	12.00m	39ft 4in
Height overall	4.43m	14ft 6in

Weights
Empty equipped	5,061kg	11,157lb
Normal loaded	8,762kg with	19,316lb with
	3,900 litres of fuel	857 gallons
Max wing loading	398kg/m²	81.5lb/ft²

It is questionable whether the Technische Amt (Technical Office) would have been happy with the above figures, which were extremely high for those days. To achieve any sort of acceptable take-off performance the use of jettisonable rocket assistance would have been unavoidable.

Performance
No calculated performance figures are available. The data below are from a British source.

Max speed	805km/h	500mph
	at 9,100m	at 30,000ft
Service ceiling	9,810m	32,000ft
Range	1,340km at	832 miles at
	6,000m without	20,000ft without
	additional fuel	additional fuel

Armament
Fighter I with several smaller weapons
Version A Four 30mm MK 108 cannon
Version B Two 30mm MK 103 cannon
Version C Two 30mm MK 108 cannon, plus two 30mm MK 103 cannon

Armament was arranged in the forward fuselage below the crew cabin. All versions had provision for a maximum 2,150 litres (473 gallons) of additional fuel.

Armament
Version A: One 30mm MK 108 cannon, plus one 55mm MK 112 cannon. Provision for a maximum of 2,000 litres (440 gallons) of additional fuel. Version B: One 50mm MK 214 cannon. Provision for a maximum of 1,500 litres of additional fuel. Arrangement of armament as Fighter I above.

Radio Equipment
Funkgerät (FuG radio or radar set 16ZY) (VHF/RT), Peilgerät (PeilG - direction finding equipment) VI (D/F and homing receiver), FuG 101 (radio altimeter), Funk-Blindlandeanlage (FuBl - radio blind-running equipment) 2 (ALS) and FuG 25 (IFF).

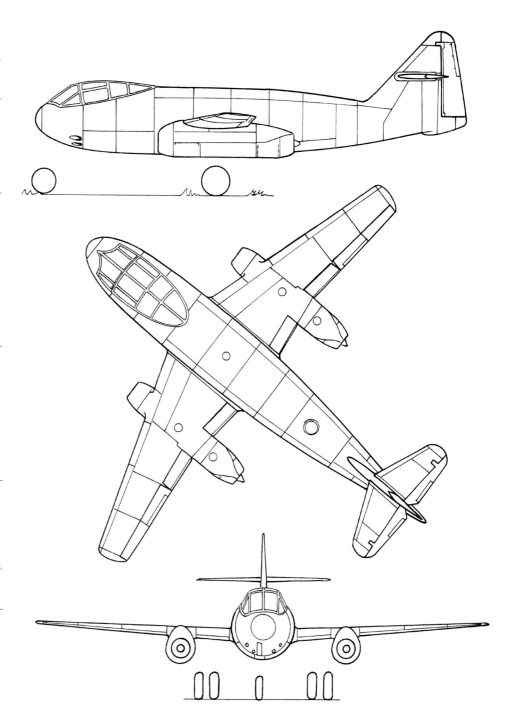

Messerschmitt P.1101

It is not known whether work on this project continued beyond March 1944. Messerschmitt was subsequently to use the basic design for his very similar P.1100 fast bomber project. This in turn led to a comprehensive series of studies for aircraft fulfilling a diversity of roles contained under the project number P.1101.

In the summer of 1944 Messerschmitt abandoned all further development upon the instructions of the Jägerstab (Fighter Staff)

and concentrated instead on the production of a single-jet high performance fighter to be powered by the HeS 011. This then took over as project number 1101.

Chapter Four

'People's fighter' versus 'People's aircraft'

By the summer of 1944, when the general collapse of Germany's daylight fighter arm could no longer be ignored, the threat of attack by ever-increasing numbers of low flying Allied fighters was beginning to pose serious problems. Germany's standard fighters, the Messerschmitt Bf109 and Focke-Wulf Fw190, were no longer in a position to combat the wide-ranging low level sweeps by North American Mustangs, Lockheed Lightnings, Republic Thunderbolts and de Havilland Mosquitos. Such incursions were not only highly demoralising to civilian and soldier alike, they also rendered any offensive movement by German ground forces all but impossible.

In an attempt to remedy this situation, and co-incident with the activation of the Volkssturm (Germany's 'Home Guard'), Albert Speer's Reichsministerium für Rüstung und Kriegsproduktion (RfRuk – Reich Ministry of Armament and War Production and the Reichsluftfahrtministerium (RLM – Reich Air Ministry) came up with the idea of a light-weight, easy-to-build, easy-to-fly, but none-theless high performance aircraft, which could be mass produced and which would be able to take-off from even the smallest of landing strips.

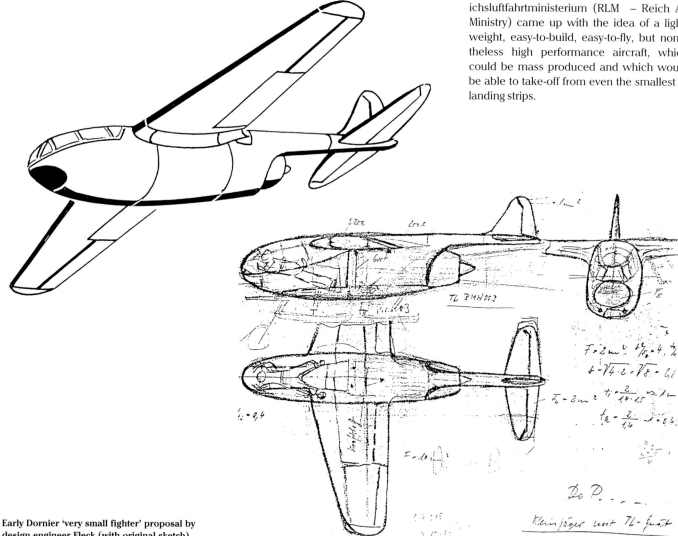

**Early Dornier 'very small fighter' proposal by
design engineer Fleck (with original sketch).**

Winner of the Volksjäger competition: the Heinkel He162.

With a wingspan of 7.2m (23ft 6in) the Heinkel He162A-1 was an exceptionally compact fighter.

The man behind this scheme was presumably Karl-Otto Saur, Albert Speer's deputy at the RfRuK. For as the managing director of the Ernst Heinkel AG, Dipl-Ing Karl Frydag, was to explain to Professor Willy Messerschmitt on 11th April 1945:

I never campaigned for the single-jet fighter (by which he meant the Volksjäger – Authors). Quite the opposite, I always spoke out against it. The decision to build the single-jet fighter with all possible haste was the result of discussions between Herr Saur, Herr Oberstleutnant Knemeyer and a large number of gentlemen in the Air Ministry.

On the evening of 7th September 1944 Drs Heinkel, Günter and Meschkat in Vienna received a top priority blitz (lightning) telegram from Oranienburg. It contained precise specifications and delivery dates for a 'very small fighter'. By the time the Arado, Blohm und Voss, Fieseler, Focke-Wulf, Junkers and Siebel

companies had officially received their copies of the specifications from the RLM on 10th September, Heinkel had already produced their first designs and calculations based upon their earlier P.1073 (P – Projekt) project.

At an internal meeting 24 hours later Heinkel was already making firm plans for the construction of a prototype and commencement of series production of the P.1073, soon to be known as the He162.

So when, by mid-September, the other manufacturers who had been invited to tender had completed and submitted their projects for discussion, Heinkel AG already seem to have been assured of the go ahead.

Even the circle of Volksjäger supporters surrounding the influential Saur obviously knew from the start exactly what, and who, it was he wanted. With production of the He 177 Greif (Griffon) heavy bomber virtually at a

halt, and that of the He 219 Uhu (Owl) about to follow suit, Heinkel appeared to be the obvious choice.

Which begs the question as to why – at this late stage of the war and simply to keep up appearances with the industry – did the RLM permit such a farce?

Saur knew exactly how to use his influence to push through his own ideas on schemes like this against numerous opponents such as, amongst others, Dipl-Ing Robert Lüsser, Messerschmitt and Adolf Galland. On 30th September 1944 the RLM officially awarded the contract to Heinkel, who by then had already built a full-scale mock-up.

The He162V1 successfully completed its maiden flight on 6th December. After a few minor modifications the aircraft began to show great promise as a fighter. It entered mass production and a number of examples even saw operational service.

ARADO

Arado E.580

12th September 1944

Powerplant

One BMW 003A-1 rated at 800kP (1,763lb) static thrust.

Dimensions

Span	7.75m	25ft 5in
Wing area	10m²	107ft²
Aspect ratio	6.0 : 1	
Length overall	8.00m	26ft 3in
Height overall	2.50m	8ft 3in

Weights

Empty equipped	1,955kg	4,309lb
Loaded	2,635kg with	5,809lb with
	500kg of fuel	1,102lb of fuel
Max wing loading	263kg/m²	53.9lb/ft²

Performance

Max speed	750km/h at 6,000m	466mph at 20,000ft
Initial rate of climb	17.5m/sec	57ft/sec
Service ceiling	12,000m	39,400ft
Time to 6,000m (20,000ft)	7.4 minutes	
Time to 10,000m (32,800ft)	17.9 minutes	
Endurance at 100% thrust	35 minutes at 6,000m	
Range at 100% thrust and at 6,000m		
	403km	250 miles
Take-off run	570m	1,870ft
Landing speed	154km/h	95.6mph

Armament

Two 30mm MK 108 cannon in the nose.

Arado had just two days to complete its design proposal, as since recorded by the head of the company's aerodynamic design department, Rüdiger Kosin:

One day in mid-September 1944, without any prior warning, a representative of the Technische Amt arrived at Arado's design department which had recently relocated to Landeshut in Silesia. He wanted us to produce a design for a lightweight fighter, to be powered by a BMW 003 turbojet, within a matter of days. He seemed to know exactly what the final design should look like. He didn't budge from the department for two whole days and tried throughout that time to steer the project in the direction he wanted it to go. (From *Die Deutsche Luftfahrt,* Vol. 4 – The Development of the German Fighter – Bernhard and Graefe Verlag, published in Bonn, 1983).

The design thus arrived at showed certain parallels to the He 162, albeit with a low-mounted wing. One great risk inherent in the E.580 was the positioning of the cockpit canopy immediately ahead of the engine air intake. (The Arado company use for a while 'E' – Entwurf – as a prefix for their projects, instead of the more universally adopted 'P' – Projekt.) Even the smallest airflow vortices would have resulted in a not inconsiderable loss of performance. As the Rechlin test pilot Heinz Borsdorff once explained to Walter Schick, during one flight he had suffered a 10% performance loss brought about by a vortex caused by a small gap where the canopy of his He 162 had not been completely closed. Determining the exact shape of the E.580's air intake would have required some considerable time spent on wind tunnel tests; time which simply was not available.

The fuselage of the E.580 was constructed primarily of steel. The wing, as laid down in the specification, was built of wood.

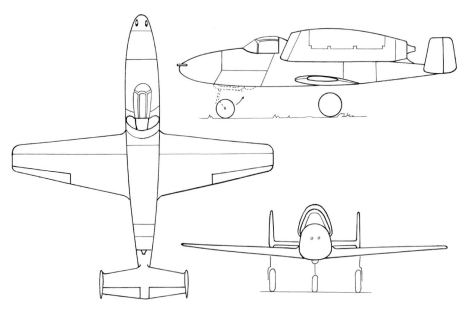

BLOHM UND VOSS

After some initial hesitation about participating in the Volksjäger tender, Dr Richard Vogt, assisted by Dipl-Ing Hans Amtmann, then went on to produce three unusual and widely differing proposals in about as many weeks. In a first comparison study he considered the merits of the tail-less P.210, which had been developed out of the P.208, against those of the more conventional P.211 with its swept wing and tail surfaces.

The development risks associated with the former decided Dr Vogt to submit project number 211.

The simple and cheap method of construction, typical of so many Blohm und Voss designs, found wide support among those experts present at the discussions held on 14th and 19th September. But Heinkel's P.1073, while not quite meeting the specifications in terms of endurance, was appreciably lighter and possessed a better overall performance. In addition, a more powerful or alternative engine could be installed in the Heinkel design much more easily and with far fewer complications; as Siegfried Günter was to demonstrate on more than one occasion.

When it became clear that, for the speeds envisaged, a swept wing offered little additional advantage, but rather increased overall weight and added to the development risks, Blohm und Voss reworked their project giving it completely straight, constant-chord, wing and tail surfaces. But time was running out for the Hamburg team and, furthermore, such an uncompromisingly basic aircraft would have been hard put to come even close to the performance figures offered by the He 162. This point should not be overlooked when reviewing the whole decision-making process.

Blohm und Voss P.210

14th September 1944

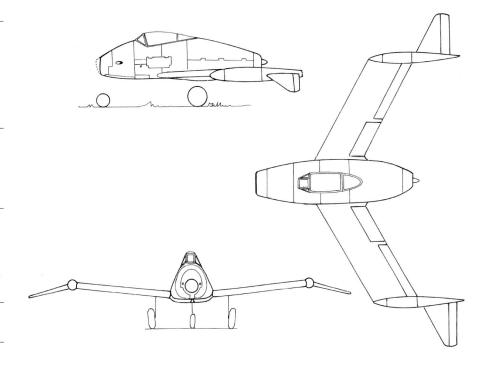

Constructed mainly of steel, this aircraft's load-bearing structure took the form of Blohm und Voss's usual tubular spar, which also served as the intake duct for the engine. To this central member were attached all the other assemblies and components. The remainder of the airframe was similar to that developed for the P.208.

Powerplant
One BMW 003A-1 rated at 800kP (1,763lb) static thrust; optional rocket take-off assistance.

Dimensions (partly reconstructed)
Span	8.40m	27ft 6½in
Sweep	30° at 0.25 chord	
Wing area	15.00m²	161ft²
Aspect ratio	4.7 : 1	
Length overall	7.10m	23ft 3 1/2in
Height overall	2.60m	8ft 6in

Weights
Empty Equipped	2,480kg	5,467lb
Loaded	3,400kg with	7,495lb with
	750kg of fuel	1,653lb of fuel
Max wing loading	227kg/m²	46.5lb/ft²

Performance
Figures would probably have slightly exceeded specifications. Precise data not available. Due to its relatively high loaded weight, the project would have had some difficulty meeting the required take-off run (500 m/1,600ft). Without rocket assistance take-off run amounted to 1,020m (3,346ft).

Armament
Two 30mm MK 108 fixed forward firing cannon in the nose.

Blohm und Voss P.211/01

14th September 1944

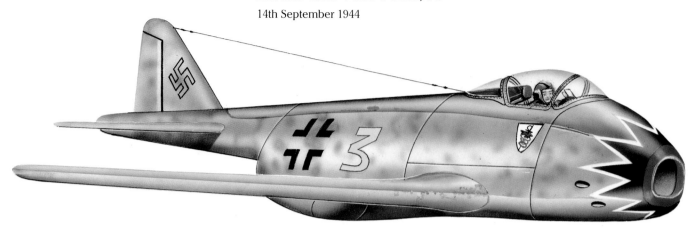

Powerplant

One BMW 003A-1 rated at 800kP (1,763lb) static thrust.

Dimensions

Span	8.40m	27ft 6½in
Sweep	30° at 0.25 chord	
Wing area	15.00m²	161ft²
Aspect ratio	4.7 : 1	
Length overall	8.70m	28ft 6in
Height overall	2.70m	8ft 9in

Weights

Empty equipped	2,580kg	5,687lb
Loaded	3,500kg with	7,716lb with
	750kg of fuel	1,653lb of fuel
Max wing loading	233kg/m²	47.7lb/ft²

Performance

No works data are available; those given below, whose accuracy cannot be guaranteed, have been taken from previously published sources.

Max speed	860km/h at 8,000m	534mph at 26,250ft
Initial rate of climb	17.8m/sec	58ft/sec
Service ceiling	11,100m	36,500ft
Take-off run (on grass)	800m	2,600ft

Armament

Two 30mm MK 108 fixed forward firing cannon in the nose.

A more conventional alternative to the tailless P.210, in which, however, Dipl-Ing Amtmann again made use of the basic structural design and constant-chord swept wing of the P.210, but here the load-bearing element, the welded tubular steel spar, was simply extended aft to form a tail boom.

Had it been awarded a production contract, this aircraft would have been the first fighter in the world to use wing sweep effect as a design basis. It therefore contained a certain element of risk. But in his proposal Dr Vogt emphasised rather the simplicity of construction and the use of 'non-essential' materials. He summarised by arguing that;

... the designs submitted must result in an aircraft that will ease the burden once and for all on the light alloy sector of our raw material production and, at the same time, reduce labour costs.

He also pointed to the ease of maintenance and a consequent high degree of operational availability – these concepts found widespread approval. But official circles delayed the announcement of a decision and Dr Vogt was kept waiting.

In order to eliminate any uncertainty and also be able to keep to the tight schedules, Dr Vogt greatly simplified the aerodynamic concept of the P.211/01. In so doing he made full use of his previous experience with the BV 40 glider-interceptor which had employed similar wing and tail surfaces to those now proposed.

To provide a comparison with the Blohm und Voss data given, figures taken from Heinkel Report No.105/44 of 23rd September 1944, 'The P.1073 Jet Fighter', are also listed on the opposite page.

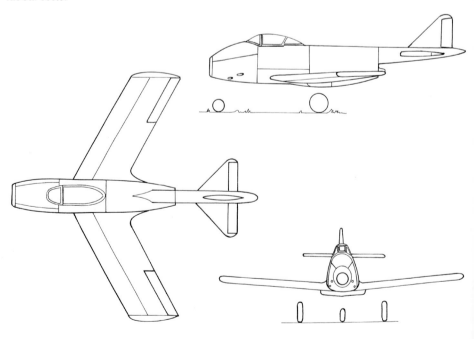

Blohm und Voss P.211/02

29th September 1944

Powerplant

One BMW 003A-1 rated at 800kP (1,763lb) thrust.

Dimensions

Span		7.60m	24ft 10in
	P.1073	7.20m	23ft 7in
Wing area		12.87m	42ft 2in
	P.1073	11.16m	36ft 7in
Aspect ratio		4.49 : 1	
	P.1073	4.65 : 1	
Length overall		8.06m	26ft 5in
	P.1073	8.65m	28ft 4in

Weights

Empty equipped		1,930kg	4,254lb
	P.1073	1,868kg	4,118lb
Loaded		2,760kg with	6,064lb with
		420kg of fuel	925lb of fuel
	P.1073	2,571kg* with	5,667lb* with
		420kg of fuel	925lb of fuel
Max wing loading		214.5kg/m²	43.9lb/ft²
	P.1073	230kg/m²	47lb/ft²

* The Heinkel figure above was hand altered to read 2,750kg (6,062lb).
The actual loaded weight of the He162A-1 was 2,805kg (6,183lb).
The P.211/2 could accommodate an additional 490 litres (107.7 gallons)
of fuel in the wings.

Performance

Max speed		767km/h at 6,000m	476mph at 20,000ft
	P.1073	840km/h at 6,000m	521mph at 20,000ft
Initial rate of climb		14.05m/sec	46ft/sec
	P.1073	21.5m/sec	70ft/sec
Service ceiling		11,000m	36,000ft
	P.1073	11,700m	38,400ft
Time to 6,000m		10 minutes	
	P.1073	6.6 minutes	
Max range		550km (341 miles) without extra fuel	
	P.1073	660km (410 miles) without extra fuel	
Take-off run on grass.		800m (2,624ft)	P.1073 same.†

† This could be considerably reduced by employing take-off assistance.

Armament

Two 30mm MK 108 fixed forward firing cannon in the nose.

Despite the undisputed advantages in terms of construction and assembly, the Blohm und Voss project also displayed certain disadvantages when compared to the P.1073 (He 162).

An inferior performance could probably be expected, caused, in part, by the 2.5m (8ft 3in) long engine air intake duct, also the significant amount of drag induced by its 'rectangular' construction.

As the air intake was only some 1.2m (3ft 10in) above ground level, there was a real danger of foreign bodies being ingested, particularly on unprepared forward landing strips as well as the high risk of engine damage in a belly landing.

Although the contract was officially awarded to Heinkel on 30th September, Dr Vogt continued work on this project until 4th October 1944.

Taking everything into consideration, not just the suitability or otherwise of the individual proposals themselves, but seen in the light of the situation, the decision of the Air Armaments Staff to opt for the He 162 must be regarded as justifiable.

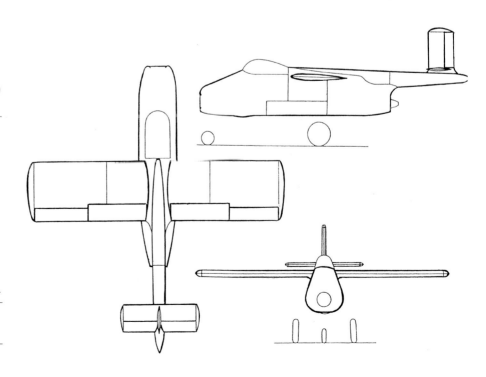

FOCKE-WULF

The company's technical director, Kurt Tank, whose stance on the whole Volksjäger concept was, if anything, more anti- than pro-, nevertheless presented the Technische Amt (RLM Technical Office) with two proposals based upon his previous research and development activities.

Together with a Volksflitzer (People's whizzer or darter, or jet fighter) project which, apart from the powerplant, was taken directly from the earlier twin-boom Flitzer models, his design department also began work on a new, so-called Volksflugzeug (People's Aircraft) which had its origins in Focke-Wulf's Design No.5 of January 1944.

Tank intended to use the Volksflugzeug more for purposes of comparison in order to promote his idea for a 'standard jet fighter' based upon the Flitzer. For although this latter had not particularly shone in a first round of discussions on the subject of a single-jet successor to the Messerschmitt Me 262, Tank still hoped at this stage to improve the performance of the Flitzer by such measures as reductions in weight and surface area.

Focke-Wulf's design leaders foresaw considerable drawbacks to the Volksjäger programme as proposed by the powers-that-be:

By the time it reaches the front in any meaningful numbers (third quarter of 1945), any Volksjäger-type aircraft is certain to be inferior to enemy jet fighters (eg Lockheed P-80 Shooting Star or Gloster Meteor – authors) and its operational life span would be brief because: the BMW 003 is too weak a powerplant; the lack of wing sweep, dictated on production grounds, will limit dive speed and impair combat performance; there is no design capacity for improvements in armament, armour or other equipment.*

This stance effectively put the company beyond the pale as far as the strict guidelines as laid down by Karl-Otto Saur went, and so Tank's dream of producing a Volksflitzer remained just that.

A somewhat lavish design for an 'emergency solution' aircraft, the Volksflugzeug featured a long, loss-inducing intake duct which added to both overall weight and surface area. An alternative layout featured an unswept wing somewhat similar to that of the He 162. Data quoted is for the swept version.

Focke-Wulf Volksflugzeug

18th September 1944

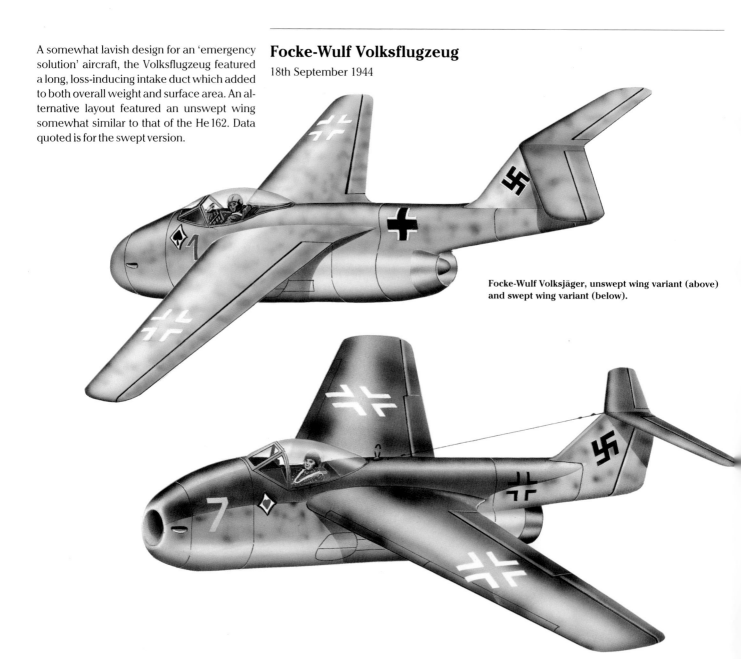

Focke-Wulf Volksjäger, unswept wing variant (above) and swept wing variant (below).

Powerplant

One BMW 003A-1 rated at 800kP (1,763lb) thrust.

Dimensions

Span	7.50m	26ft 7in
Sweep	35° at 0.25 chord	
Wing area	13.5m²	145ft²
Aspect ratio	4.0 : 1	
Length overall	8.80m	28ft 9½in
Height overall	2.85m	9ft 4in

Weights

Loaded	3,050kg with	6,723lb with
	660kg of fuel	1,455lb of fuel
Max wing loading	226kg/m²	46lb/ft²

Performance

Max speed	820km/h at 6,000m	509mph at 20,000ft
Initial rate of climb	14.5m/sec	47ft 6in/sec
Endurance	0.5 hrs at ground level	
Endurance	0.7 hrs at 10,000m	32,800ft
Take-off run, approx	1,000m	3,280ft

Armament

Two 30mm MK 108 fixed forward firing cannon in the nose.

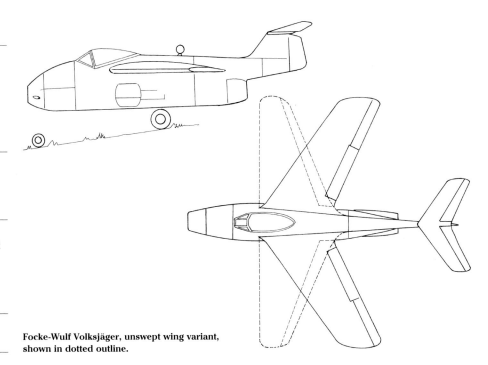

Focke-Wulf Volksjäger, unswept wing variant, shown in dotted outline.

OTHER DESIGNS

The performance of the Volksflitzer would have been markedly inferior to that of the Volksflugzeug in certain respects. Although it may have met the requirements of the specifications – at least when based on purely mathematical calculations – the design in fact stood no chance of being realised due to the technical difficulties of the production and because of the tight scheduling. Focke-Wulf showed manifestly little interest either way.

Information on all other submissions to the Volksjäger project is very patchy. The Junkers design, the EF.123 or EF.124, is known only through photographs of a model. (Junkers tended to use the prefix 'EF' – Entwicklungflugzeug, development aircraft – instead of the more universally adopted 'P' – Projekt – prefix. Exact dimensions and performance data are not available. The aircraft bore a certain similarity to the He 162, but by featuring a ventral powerplant was able to make use of a single-fin tail unit.

For the Fieseler Volksjäger, on the other hand, there are some data but no known illustrations. Fieseler's head of design, Lüsser, who was very sceptical of the whole concept, determined a loaded weight of 2,900kg (6,393lb) with a wing area of 13.00m² (140ft²). The stated take-off run of just 580m (1,640ft) is surprisingly short. Further details have been unobtainable.

As far as is known, neither illustrations nor technical data exist for the Siebel proposal.

Model of the Junkers Volksjäger design.

Artist's impression of the Junkers contender.

Chapter Five

Night and all weather fighters

It was not until 1940, when Germany's anti-aircraft ground defences had proved incapable of effectively combating the growing strength of the night raids being mounted by RAF bombers on targets within the Reich, that the Luftwaffe leadership recognised the necessity for an aircraft specially equipped for nocturnal pursuit operations.

The first aircraft delivered to the fledgling night fighter arm were re-equipped Messerschmitt Bf 110 Zerstörer and suitably converted bomber types such as Dornier's Do 17 and Do 217 and the Junkers Ju 88. When the enemy began to introduce new and improved aircraft capable of flying faster and at higher altitudes, these 'auxiliary night fighters' were soon being stretched to the limit of their capabilities. Then at the beginning of 1942, the de Havilland DH.98 Mosquito appeared, an aircraft that was to prove extremely difficult – if not impossible – to intercept.

At a meeting with representatives of the industry held in the summer of 1942, and with the horse long since bolted, the Reichsluftfahrtministerium (RLM – Reich Ministry of Armament and War Production) attempted belatedly to shut the stable door by demanding a dedicated night fighter which should not only carry the 'heaviest' armament, but also, and even more importantly, be faster than the enemy's night bombers. As Göring explained on 12th September 1942: *It is not right that I should continually be having to borrow from the bomber arm. Neither the bomber nor the day fighter is suited 100% for re-employment in the night fighter role.*

With the Heinkel He 219 Uhu (Owl), which successfully completed its maiden flight on 6th November 1942, the right aircraft for the job seemed at first to have been found. Internal squabbles and disagreements between the RLM, the Luftwaffe and the industry prevented its entering service with the night fighter force either rapidly enough or in sufficient numbers to be effective.

By mid-1944 it had become apparent that this aircraft, too, had its limitations in the struggle against the RAF's Mosquitos. Dipl-Ing Karl Francke, Heinkel's technical director

since 1942, was forced to admit on 15th August 1944: *The He 219 is currently the best and fastest night fighter we possess. But its performance is today no longer sufficient to catch the Mosquitoes/Griffon* (sic).

Initially the Focke-Wulf Ta 154, which first flew on 1st June 1943, was intended solely and specifically for this role. But on 1st July 1944 this aircraft was cancelled as part of the Jägerstab's (Fighter Staff's) type standardisation programme. The wooden construction of Germany's 'Moskito' was by then already posing great problems. The difficulties arising from the type of cold glue being used in its manufacture could not be overcome due to the debilitating effects on German industry of the very bombing campaign that the aircraft was intended to combat.

It was against the background of this most unsatisfactory and, for the Reich, highly dangerous state of affairs that concrete plans were formulated to convert Messerschmitt Me 262 Schwalbe (Swallow) and Arado Ar 234 Blitz

Test flight by a development Arado Ar 234 towing a Deichselschlepp (air trailer) auxiliary fuel tank.
Ken Ellis collection

(Lightning) jets and the high speed Dornier Do 335 Pfeil (Arrow) piston-engined fighter, for operational deployment as short range night fighters. All three machines seemed capable of bringing the Mosquito plague to an end.

As a first step, the two-seat Me 262B-1a trainer was to be modified as the Me 262B-1a/U1 interim night fighter. The definitive night fighter version, the Me 262B-2a, would then come somewhat later based upon the experience gained from the interim model.

Arado followed a similar route. But as the Ar 234 housed its crew in a fully-glazed nose compartment in keeping with its intended reconnaissance role, development was not quite so straightforward. The Ar 234B-2/N interim night fighter would have to evolve through a number of stages, via the Ar 234C-3/N and proposals such as the Ar 234C-7, 'P-1, 'P-2, 'P-3 and 'P-4, before the definitive 'P-5 finally emerged.

Dornier also initially envisaged an interim solution with the Do 335A-6, which in the event was rendered superfluous by the advent of the definitive Do 335B-6 night fighter design. Because of its markedly inferior maximum speed when compared to the two jet types, however, and with the forward engine

precluding any possibility of installing the latest Funkgerät (FuG - radio or radar set) 244 'Bremen 0' search radar in the nose, this aircraft really stood very little chance.

Later, in March 1945, the Horten brothers entered the ring by offering the Luftwaffe a night fighter variant of their two-seat 8-229 (Horten Ho IX / Gotha Go 229) multi-purpose aircraft as an 'immediate solution'. (The '8' being an RLM prefix to a sequence of numbers allocated to designs of aircraft and missiles. '8-' numbers were generally allocated in batches, although there were exceptions, as in this case; the 'neighbours' of the 8-229 being the DFS 228 high altitude rocket-powered research aircraft and the DFS 230 assault glider. In a similar system, piston engines were prefixed '9-', turbojet and rocket engines '109-'.) With the exception of this last named proposal, all of the 'interim night fighter' designs resulted in prototypes being built and tested.

The Me 262B-2a was by far the most promising contender for the rapid production of a 'definitive' short range night fighter. A low all-up-weight, scope for further development and a good performance were not the only things in its favour. There was also the invaluable operational experience gained in the meantime on the Me 262A-1a and Me 262B-1a/U1 by the experimental Kommando (special duties unit) Welter (the later 10/NJG 11). A first prototype of the definitive Me 262B-2a was nearing completion by April 1945. The Hortens also began construction of the two-seat Ho IX V6, and four trials models of the Do 335B-6 had come off Dornier's production lines before the capitulation. The Arado Ar 234 P-5 was scheduled to make its maiden flight by June 1945 at the latest, with operational trials commencing in the autumn.

None of the above was suited for long range night fighter operations, which called for the enemy bomber stream to be engaged, if possible, during assembly and approach and thence while being 'escorted' across Reich airspace.

Parallel to their development of the short range night fighter, Focke-Wulf and Dornier – the latter again using the Do 335 as a basis – therefore began work on mixed powerplant night fighter and Zerstörer projects combining a high speed dash capability with extended range and endurance. Arado's Professor Walter Blume proposed increasing the range of the Ar 234C-7 night fighter by use of an expendable long-range fuel tank towed behind the aircraft by means of a semi-rigid tube; the so-called Deichselschlepp (air trailer). But at the beginning of 1945 work on extended range night fighters was cancelled on 'capacity grounds'. Only Dornier, who had received a development contract for the Do 435 (a side-

Radar operator's station and equipment in the Me 262B-1a/U1 auxiliary night fighter as used in the night and all weather roles.

by-side two seater version of the Do 335), is known to have continued work into February 1945.

That was not the end of the story: incredible as it may seem, the Luftwaffe began to plan for the night fighter of the future. On 27th January 1945 the Technische Luftrüstung (TLR – Technical Air Armaments Board) issued a specification, numbered 12376/45, for the future, the 'optimum', night fighter, which was ultimately to replace all present types: the auxiliary, the interim and the 'immediate solution' night fighters.

Combining a speed of 900km/h (559mph) at 9,000m (29,500ft) with an overall endurance of four hours, the machine was to be armed with four cannon and equipped with 'Bremen 0' radar. Contemporary thinking obviously still regarded a two-man crew and purely offensive armament as sufficient.

Arado, Blohm und Voss, Dornier, Heinkel and Messerschmitt were initially invited to compete for the development contract; Focke-Wulf and Gotha adding their names later.

On 26th February 1945 a first meeting was held at the Focke-Wulf facility at Bad Eilsen to discuss initial submissions for the proposed night fighter projects. Focke-Wulf's technical director, Dipl-Ing Kurt Tank, also headed the Entwicklungssonderkommission (ESK – Special Development Commission) for night and all weather fighters, one of the numerous divisions of the Entwicklunghauptkommission

(EHK – Main Developments Commission). Along with top speed and armament, the question of maximum achievable endurance began to assume growing importance as one of the main criteria.

A few days later the industry received revised specifications. The Luftwaffe was now demanding an enormous increase in armament, including defensive weaponry, and a greatly extended endurance. As a logical consequence of this, provision for a third crew member had become indispensible. These new requirements went way beyond the present projects and forced the companies either to rework or completely redesign their proposals. But the modified and new projects which emerged were still far from satisfactory for their intended operational role in terms of dimensions and weights.

This fact had to be accepted by the participants in a final round of discussions on the subject which took place on 20th and 21st March 1945 again at Bad Eilsen. Represented by Oberstleutnant Siegfried Knemeyer, the TLR withdrew the controversial new requirements and promised yet a third set of specifications for the 2nd April 1945. At the same time the number of firms to be involved in the continued development of the future night fighter was reduced to just three: Arado, Blohm und Voss and Gotha.

Time was running out fast. In the east Gotenhafen and Danzig had been lost to the rapidly advancing Soviets. The fall of Vienna was imminent. In the west the Allies had crossed the Rhine and the German 'West Front' had collapsed along its entire length from Emmerich to Mannheim.

Dish antenna of the FuG 240 'Berlin' radar, predecessor of the FuG 244 'Bremen 0' model.

Two MK 1088 30mm cannon protruding from the fuselage of a Junkers Ju88G-6 – the upward-firing Schräge Musik anti-bomber weapon.

Ground/Air Radio Communications:
FuG 24SE (Funkgerät) radio or radar set, with ZVG 15 (Zielflugvorsatzgerät) homing device.
FuG 29 ground-to-air control. 'Reportage' airborne situation report receiver.
EiV 125 (Eigenverständigungsanlage) crew intercom system.

Identification Equipment:
FuG 25a or 'c 'Erstling' ground-to-air identification, friend or foe (IFF).
Combined ground-to-air and air-to-air IFF devices (eg FuG 226 'Neuling') were under development.

Navigation Equipment:
FuG 120K simplified version of the 'Bernhardine' radio beacon receiver.
Peil G6 'Ludwig' with APZ 6 (Automatischer Peilzusatz) – automatic supplementary direction finding equipment.
D/F Direction finding homing receiver.

Airborne Search Radar:
FuG 244 'Bremen 0', active homing device with concave mirror antenna, range 0.2 to 50km (1,500ft to 30 miles).
FuG 350Zc 'Naxos', passive receiver, reactive to H2S radar emissions from enemy aircraft, maximum range 50km (30 miles).
FuG 280 'Kiel Z', infra-red homer, range 4km (2.5 miles) as an additional option.

Bad-weather Landing Aids:
FuG 125 'Hermine', radio beacon receiver.
FuG 101a precision altimeter.
FuBl 3 (Funk-Blindlandeanlage) blind-landing radio equipment.

Other devices used, but not listed above, are covered briefly in the individual project descriptions.

After this 'closing' conference only one or two sporadic instances of further night fighter development have been recorded.

The only practical result of these endeavours was the handful of Me 262B-1a/U1 interim night fighters of Kurt Welter's 10/NJG11 which continued to combat Allied bombers throughout March and into April. A prototype of the definitive night fighter, the Me 262B-2a, was nearing completion at the time of the capitulation. It, and much else, provided welcome booty for the victorious Allies.

The aircraft to be produced under the 'immediate solution' were specifically adapted for the night fighting role, but were based upon types already flying in order to keep production costs and development risks to a minimum.

Front line units were to receive their first operational machines in the autumn of 1945. To have any chance of meeting this target date, the first prototypes needed to commence flight testing in the early summer of 1945. The performance of these short range night fighters would be superior to any enemy machine. They were intended to bridge the gap until the entry into service of the 'optimum solution' aircraft.

In the space of just a few years, the night fighter had evolved from a standard day fighter operating on a makeshift basis under cover of darkness, via suitably modified Zerstörer and bomber aircraft, into a highly specialised machine, equipped with sophisticated electronics and armament, which in 1945 represented the pinnacle of aviation technology.

Together with an increased fuel capacity and an armament installation designed to meet the needs of nocturnal operations, the night and all weather fighter of the closing months of the Second World War was characterised by a comprehensive radio and electronics fit used for target search and ranging, to warn of enemy radar and to ensure accurate navigation. Typical equipment for a night fighter of 1945 consisted of:

ARADO

In August 1943, as part of the 'two-seater study', Arado's chief project engineer, Wilhelm van Nes, had suggested a night fighter variant of the 'TL-1500' jet-powered multipurpose aircraft. It was not until a good 12 months later that concrete plans, based instead upon the Ar 234, were drawn up.
The first model to be built was the Ar 234B-2N auxiliary night fighter, a few examples of which began development trials. No operational successes were achieved however.

Almost at the same time Arado's design department used the single-seat Ar 234C-3 and the two-seat 'C-5 as bases to propose, respectively, the Ar 234C-3N, an interim solution which could be produced fairly rapidly, and the improved – albeit more costly – Ar 234C-7 (initially known as the Ar 234C-5N).

The Luftwaffe voiced strong criticism, principally of the Ar 234C-3N. Its fully-glazed nose, they argued, would subject the pilot to additional danger from glare while offering absolutely no protection from flying debris. Further doubts were expressed regarding the armament.

Professor Blume could see his chances fading. At the beginning of January 1945 he therefore instructed his two designers, Meyer and Rebeski, to start work on a new series of night fighters to be developed out of the Ar 234C-7. The new model was to be designated the 'P', and by 19th January 1945 four projects, the Arado Ar 234P-1, 'P-2, 'P-3 and 'P-4 had appeared in very short order. This quartet differed primarily in accommodation for the two-man crew and in powerplant detail.

After discussions with the TLR, the Luftwaffe General Staff finally cancelled the Ar 234C-3N altogether on 24th January, but gave the go ahead for the Ar 234P-2 proposal, which was now to be fitted with additional oblique upward-firing armament. (This was known as Schräge Musik – literally oblique or jazz music.) Blume wanted to commence flight trials with his revised project, now designated the Ar 234P-5, as quickly as possible; if necessary using FuG 218. But he had only a few weeks in which to do so...

Arado Ar 234P-5

10th February 1945

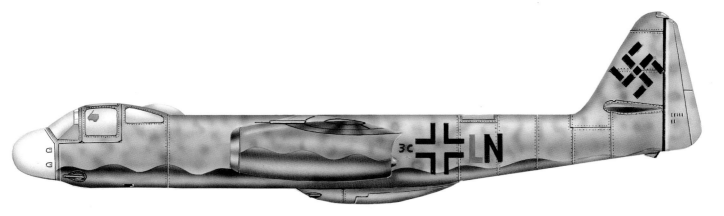

Crew
Pilot and navigator in two-man cabin, radar-operator in rear fuselage.

Powerplant
Two HeS 011A turbojets each rated at 1,300kP (2,865lb) static thrust.

Dimensions
Span	14.40m	47ft 3in
Wing area	27.0m²	290.6ft²
Length overall	13.30m	43ft 7in
Height overall	4.15m	13ft 7in

Weights (recalculated)
Empty equipped	6,400kg	14,109lb
Loaded	11,000kg with	24,250lb with
	3,300 litres	726 gallons
	internal fuel,	internal fuel,
	plus two 600 litre	plus two 131 gallon
	jettisonable tanks	jettisonable tanks
Maximum loaded with take-off assistance		
	11,400kg	25,132lb
Max wing loading	411kg/m²	84lb/ft²

The Special Development Commission adjudged weights of this order to be 'almost intolerable'.

Performance (recalculated)
Max speed	820km/h at 7,000m	509mph at 23,000ft
Service ceiling	11,500m	37,750ft
Time to 10,000m (32,800ft)	13.6 minutes	
Max endurance	at 9,000m	29,500ft
	2hrs 23 mins at max reduced throttle	
	1hr 30 mins at full thrust	

Armament
Two 20mm MG 151/20 cannon in nose, plus two 30mm MK 108 oblique upward-firing cannon at or near aircraft centre of gravity. Additional conversion set of two 30mm MK 108 cannon below the fuselage. Weapon load: Two 500kg bombs or two 600 litre (131 gallon) fuel tanks on ETC 504 racks below each engine.

Electronic equipment
FuG 15 VHF R/T with EiV 7 crew intercom, FuG 25a IFF with FuG 136 'Nachtfee' command transmission facility; FuG 142 emergency D/F receiver, FuG 120a 'Bernhardine' and FuG 125 radio beacon receivers, FuG 130 autopilot; FuG 244 active search radar (first prototypes with FuG 218 if necessary), FuG 350Z passive receiver.

Evidence of two different sets of proposals for this night fighter project has survived. With the first Ar 234P-5 of 31st January 1945 the use of four engines gave rise to strong reservations:

– Too high a fuel consumption.
– Aerodynamically unfavourable arrangement.
– Unlikely to meet stringent state-of-readiness requirements.

These, and similar, arguments finally forced the company to rethink their proposal.

For the second Ar 234P-5 Dipl-Ing Rebeski used the Ar 234P-1 design as a basis. He added the oblique upward-firing gun armament, made provision for a third crew member and exchanged the four BMW 003 turbo-jets for two Heinkel HeS 011s.

The performance of the 'P-5 was slightly inferior to that of the Messerschmitt Me 262B-2 but the aircraft proposed by Dipl-Ing Blume's team did have other advantages: protected fuselage fuel tanks and better protection for the crew.

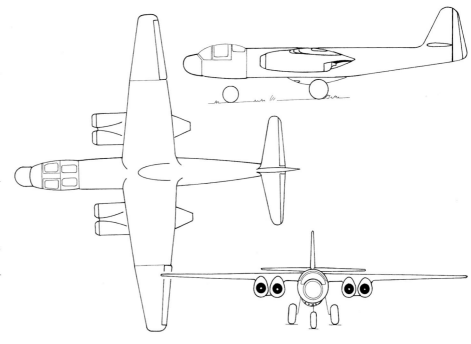

Arado Ar 234C-7

Horten Ho IXb (8-229B-1/Go 229B)

1st March 1945

The Horten brothers submitted a proposal for a two-seat version of their Horten HoIX intended, among other roles, for service as a night fighter. Shortly thereafter this small company received specifications from the TLR for an 'all-weather day and night fighter'

As an 'immediate solution' the night fighter variant of the two-seat multi-purpose aircraft had a decided advantage over such types as the Ar234P-5, Do335B-6 or Me262B-2 in that it would be built almost entirely of tubular steel and plywood and thus at appreciably less cost. Nor was that by any means all. In 1950 Dr Reimar Horten was to say of his design: *As wooden surfaces offer very little reflection to electric waves, they are almost invisible on the radar screen. And as a fighter pilot must, and should, utilise the element of surprise to the full, especially by night, so should his aircraft be constructed of wood ...*

The Hortens had also listed other advantages in their original submission, such as higher speed, lower wing loading, good climb capability and, not least, considerably extended endurance; each and every one of particular import for a night fighter.

The Horten HoIX V6 was to be the prototype for the two-seater variant. Partial assembly had already begun prior to the Reich's capitulation. Under even halfway normal circumstances, the chances of series production would not have been bad. Göring for one was a firm believer in the two brothers' work.

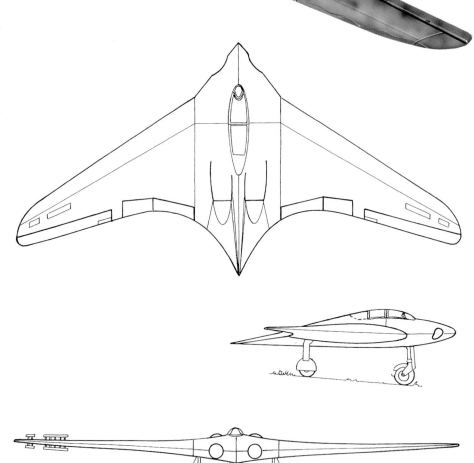

Crew

Pilot and radar operator/observer in ejection seats in armoured pressure cabin.

Powerplant

Two Junkers Jumo 004B-2 turbojets each rated at 910kP (2,006lb) thrust. Alternative option of two BMW 003A-1 each rated at 800kP (1,763lb) static thrust. (For structural reasons installation of the Heinkel HeS 011 could only have been carried out with the greatest difficulty.) Two 1,000kP (2,204lb) take-off rockets as additional field conversion set.

Dimensions

Span	16.76m	54ft 10½in
Sweep	28°	
Wing area	53.6m²	576.9ft²
Aspect ratio	5.2 : 1	
Length overall, approx	8.50m	27ft 10½in
Height overall	3.05m	10ft 0in

Weights

Empty equipped	5,200kg	11,463lb
Normal loaded	8,650kg with	19,069lb with
	1,850kg of fuel	4,078lb of fuel
Max loaded	10,500kg with	23,148lb with
	3,500kg of fuel	7,716lb of fuel
Max wing loading	196kg/m²	40lb/ft²

Performance

At normal take-off weight with two Jumo 004s.
Max speed at ground level

approx	950km/h	590mph
Initial rate of climb	16.4m/sec	53.8ft/sec
Service ceiling*	15,000-16,000m	49,000-52,500ft
Range	2,080km	1,292 miles
Range with max fuel load	4,600km	2,858 miles

*Powerplant data insufficient to determine exact ceiling.

Armament

Four 30mm MK 108 fixed forward firing cannon, additional 24 to 36 R4M unguided air-to-air rockets optional.

Electronic equipment

The Oberkommando der Luftwaffe (OKL – Luftwaffe High Command) specified that FuG 244 'Bremen 0' search radar was to be installed. This could be accommodated quite easily in the nose section.

Braking

Saw-toothed ventral brake under centre-section. Braking parachute reefed (gathered in) and unreefed.

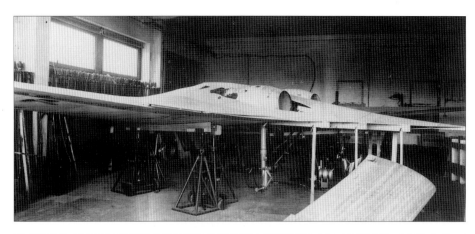

Top right: **Ho IX second prototype under construction.**

Centre right and bottom right: **Two views of the uncompleted Ho IX V3 centre section. This is held in storage at Silver Hill, Maryland, by the US National Air and Space Museum.**

MESSERSCHMITT

Thanks mainly to its Bf110G-4 night fighter, developed out of the original Zerstörer, the south-German company already had vast experience in the production and building of such specialised aircraft. At the same time the inherent inadequacies of the Bf110 meant that Messerschmitt had to contend at first hand with all the problems and the ever rising demands of the night fighter war.

The attempt to use the Bf110's successor, the Me 410 Hornisse (Hornet), in the night fighting role foundered on the latter's unsatisfactory performance; only a few examples of the type being employed on long range night fighter operations.

The Augsburg team had considered a night fighter version of the Me 262 as early as 1943 but expensive trials to develop and perfect an audio search system came to nothing. In May 1943, as part of his effort to create a true multi-purpose aircraft, Messerschmitt himself had

put a proposal before the RLM outlining the P.1092E (P – Projekt, project), a specialised jet-powered night fighter based upon the Me 262. In this he was unsuccessful.

Recognising the urgency of the situation, Messerschmitt did not let it rest there. In February 1944 his project bureau came up with the P.1099, an Me 262 with an enlarged fuselage. As well as heavy fighter and Zerstörer variants, they proposed a night fighter model which would have more than double the fuel capacity of the Me 262. But this too was to remain just a project. It was not until six months later that Berlin finally began to apply the sort of pressure that had long been called for.

As already described, Messerschmitt – like Arado and Dornier – intended to create his short range night fighter in two stages.

Stage 1: Production of the Me 262B-1a/U1 auxiliary night fighter, an aircraft which was to see operational service in limited numbers with 10/NJG 11 mainly in the Berlin area during the closing weeks of the war. Oberleutnant Kurt Welter, the Kommandeur of this unit, had already demonstrated almost single-handedly that even a minimally modified Me 262A-1a could be turned into a useful night fighter. In December 1944 Welter had

started to fly the day fighter version on Wilde Sau (Wild Boar) sorties (Short range night fighter missions devoid of any radar aids and relying solely on visual target contact in collaboration with ground searchlights.) He achieved considerable success; his victims including several Mosquitos.

The conversion of the Me 262B-1a two-seat trainer into an auxiliary night fighter was carried out by the Lufthansa facility at Berlin-Staaken, whose engineers were soon offering their own suggestions on how best to adapt the aircraft to take the then latest in electronic equipment.

Stage 2: Designing and building the 'definitive' Me 262B-2 night fighter. Externally this differed from its predecessor in its lengthened fuselage, redesigned centre section and aerodynamically refined cockpit canopy. In terms of performance it possessed, above all, an increased range and incorporated the option of fitting oblique upward-firing Schräge Musik armament.

Even while the first prototype was under construction, this aircraft too underwent further development; its performance being upgraded by the installation of two HeS 011 turbojets and 'Bremen 0' radar.

Messerschmitt P.1099 night fighter.

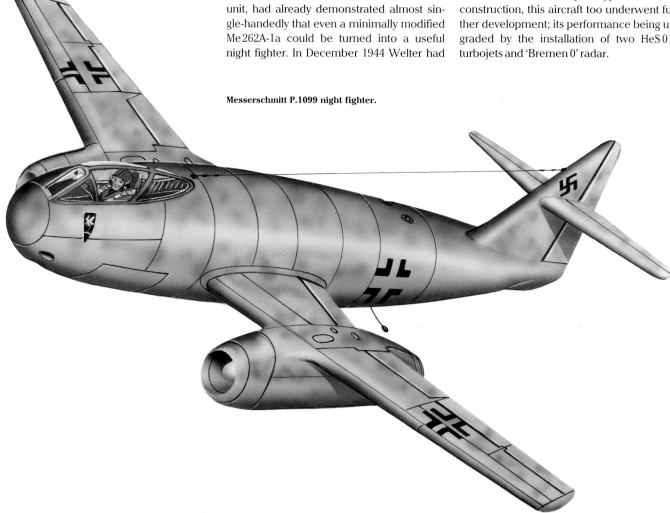

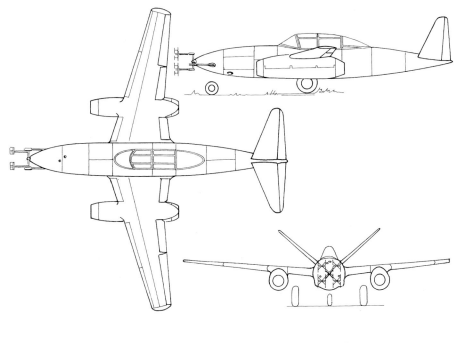

Above: **The jet night fighter 'ace of aces':
Oberleutnant Kurt Welter.**

Above left and left: **Messerschmitt P.1092E
specialised development of the Me262.**

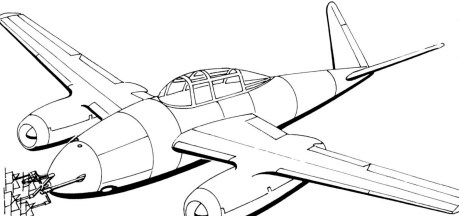

Below: **Messerschmitt Me262B-1a/U1 auxiliary
night fighter. 'FE-610' identifies it as one of the
aircraft assessed by the US Foreign Aircraft
Evaluation Centre, Freeman Field, Indiana.**

Messerschmitt Me 262B-2a

Project description of 18th January 1945

Crew

One pilot and one radar-operator/navigator seated in tandem in (optionally pressurised) cabin.

Powerplant

Two Junkers Jumo 004B-2 turbojets each rated at 910kP (2,006lb) static thrust; or two Junkers Jumo 004D each rated at 930kP (2,050lb) static thrust, plus an additional four 500kP (1,102lb) RI-502 take-off rockets (with six seconds of combustion); or two 1,000kP (2,204lb) RI-503 take-off rockets.

Dimensions

Span	12.56m	41ft 2in
Sweep	18.5° at 0.25 chord	
Wing area	21.7m²	233.5ft²
Aspect ratio	7.27 : 1	
Length overall	11.70m	38ft 4½in
Height	3.83m	12ft 7in

Weights

Empty equipped	4,764kg	10,502lb
Take-off weight	7,770kg with	17,129lb with
	3,100 litres of fuel	681 gallons of fuel
Max wing loading	358kg/m²	73.3lb/ft²

Loaded weight could be increased to 9,200kg (20,282lb), but only if a strengthened undercarriage was used. This would increase the wing loading at take-off to 425kg/m² (87.0lb/ft²). It was hoped that the long take-off run which this in turn necessitated could be kept within reasonable limits by use of rocket assistance.

Performance

At 7,770kg (17.129lb) loaded weight and with two Jumo 004B-2s.

Max speed	841km/h at 6,000m	522mph at 20,000ft
Initial rate of climb	16.0m/sec	52ft/sec
Service ceiling	10,500m	34,500ft
Endurance*	2.25 hours at 6,000m	
Range, at optimum throttle	1,300km	807 miles

* With additional fuel in external tanks, a maximum endurance of four hours should have been possible.

Armament

Four 30mm MK 108 cannon similar to the Me 262A-1, or two 30mm MK 103 cannon, plus two MG 151 or two MK 108 likewise in the nose. Alternative: Two 30mm MK 108 cannon in nose cone, plus two oblique upward-firing MK 108 cannon either side of cockpit.

Electronic Equipment

FuG 16 ZY with AFN (later FuG 24) VHF R/T with homing device; FuG 25a, FuG 125, FuG 120a; FuG 218 search and range-finding radar with Siemens 'Antler' nose antennae.

The project bureau passed their drawings to the assembly shop on 8th October 1944, only days after delivering those for the auxiliary night fighter. On 7th December the mock-up was ready for inspection by representatives of the TLR, of the Rechlin and Werneuchen test centres and by the one 'practical' expert, Kurt Welter. Only a few minor alterations were requested.

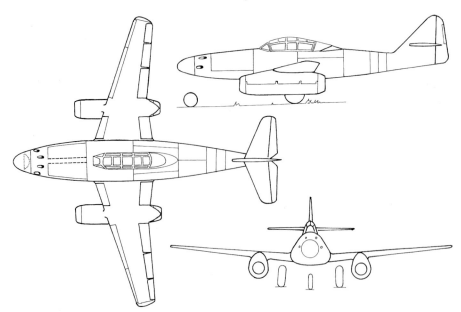

On 22nd January 1945 the Technische Amt (RLM Technical Office) commented apropos the use of FuG 218, 'The intention to use the FuG 218 as an interim solution on an aircraft with a maximum speed approaching 800km/h is not justifiable.' In autumn 1944 Messerschmitt had already carried out trials with this nose antenna array on the Me 262 V056. There had been no stability problems and by profiling the antennae support rods the loss of speed had been kept down to just 20km/h (12.4mph). At any higher operating speeds the use of such an array would be unacceptable and the aerodynamicists in particular – always mindful of the smallest percentage drop in performance – preferred to see a reflector antenna contained entirely within the contours of the fuselage.

(In a development report prepared for the Americans in June 1945 the Me 262B-2 was declared 'ready for take-off'. No maiden flight ever took place; nor even any further testing.) Prior to this, back in January 1945 official circles had expressed great interest in improving the performance of the Me 262 night fighter. Even at that late stage of the war, development of new engines, equipment and armament had been proceeding at breathtaking speed and Messerschmitt's 'Upper Bavarian Research Institute' was continually trying to improve the 'immediate solution' night fighter, even to the extent of attempting to comply with the new specifications issued on 27th January 1945. As before, Messerschmitt's aim was to avoid as far as possible unnecessary parallel developments and to achieve quick results by making extensive use of existing components.

In February 1945 Messerschmitt proposed equipping the Me 262B-2 with Daimler-Benz DB 021 turboprop engines. These promised a shorter take-off run and extended endurance. But this powerplant was also still in its infancy and so, on 17th March 1945 – just four weeks before his offices and workshops were occupied by the Allies – Messerschmitt submitted details of an improved version powered by HeS 011 turbojets.

Messerschmitt Me 262B-2 with two HeS 011s

17th March 1945

As well as the change in powerplant, this project was also to feature a strengthened undercarriage, improved electronics and increased armament.

Crew

One pilot and one radio-operator.

Powerplant

Two HeS 011A-0 turbojets each rated at 1,300kP (2,865lb) static thrust. At a later date two HeS 011B turbojets each rated at 1,500kP (3,306lb) static thrust, plus two 500kP (1,102lb) RI-502 take-off rockets or two 1,000kP (2,204lb) RI-503 take-off rockets.

Dimensions

Span*	12.56m	41ft 2in
Sweep*	18.5° at 0.25 chord	
Wing area*	21.7m²	233.5ft²
Aspect ratio	7.27 : 1	
Length overall	11.70m	38ft 5in
Height overall	3.85m	12ft 7in

* The wing of the Me 262B-2 was the same as that of the Me 262A.

Weights

Data below given to include the following options; internal fuel only (1); with two 600 litre (132 gallon) Doppelreiter ('Double rider', wing fuel fairings, precursors of the conformal tank) auxiliary fuel tanks faired into the wing upper surfaces (2); with two 600 litre (132 gallon) Doppelreiter auxiliary fuel tanks faired into the wing upper surfaces and two 300 litre (66 gallon) external auxiliary tanks (3).

Empty equipped, with six MK 108			
	(1)	5,149kg	11,351lb
	(2)	5,289kg	11,660lb
	(3)	5,329kg	11,748lb
Loaded	(1)	8,124kg with	17,910lb with
		2,890 litres of fuel	635.7 gallons of fuel
	(2)	9,264kg with	20,423lb with
		4,090 litres of fuel	899.6 gallons of fuel
	(3)	9,804kg with	21,613lb with
		4,690 litres of fuel	1,031.6 galls of fuel
Max wing loading	(1)	368kg/m²	75.3lb/ft²
	(1)	423kg/m²	86.6lb/ft²
	(1)	446kg/m²	91.3lb/ft²

The above wing loadings would have required not only intact airfields with long, undamaged concrete runways, but also pilots experienced enough to be able to get such a heavy machine into the air, with rocket assistance, by night, without undue difficulty. In the Germany of 1945 both these items were in short supply.

Performance (with HeS 011A-0)

Max speed		at 6,000m	20,000ft
	(1)	930km/h	577mph
	(2)	862km/h	535mph
Initial rate of climb	(1)	22.2m/sec	72.8ft/sec
	(2)	18.3m/sec	60.0ft/sec
	(3)	16.0m/sec	52.4ft/sec
Service ceiling		12,300m	40,350ft
Max endurance, optimum throttle			
	(1)	2.44 hours at 12,000m (39,300ft)	
	(2)	3.44 hours at 12,000m (39,300ft)	
	(3)	3.68 hours at 9,800m (32,000ft)	
Max range	(1)	1,480km at 12,000m	919 miles at 39,300ft
	(2)	2,220km at 12,000m	1,379 miles at 39,300ft
	(3)	2,260km at 10,200m	1,404 miles at 33,500ft
Take-off run (type 3)			
without assistance		1,400m	4,593ft
with 1,000kg assistance		1,150m	3,772ft
with 2,000kg assistance		950m	3,116ft

Armament

Four 30mm MK 108 cannon as exchangeable weapon pack in nose, plus two oblique upward-firing cannon to left and right of cockpit (conversion set). Alternatively: one 50mm MK 214 (Rheinmetall BK 5) cannon for use in Pulkzerstörer – heavily-armed anti-bomber aircraft – role against enemy bomber formations, plus (as conversion sets): two 24 R4M unguided air-to-air rockets, or two R 100 BS large-calibre unguided air-to-air rockets.

Electronic Equipment

Fug 24 SE with ZVG 15, FuG 29, EiV 125, FuG 25a or 'c, FuG 120 K, Peil G6 with APZ 6, FuG 244, FuG 350 Zc, FuG 125, FuG 101a.

Interim solution – extended endurance

In 1941 the Junkers Ju 88C and Dornier Do 17Z intruders of I Gruppe/NJG 2 were proving highly effective against aircraft of RAF Bomber Command over the British Isles. Inexplicably, however, the Luftwaffe abandoned these long range night fighter sorties in October 1941 by express 'Order of the Führer'. From that point on, much to the relief of the British and later the Americans, the absence of such missions remained a dangerous gap in Germany's aerial defences.

As part of the plans being drawn up from about mid-1944 onwards for a new, superior night and all weather fighter, the Luftwaffe – conscious of the speeds being attained by enemy bombers – demanded an aircraft which itself combined a high maximum speed with the extended endurance necessary for effective night operations. The aircraft development department within the TLR came to the conclusion that these requirements could only be met by a mixed power-plant machine featuring both piston and jet engines. The Technisches Amt specified a flying time of 5 hours, 20 minutes at an altitude of 8,000m (26,250ft). Twenty minutes of this total had to be maintainable at full emergency boost for the piston engine with simultaneous full throttle of the turbojet.

Such an aircraft would be used primarily for the following purposes:

– As a long range night fighter to engage enemy bombers in their assembly areas.
– For nocturnal patrolling to 'escort' the approaching and departing bomber streams, and as an airborne command and control aircraft to direct the Luftwaffe's own night fighter units.

The role of the short range night fighter was to be taken over by suitably modified high performance aircraft such as the Ar 234, Me 262 and Do 335.

In January 1945 the dedicated long range night fighter was abandoned on 'capacity grounds' and shortly thereafter, on 27th January, the Technisches Amt issued the specifications for the night fighter of the future.

DORNIER

Dornier P.254 (Do 435)

February 1945

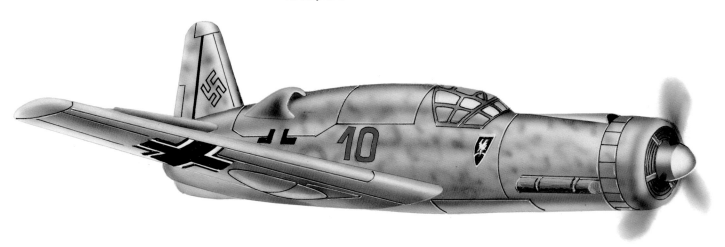

Dornier P.254 (Do 435) night fighter with extended endurance.

The Friedrichshafen company, perhaps the most conservative of the German aircraft manufacturers, based all its projects of the final war years on the extremely fast and aerodynamically proven Do 335 piston-engined fighter.

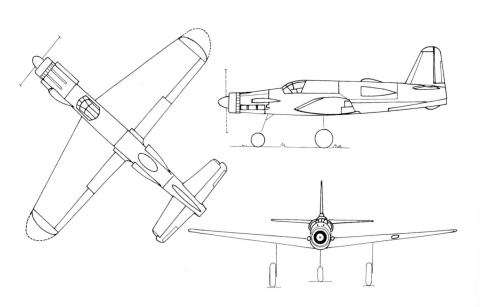

This aircraft was designed for operation both as a night fighter and Zerstörer. In May 1943, even before the first flight of the Do 335, the company had been working on Projekt P.232 for a fast mixed powerplant bomber. The design department's intention in combining a piston engine with a turbojet was to utilise the advantages of each system:

– To achieve long range capability at increased cruise speed by use of the piston engine alone,
– To offer the highest combat performance when in contact with the enemy by cutting in the turbojet and, not least
– To reduce take off and landing runs.

With the P.254, Dornier were to return to this earlier concept. Known as the Do 435 (a designation originally used to cover work on a high altitude Zerstörer version of the Do 335), the forward fuselage of the new aircraft was similar to the Do 335. Construction plans for the laminar wing had already been completed. The undercarriage was identical in all respects to that of the Do 335. Dornier were thus able to keep the development risks, and tooling costs should a contract for series production be awarded, well within acceptable limits.

Despite its extended endurance, the aircraft was not really suited to the long range night fighter role due to the lack of a third crew member. Dornier then offered the Do 435 as a performance-enhanced Do 335 within the remit of the 'immediate solution night fighter for combating the Mosquito'. The most telling argument in favour of the aircraft was undeniably its endurance, which the younger Dornier and Dipl-Ing Reidenbach were constantly bringing to the attention of the Main Development Commission. On 18th January 1945 Dornier submitted the project in Berlin and received a development contract. The Technische Amt obviously wanted the Jumo 213J engine as a possible alternative to the DB 603LA, as is evident from the upgraded specification of 2nd February 1945.

The maiden flight of a first prototype was planned for May 1945, with the first production machines being completed by the year's end.

Note:
The Do 435 as often illustrated with tandem piston engines and full-vision canopy is in all likelihood a 'post war development' which originated in some magazine's editorial office – not the only example of its kind!

In the United States the US Navy used a mixed powerplant configuration for two of its earliest post war carrier aircraft, albeit for only a very short time. These were the Ryan FR-1 Fireball and the Curtiss XF15C-1; the latter being only slightly smaller than the Do 435. With a powerplant of almost equal output, the American machine achieved a maximum speed which was about 100km/h (62mph) below that calculated for the Do 435.

Crew
One pilot and one radar operator in ejection seats in separate cabins.

Powerplant
(1). One Daimler Benz DB 603LA, take-off power 1,715kW (2,300hp), with 3.5m (11ft 6in) diameter three-bladed Me P8 variable pitch propeller plus additionally one Heinkel HeS 011A turbojet rated at 1,300kP (2,865lb) static thrust in rear fuselage.
(2). Alternatively, one Junkers Jumo 213J high altitude engine, take-off power (at full emergency boost with MW 50) 1,939kW (2,600hp) plus additionally one Heinkel HeS 011A turbojet rated at 1,300kP (2,865lb) static thrust in rear fuselage.

Dimensions
Span	15.40m	50ft 6in
Wing area	41.0m²	441.3ft²
Aspect ratio	5.8 : 1	
Length overall	13.40m	43ft 11¼in
Height overall	5.60m	18ft 5in

Weights
Empty equipped	(1)	7,585kg	16,721lb
	(2)	7,725kg	17,030lb
Loaded	(1)	10,500kg	23,148lb
	(2)	10,640kg	23,456lb
Wing loading	(1)	256kg/m²	52.4lb/ft²
at take-off	(2)	260kg/m²	53.2lb/ft²

Performance
Max speed	(1)	822km/h at 7,500m	510mph at 24,600ft
	(2)	865km/h at 11,200m	537mph at 36,750ft
Initial rate of climb	(1)	11.3m/sec	37ft/sec
	(2)	14.0m/sec	46ft/sec
Time to height		8,000m	26,250ft
	(1)	13.5 minutes	
	(2)	12 minutes	
Time to height		10,000m	32,800ft
	(1)	18 minutes	
	(2)	16.5 minutes	

Endurance
(Endurance figures for the DB 603LA-powered version.)
Approx two hours at 9,500m (31,000ft), climb at combat rating and constant power with turbojet throughout. Approx 4.9 hours at 7,000m (23,000ft) at constant power with turbojet in use for 30 minutes.
Approx nine hours at 4,000m (13,000ft) and 10.8 hours at ground level with piston engine alone at optimum throttle.

Armament
Two 20mm MG 151 cannon in fixed barbette above front engine, one 30mm MK 108 engine-mounted cannon, and two oblique upward firing 30mm MK 108 cannon in mid-fuselage.
Weapon load: One 500kg bomb as conversion set.

Electronic equipment
FuG 15 with EiV 15, FuG 25a, FuG 125, FuG 120, FuG 218, FuG 350 and FuG 101a.
Installation of the modern FuG 244 'Bremen 0' would hardly have been possible given the limited space.

FOCKE-WULF

On the basis of previous experience, Dipl-Ing Kurt Tank wanted to put night fighting on an altogether broader footing. Auxiliary and intermediate solutions did not interest him. For him the future of the night fighter arm came in the form of a relatively large aircraft, carrying a crew of three and equipped with the latest radar and navigational aids, which would be capable of staying aloft for some five to eight hours.

The design department's initial deliberations led in September/October 1944 to three studies which differed markedly in layout and powerplant. For the third of these preliminary designs a mixed powerplant of one Argus As 413 and two BMW 003s had already been mooted. It was on this basis that work went ahead. At the end of December 1944 during a meeting of the EHK, Generalmajor Ulrich Diesing, head of the TLR – the body which had been established the previous July to replace the Department of the Chief of Aircraft Procurement and Supply – concurred with Tank's point of view. But as is now known, this expensive scheme was then deferred in the light of the existing situation. Berlin wanted first to await the final victory before progressing any further.

Focke-Wulf mixed powerplant night and all-weather fighter

4th January 1945

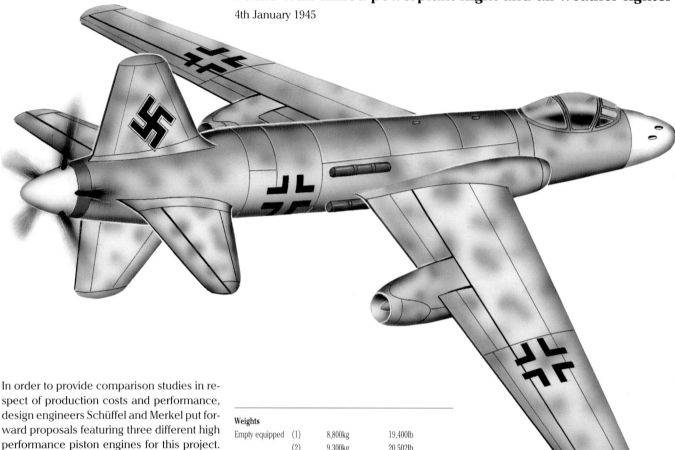

In order to provide comparison studies in respect of production costs and performance, design engineers Schüffel and Merkel put forward proposals featuring three different high performance piston engines for this project. Otherwise, all three designs were of the same basic layout and identical in terms of equipment, armament and endurance.

Crew

Pilot, radar operator and navigator together in one pressure cabin.

Powerplant

(1): One DB 603N, take-off power 2,051kW (2,750lb), with 3.4m (11ft 2in) diameter four blade propeller, or

(2): One Jumo 222C/D 24-cylinder four row radial engine, take-off power 2,238kW (3,000hp) with 3.4m (11ft 2in) diameter five blade propeller plus additional two BMW 003A turbojets each rated at 800kP (1,763lb) static thrust, or

(3): One Argus As 413, take off power 2,984kW (4,000hp), with two 3.1m (10ft 2in) diameter four blade propellers plus additional two BMW 003A turbojets each rated at 800kP (1,763lb) static thrust .

Dimensions

Span	(1)	20.40m	66ft 10½in
	(2)	21.00m	68ft 10in
	(3)	22.80m	74ft 9⅓in
Sweep		25°	
Wing area	(1)	52.0m²	559.7ft²
	(2)	55.0m²	592.0ft²
	(3)	65.0m²	669.6ft²
Length overall	(1)	16.65m	54ft 7in
	(2)	16.55m	54ft 4in
	(3)	18.10m	59ft 5½in
Height overall	(1)	4.99m	16ft 5in
	(2)	4.66m	15ft 4in
	(3)	4.90m	16ft 0in

Weights

Empty equipped	(1)	8,800kg	19,400lb
	(2)	9,300kg	20,502lb
	(3)	11,755kg	25,914lb
Normal loaded	(1)	11,500kg	25,352lb
	(2)	12,000kg	26,455lb
	(3)	15,000kg	33.068lb

Provision for increased fuel load as long range fighter:

Max loaded	(1)	13,000kg with	28,659lbs with
		3,000kg of fuel	6,613lb of fuel
	(2)	14,000kg with	30,806lbs with
		3,400kg of fuel	7,495lb of fuel
	(3)	19,000kg with	41,887lbs with
		5,300kg of fuel	11,684lb of fuel

Max wing loading at normal loaded weight

(1)	221kg/m²	45.2lb/ft²
(2)	218kg/m²	44.6lb/ft²
(1)	231kg/m²	47.3lb/ft²

Performance (As long range night fighter)

Max speed	(1)	816km/h at 11,500m	
		507mph at 37,750ft	
	(2)	848km/h at 10,500m	
		526mph at 34,500ft	
	(3)	850km/h at 10,500m	
		528mph at 34,500ft	
Initial rate of climb	(1)	15.6m/sec	51ft/sec
	(2)	16.5m/sec	54ft/sec
	(3)	15.6m/sec	51ft/sec
Service ceiling	(1)	13,400m	44,000ft
	(2)	14,000m	46,000ft
	(3)	13,000m	42,700ft
Time to 8,000m	(1)	11.3 minutes	
(26,250ft)	(2)	9.3 minutes	
	(3)	10.4 minutes	

Endurance

With turbojet shut down and piston engine at half throttle ('economical power'), and with a normal fuel load [ie 2 tonnes (1), 2 tonnes (2) and 2.5 tonnes (3)] flight durations of up to eight hours were possible. Figures with increased fuel capacity are not available.

Armament

Four fixed forward-firing 30mm MK 108 cannon in nose. By exchanging the weapons pack the following combinations were also possible: Two 30mm MK 103 plus two 30mm MK 213 cannon, or one 55mm MK 112 plus two 30mm MK 108 cannon. Two oblique upward-firing 30mm MK 108 cannon could be retrofitted in place of the two 85 litre MW50 booster tanks. Weapon load: Two 500kg (1,102lb) bombs as conversion set at outer wing stations.

Electronic equipment

FuG 24, FuBl 3F, FuG 130, FuG 101a, Peil G6, FuG 244, FuG 226 (25a) with FuG 139 'Barbarossa' command relay equipment, FuG 280.

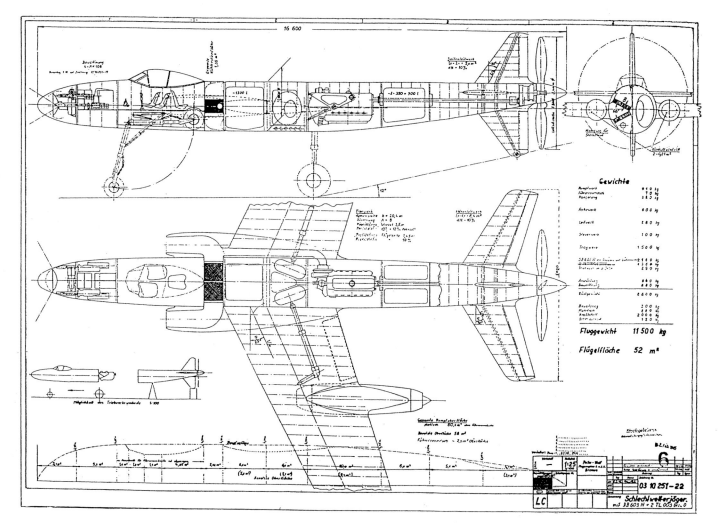

Focke-Wulf mixed-powerplant night and all weather fighter of January 1945, Design II.

Douglas XB-42 Mixmaster mixed-powerplant bomber.

Before the war's end a bomber powered by a pusher piston engine had been flown in the USA. To improve its performance, two Westinghouse 19B-2 turbojets were later added. The aircraft in question, the Douglas XB-42 Mixmaster, was thus equipped with a powerplant of almost equal output to that of the Focke-Wulf project. Despite it being very nearly the same size, the US machine's maximum speed of 487mph (785km/h) was appreciably lower than that of the German design.

Optimum solution – the next generation

With the specifications issued to the industry on 27th January and 27th February 1945, the TLR encapsulated the Luftwaffe's requirements for the 'optimum solution' night fighter which were intended to replace all previous auxiliary, immediate and intermediate solution designs.

The Heinkel (Heinkel-Hirth) HeS 011 (or 109-011A) powerplant for the night and all-weather fighter 'optimum solution' designs.

ARADO

Arado's chief designer, Professor Blume, submitted two very different proposals in response to the specification issued. Unlike Dornier's or Messerschmitt's offerings, for example, neither the tail-less Arado P.I design, nor the more conventionally configured Arado P.II project, resorted to types which were already flying as their starting point. Rather, both represented almost totally new designs, albeit with the advantage of having access to extensive earlier research. Work was undertaken on several different studies of each, which does not simplify matters for a review of this kind.

Some sources would seem to indicate that all of Arado's 'future night fighter' development work was carried out under the blanket designation E.583.

Clearly influenced by Arado and Messerschmitt: the Vought F7U-3 Cutlass carrier-based fighter of the US Navy.

Arado Project I

January-March 1945

Arado Project I (E.583) early design.

Crew

Pilot, radar operator and navigator in ejection seats together in one pressure cabin.

Powerplant

Two Heinkel HeS 011A turbojets each rated at 1,300kP (2,865lb) static thrust, semi-buried in rear fuselage.

Dimensions

Span	18.40m	60ft 4in
Sweep	35° at 0.25 chord	
Wing area	75.0m²	807ft²
Aspect ratio	4.5 : 1	
Length overall	12.95m	42ft 6in
Height overall	3.80m	12ft 6in

Weights

As per the Arado tender

Empty equipped	9,300kg	20,502lb
Normal loaded	14,700kg with	32,407lb with
	5,400 litres of fuel	1,187 gallons of fuel
Max loaded	15,700kg with	34,611lb with
	6,600 litres of fuel	1,451 gallons of fuel
Max wing loading	209kg/m²	42.8lb/ft²

Performance

According to EHK comparison figures calculated with a standard specified fuel load of 4,000kg or 4,800 litres (8,818lb/1,055 gallons).

Max speed	810km/h at 9,000m	503mph at 29,500ft
Initial rate of climb	11.6m/sec	38ft/sec
Service ceiling	12,600m	41,300ft
Max endurance* 3.15 hrs	at 450km/h	at 279mph
	at 6,000m	at 20,000ft

* With one engine shut down

Armament (definitive version)

Two fixed forward-firing 30mm MK 213 cannon in nose, two oblique upward-firing 30mm MK 108 cannon near aircraft centre of gravity, two rearward-firing 30mm MK 213 cannon in tail as defensive armament. Weapon load: Two 500kg (1,102lb) bombs as conversion set.

Electronic equipment

FuG 24, FuG 29, FuG 25a, FuBl 3, FuG 101, Peil G6 and APZ 6, FuG 244, FuG 280.

Aerodynamically this aircraft was based on the tail-less design studies already undertaken by Arado for the E.555 bomber project and the E.581 fighter proposal.

A characteristic of this and all other Arado tail-less night fighter designs was the wing-mounted fin and rudder assemblies which also served as boundary layer fences.

Following the 27th January specification, one of the first concepts depicted a twin-jet night and all weather fighter with an almost deltaform wingplan. In March, responding to the upgraded requirements, a larger design was completed with a broader fuselage intended to accommodate a third crew member and increased fuel capacity. This now featured a swept wing. It was in this latter form that the project was submitted by Arado to the EHK in Berlin.

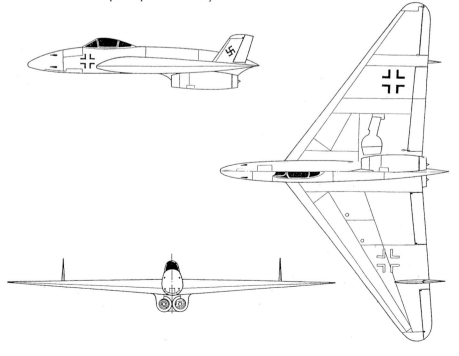

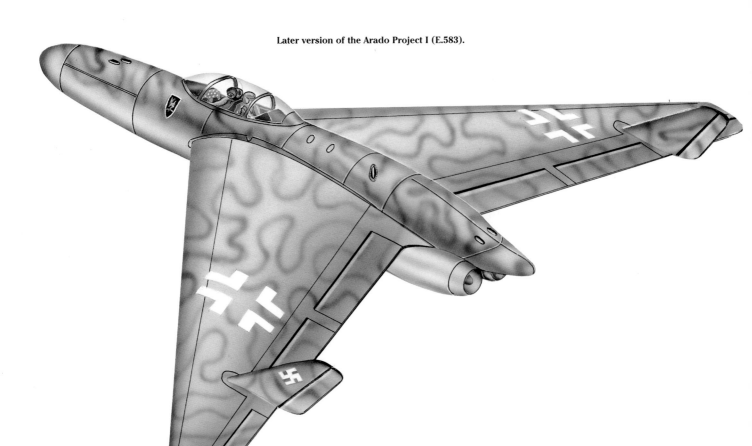

Later version of the Arado Project I (E.583).

On 20th/21st March 1945 the specialists' report criticised above all the large, drag-inducing surface area of the aircraft and the unfavourable engine installation arrangement. Immediately following on from this, yet another version was proposed. This featured a smaller, more sharply swept wing. Unfortunately, only written evidence of this latter has survived.

After the war the American manufacturer Vought utilised the Arado concept for their F7U-1 Cutlass carrier-based fighter. Powered by two Westinghouse turbojets, which delivered some 4,400hp (3,282kP) static thrust with afterburning, this lighter machine with its appreciably smaller wing achieved a top speed approaching 683mph (1,100km/h) at 20,000ft (6,000m).

Later version of the Arado Project I (E.583).

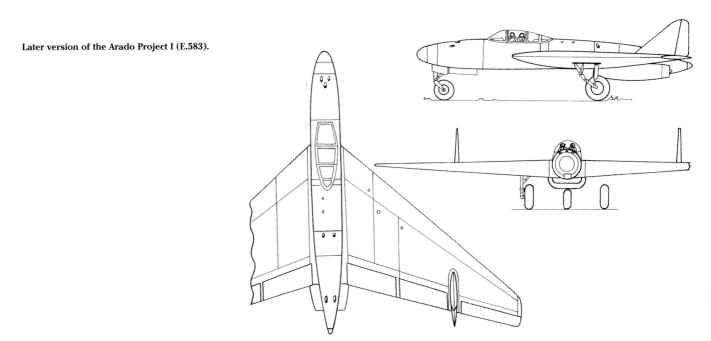

Arado Project II

March 1945

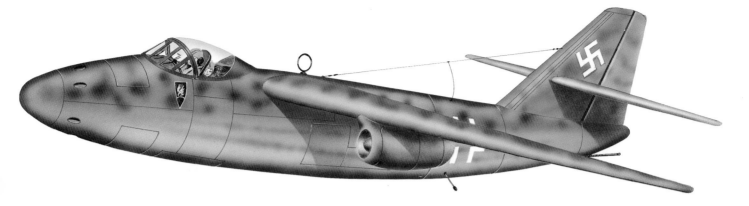

Crew

Pilot, radar operator and navigator in ejection seats together in one pressure cabin.

Powerplant

Two Heinkel HeS 011A turbojets, each rated at 1,300kP (2,865lb) static thrust, in underwing nacelles.

Dimensions

Span	14.98m	49ft 1½in
Sweep	35° at 0.25 chord	
Wing area	50.0m²	538ft²
Aspect ratio	4.5 : 1	
Length overall	17.30m	56ft 9in
Height overall	5.5m	18ft 0in

Weights

As per Arado tender

Normal loaded	14,300kg with	31,525lb with
	5,400 litres of fuel	1,187 gallons of fuel
Max wing loading	286kg/m²	58.5lb/ft²

Performance

According to EHK comparison figures calculated with 4,000kg (8,818lb) fuel.

Max speed	775km/h at 7,000m	481mph at 23,000ft
Initial rate of climb	11.5m/sec	37ft/sec
Service ceiling	11,400m	37,400ft
Max endurance* 2.3 hrs	with both engines at optimum throttle	
	at 450km/h	at 279mph
	at 6,000m	at 20,000ft

* It was not possible to shut down one engine for cruise.

Armament

As per the 27th February specifications:
Four or six fixed forward firing 30mm MK 108 cannon in nose,
two oblique upward-firing 30mm MK 108 cannon in fuselage, two
rearward-firing 20mm MG 151 cannon in tail as defensive armament.
Definitive version:
Two or four fixed forward-firing 30mm MK 213 cannon in nose,
two oblique upward-firing 30mm MK 108 cannon in fuselage, two
rearward-firing 30mm MK 213 cannon in tail as defensive armament.
Weapon load: Three 500kg (1,102lb) bombs as conversion set.

Electronic equipment

FuG 24, FuG 29, FuG 25a, FuBl 3, FuG 101, Peil G6 and APZ 6, FuG 244,
FuG 280.

Concurrent with their P.I proposal, Arado's design department offered an alternative based on experience gained from the Ar 234 and, to a lesser extent, their TEW 16/23-43 study. By using a more orthodox construction it was hoped that significant reductions could be achieved in respect of both development risk and test expenditure. Detailed drawings of the proposal show that an experimental 'V' tail unit was also being considered.

In terms of performance the Arado P.II was the least satisfactory of all the designs submitted. Once again the experts were critical of the large surface areas and the unfavourable drag-inducing arrangement of the underwing engines.

In similar manner, Vought offered the US Navy more orthodox versions of their proposal with the V-346B and 'D before that service finally opted on 25th June 1946 for the tail-less V-346A, that became the XF7U-1 Cutlass.

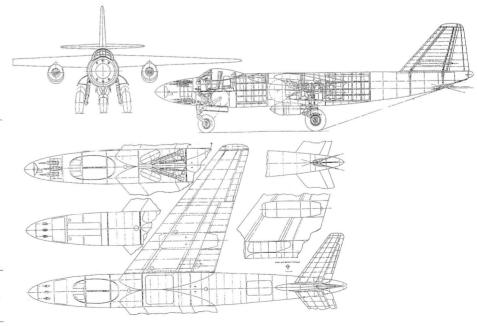

BLOHM UND VOSS

This company had little experience in the design and construction of night fighters. But at a time of far-reaching and revolutionary changes in military and aviation technology this was not necessarily any great disadvantage. Upon receipt of the specification for a new night fighter from Berlin at the end of January 1945, Dr Richard Vogt turned to his previous work on the P.212 single-jet day fighter to provide a basis for the new project. Dr Vogt, a highly unconventional designer who, almost without exception, carried out all the work himself, continued to follow a clear and self-imposed line of development which, he was convinced, was capable of meeting the continually changing demands made upon it without any significant disruption or major alterations. The only drawback to this was his use of an entirely new concept, requiring quite a lot of wind tunnel research and similar testing but which, in practice, had as yet only undergone initial trials.

Blohm und Voss P.215

March 1945

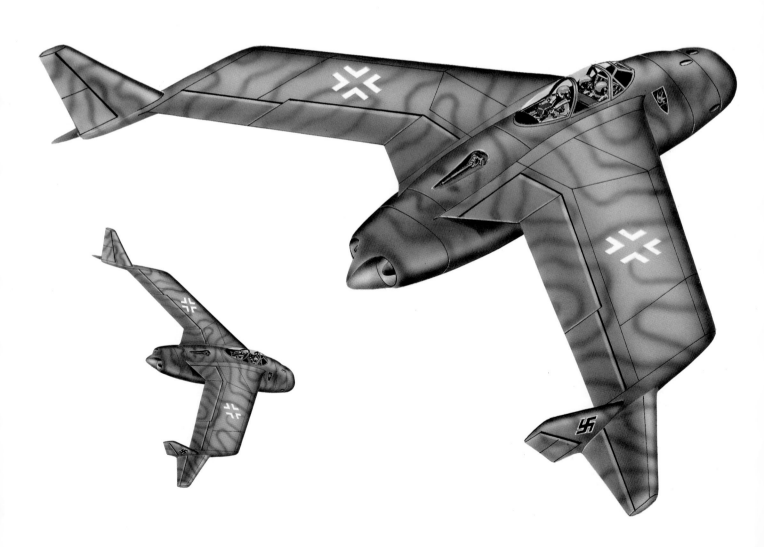

The data below refer to the P.215/02.

Crew

Pilot, radar operator and navigator/wireless operator together in one pressure cabin.

Powerplant

Two Heinkel HeS 011 turbojets each rated at 1,300kP (2,865lb) static thrust.

Dimensions

Span		14.40m	47ft 3in
Sweep	30°	at 0.25 chord, without outboard winglets	
Wing area		54.76m²	589.4ft²
Aspect ratio		3.79 : 1	
Length overall		11.60m	38ft 0in
Fuselage length		8.50m	27ft 9⅔in
Height overall		5.0m	16ft 4⅞in

In order to improve stall characteristics and to increase the stability of the swept wing, Vogt employed the 'isobaric principle', ie with a 12% profile the narrower chord outer winglets possessed a greater relative thickness than did the wingroots at 9.28%.

Weights

Empty equipped	7,400kg	16,313lb
Max loaded	14,680kg	32,363lb
	with 6,500kg	with 14,329lb
	(7,800 litres)	(1,715 gallons)
	of fuel	of fuel
Max wing loading	268kg/m²	54.8lb/ft²

Performance

According to EHK comparison figures calculated at a loaded weight of 14.7 tonnes (14.46 tons) and with 100% thrust.

Max speed		870km/h at 8,500m	540mph at 27,900ft
Initial rate of climb		10m/sec	33ft/sec
Service ceiling		12,000m	39,400ft
		14,800m	48,500ft
		possible under favourable conditions	
Time to height		25 min to 8,000m	26,250ft
Max endurance	5.2 hs	at 450km/h	at 279mph
		at 6,000m	at 20,000ft
		with one engine	with one engine
		shut down	shut down

Armament

Nose armament options: five fixed forward-firing 30mm MK 108 cannon, or five 30mm forward-firing MK 108 cannon with 0-15°elevation, or four fixed forward-firing 30mm MK 213 cannon, or two fixed forward firing 55mm MK 112 cannon, or eight by seven (=56) R4M unguided air-to-air rockets (Rocket armament could be combined with four MK 108, four MK 213 and, in some cases, with two MK 212/214), plus two oblique upward-firing 30mm MK 108 cannon in aft fuselage section and one rearward-firing FHL 151 barbette with two 20mm MG 151/20 cannon as defensive armament.

Weapon load: Two 500kg (1,102lb) bombs semi-recessed in fuselage.

Electronic equipment

FuG 244, FuG 25a, FuG 280, FuG 350 warning receiver(H2S), FuG 218R tail warning, FuG 24SE with EiV, FuBl 3E, FuG 101a, Peil G6 and FuG 29 'Reportage' for air situation reports.

The first P.215/01 design of February 1945, carrying a 4,000kg (879 gallon) fuel load, was capable of a maximum endurance of 3.5 hours. With a wing area of 50m² (538ft²) and devoid of any defensive armament, the two-seat night fighter weighed in at 12.7 tonnes (12.4 tons).

The new specification of 27th February 1945 called for some rethinking. But Blohm und Voss altered their basic design only marginally. What emerged, the P.215/02, was roughly comparable to the Junkers Ju 88G-6 night fighter in terms of wing area and loaded weight.

With the P.215 Dr Vogt again employed his familiar construction method of using a steel tube as the main structural component. Doubling up as the engine air intake, to this tube were attached all the other major components such as wings, undercarriage, armament, internal equipment and powerplant. The load bearing element of the wing was a broad box spar made of sheet steel which also served to house the fuel. Except for a few smaller components (eg the rudders), the aircraft was constructed entirely of steel and Duraluminum.

Despite what were actually quite good performance figures, the P.215 did not fully meet the 27th February specifications either. Attempts to get close to the required endurance by increasing the fuel capacity simply resulted in unsatisfactory take-off and climb capabilities. All the companies participating in the tender grappled with this self same problem of trying to 'square the circle'.

The results and the verdict were the same in every case: official insanity!

As far as the P.215 was concerned, the 'Night and All-Weather Fighter' ESK found fault with the short, broad fuselage which, it was feared, would generate airflow separation about the nose area in high speed flight. Further reservations were expressed with regard to the unusual rudder arrangement. Nevertheless, on 20th/21st March 1945 the EHK selected the Blohm und Voss proposal, together with the tail-less Arado P.I and Gotha's flying-wing project for further development. Whatever the final choice may have been, the German night fighter of the late 1940s and early 1950s would undoubtedly have displayed novel aerodynamic characteristics.

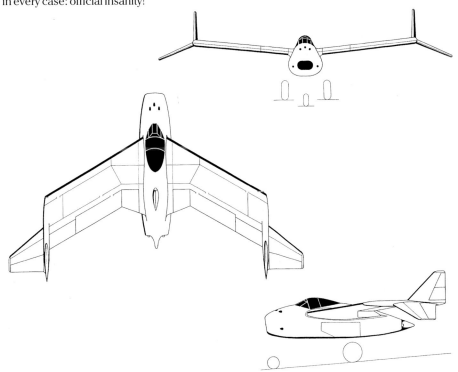

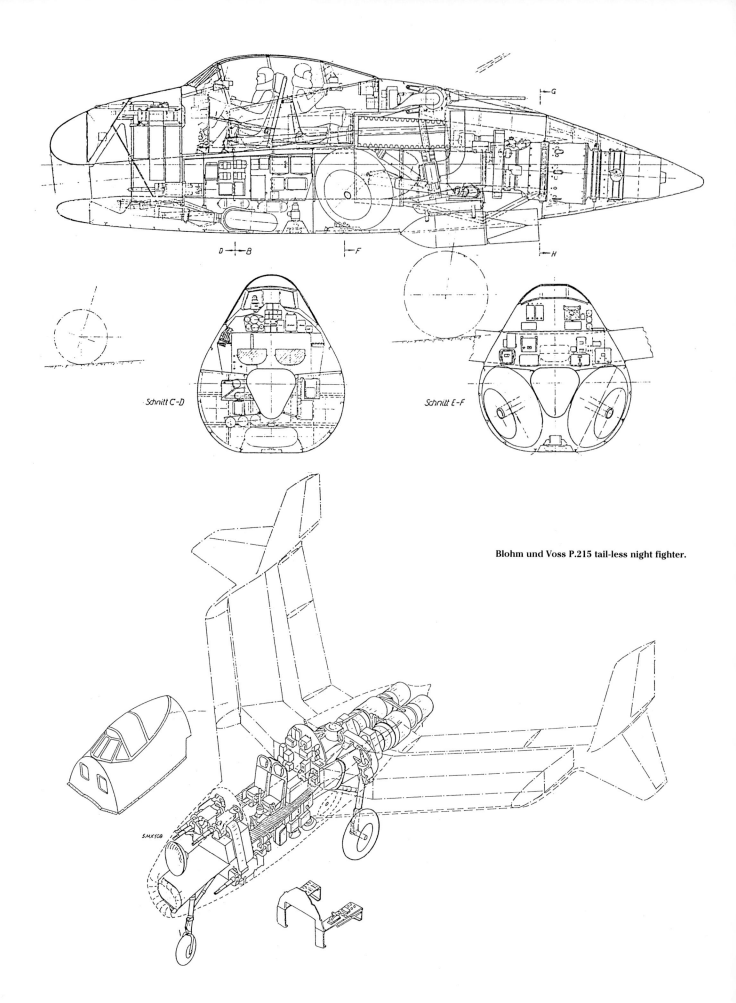

Schnitt C-D

Schnitt E-F

S.MK108

Blohm und Voss P.215 tail-less night fighter.

DORNIER

Although the required speed of 900km/h (559mph) would seem to have been attainable only by the use of jet power, Dornier attempted to utilise piston engines in the first of his aerodynamically advanced 'optimum solution' night fighter designs. After all, there were still those among the Luftwaffe's top brass who hesitated to place all their bets on the 'jet card' and who demanded parallel development of both piston and jet powerplants. Not only that, there were certain to be bottlenecks in the production of jet engines, particularly of the Heinkel HeS 011 which was intended to power so many of the projects.

But the manufacturers on the shores of Lake Constance could not get their ideas accepted. Even the pure-jet P.256 follow-up design failed to convince the experts. Dornier firmly believed that by having recourse to the Dornier Do 335, which was already flying, he could guarantee rapid construction and problem-free trials. Such advantages, he felt, should be worth a certain forfeiture in performance. In the case of the 'optimum solution' Berlin was not prepared to countenance a compromise of any sort.

Dornier P.252

February/March 1945

In the period between August 1941 and January 1942 the design department in Friedrichshafen had been occupied in producing a series of comparative studies for a night fighter. The resulting projects, the P.202, P.208, P.215 and P.217 were all characterised by a pusher propeller powerplant and tricycle undercarriage. Such a configuration allowed for a battery of heavy weapons to be housed in the nose. (As the Do 335 was originally envisaged as a 'very fast bomber', this consideration had not arisen during this aircraft's initial design stage.)

Some years later moreover, flight tests with the Do 335 confirmed what was already suspected: that the tractor propeller impaired the overall efficiency of the combined powerplant. For this reason the further developments of the Do 335, designated P.247 and P.252, were powered by rear engines alone. The advantages of such a layout for a night fighter were obvious: just as in a jet, the crew were afforded an excellent field of vision, and the radar, together with the armament, could be housed in the nose or forward fuselage without difficulty.

There were at least three studies made of the P252 night fighter and Zerstörer:
  – P.252/1 – a two-seat proposal of February 1945 with an unswept wing of 16.4m 53ft 9½in) span, 1,900 litres (418 gallons) fuel and a maximum speed of 900km/h (559mph).
  – P.252/2 – with lengthened fuselage to accommodate a third crew member, wings with 35° sweep and 18.4m (60ft 4½in) span.

  – P.252/3 – with reduced sweep and increased fuel capacity.
The Zerstörer version featured a shortened fuselage.

When the Dornier representative submitted the P.252/1 and P.252/2 projects for official evaluation on 26th February 1945, the general consensus had already swung away from the piston engine. Göring's decree of 22nd February, stipulating that only those projects powered by turbojet were to be developed further, resulted in this design being abandoned too. Nevertheless, for some unknown reason, Dornier apparently continued work on the P.252/3 project beyond this date.

In terms of performance, this heavy specialised aircraft was not inferior to the jet-powered night fighter in any respect.

Quite the opposite: its endurance, for example, could hardly be equalled by a turbojet of similar dimensions. At the same time, the highly developed P.252 was not capable of much further refinement; despite the swept propeller blades, the piston engine/propeller powerplant system had reached the very limit of its development potential.

It is interesting to compare this design with the US Northrop P-61 Black Widow heavy night fighter. Although somewhat larger and heavier than the Dornier P.252, the P-61 had a roughly comparable engine power output, yet its maximum speed at 20,000ft (6,000m) was only about 372mph (600 km/h).

The data table overleaf refers to the P.252/3 and is partially reconstructed using available manufacturers specifications.

Dornier P.252/1 with swept leading edge, but straight trailing edge (below) and P.252/2 with fully swept wing and lengthened fuselage (bottom).

Crew

Pilot, radar operator and navigator together in one cabin.

Powerplant

Two Junkers Jumo 213J liquid-cooled 12-cylinder tandem-coupled engines, take-off power 1,305kW (1,750hp) – emergency power 1,671kW (2,240hp) with MW 50 boost.

Alternative: two Daimler-Benz DB 603LA, take-off power 1,361kW (1,825hp) – emergency power 1,566kW (2,100hp) with MW 50 boost. The engines were coupled via an extension shaft, a second shaft driving the two 3.2m (10ft 6in) diameter contra-rotating, three-bladed VDM variable pitch propellers; blade sweep 50°.

Armament

Two 30mm MK 108 cannon in interchangeable nose section, and two 30mm MK 213C cannon in forward fuselage below cabin, plus two 30mm oblique upward-firing MK 108 cannon aft of cabin. Weapon load: Two 250kg (551lb) or two 500kg (1,102lb) carried externally below wings (field conversion set).

Electronic equipment:

EiV system, FuG 24SE with ZVG 24, FuBl 3 with AWG 1, FuG 218R, FuG 25a, FuG 101, FuG 139, FuG 280, FuG 350, FuG 244/245 'Bremenanlage'.

Dimensions

Span	15.80m	51ft 9½in
Sweep	22.5° at 0.25 chord	
Wing area	50.0m²	538ft²
Aspect ratio	5.0 : 1	
Length overall	17.20m	56ft 4¾in
Height overall	5.05m	16ft 6in

Weights

Empty equipped	8.600kg	18,959lb
Loaded	12,300kg	27,116lb
	with 3,400 litres	with 747.9 gallons
	of fuel	of fuel
Max wing loading	246kg/m²	50.4lb/ft²

Performance (With two Jumo 213Js.)

Max speed*		930km/h	577mph
		at 11,300m	at 37,000ft
Initial rate of climb		21m/sec	69ft/sec
Service ceiling		12,500m	41,000ft
Time to height	7.5min	to 8,000m	26,250ft
	10 min	to 10,000m	32,800ft

* Dornier's project engineers, obviously themselves surprised at figures of this magnitude, remarked of the P.252/1:

'The maximum speed of 900 km/h, which seems hardly credible for an "Otto"-engined aircraft, was substantiated by accurately calculated data'. The design could well have achieved the endurance required by the specification of 27th February 1945.

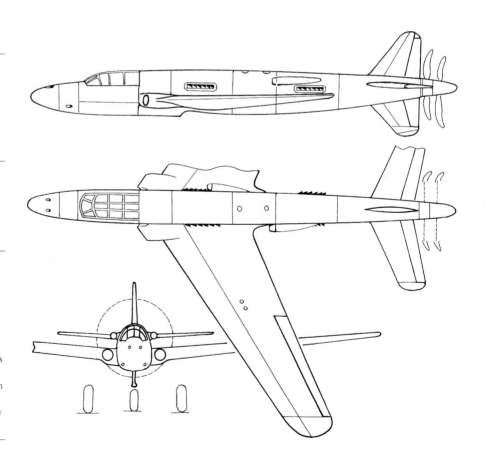

Dornier P.256

15th March 1945

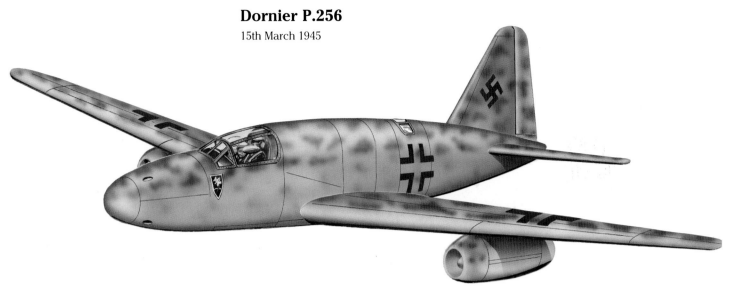

Crew

Pilot and radar operator together in one cabin, navigator in rear fuselage (the 'Arado solution').

Powerplant

Two Heinkel HeS 011 turbojets each rated at 1,300kP (2,865lb) static thrust in mid-span underwing nacelles; additional take-off assistance powerplant optional.

Dimensions

Span	15.45m	50ft 8½in
Wing area	41.0m²	441ft²
Aspect ratio	5.8 : 1	
Length overall	13.60m	44ft 7in
Height overall	5.50m	18ft 0in

Weights (As per Dornier tender)

Empty equipped	6,860kg	15,123lb
Loaded	11,300kg with	24,911lb with
	3,750kg of fuel	8,267lb of fuel
Max wing loading	276kg/m²	56.5lb/ft²

Performance (As per Dornier tender)

Max speed	882km/h	548mph
	at 8,000m	at 26,250ft
Initial rate of climb	11.2m/sec	36ft 8in/sec
Service ceiling	13,330m	43,600ft
Time to height	16.5min to 8,000m	26,250ft
	25.0 min to 10,000m	32,800ft
Max range	1,550km	963 miles
	at 630km/h	at 391mph
	at 6,000m	at 20,000ft

Max endurance*with engines throttled. (* EHK calculations)

2.6 hrs	with 4,000kg	with 8,818lb
	of fuel	of fuel

Armament

Four fixed forward-firing 30mm MK 108 cannon in detachable nose cone, plus two oblique upward-firing 30mm MK 108 cannon (field conversion set). Weapon load: Two 500kg (1,102lb) bombs as conversion set for fighter-bomber role.

Electronic equipment

FuG 24SE with ZVG 24 homer, FuG 29, EiV, FuG 25a or c, FuBl 3, FuG 101a, Peil G6 with APZ 6, FuG 280, FuG 350, FuG 244 'Bremen' with 'Elfe' and 'Gnom' automatic weapon-triggering.

After the categorical rejection of his P.252, Dornier attempted to use this proposal, a low-wing all-metal design developed directly out of the Do 335 and Do 435, to meet the Luftwaffe's requirements of 27th February 1945.

The main criticisms contained within the overall unfavourable report on the design were primarily:

- Adverse cross-sectional area distribution not conforming at all to area rule,
- Large drag-inducing surfaces, and
- The short fuselage necessitating a large tail unit.

Dornier's strength clearly lay in fast piston-engined aircraft.

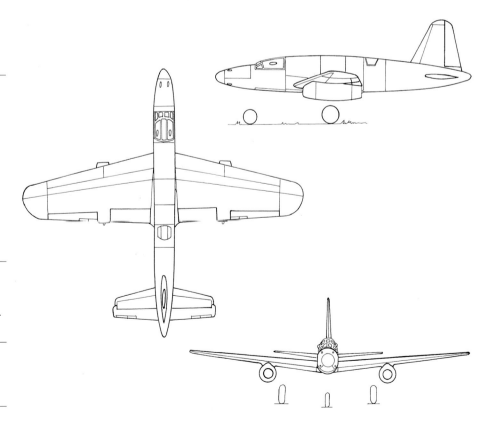

FOCKE-WULF

When Focke-Wulf started work on a new design for an all-jet night fighter at the beginning of 1945, the design bureau based it on an existing study for a twin-jet heavy fighter. By the end of January the first results of their labours were already apparent in the form of a project description and general arrangement drawing. The model as initially described and illustrated was further developed and continually improved until officially submitted for the first time on 26th February 1945. The upgrading of the specifications then resulted in a more detailed description encompassing five studies being prepared in March 1945. Professor Kurt Tank selected the two most promising of these five proposals and presented them for inspection and appraisal by representatives of the Luftwaffe and industry at Bad Eilsen on 20th/21st March 1945.

The series of designs all displayed the aerodynamically very clean, unslotted wing typical of Focke-Wulf. Experience would soon have revealed the necessity for boundary layer fences (as found by the Mikoyan-Gurevich design bureau in the USSR post-war).

The relatively low wing loading promised good take-off and landing capabilities, an equally good performance at altitude and acceptable flight characteristics at fairly low speeds.

In contrast to his project engineers Schöfel, Richter, Merkel and Bielefeld, Tank held firm for a conventional layout. He saw no particular disadvantages in this in terms of performance and construction when compared to a tail-less configuration.

A flying-wing, in Tank's view, may have proven slightly superior in performance, but it would undoubtedly have required a lengthy period of testing and trials, and there was very little previous experience upon which these could be based.

The selection of a fuselage-mounted powerplant permitted one engine to be shut down in flight, which meant a saving in fuel without having to increase drag by compensating for the thrust moment about the vertical axis. During combat the fighter would fly at full power and thus be in a position effectively to engage any enemy aircraft, even at low level.

At the 26th February conference the main criticism was aimed at the length of the engine air intake with its inherent danger of duct loss. Taking advantage of the fact that the meeting was being held at Focke-Wulf's own Bad Eilsen facility, Tank immediately had drawing No. 03 10 251-36 amended; hoping at the same time that the alteration would lead to an increase in the somewhat unsatisfactory projected maximum speed.

The mix of criticism and recommendation engendered by this project prompted Tank to continue work on the basic concept. All further proposals can, to a greater or lesser extent, be traced back to this one design. In response to Messerschmitt's proposal of 12th February 1945, which was somewhat faster, Tank pointed time and again to the low wing loading of his design; a feature of all his development work.

Design II submitted at the 20th/21st March conference, featured a Duraluminum fuselage and wooden wings with steel spars and glue-sealed fuel cells.

Focke-Wulf night fighter with two HeS 011 (Design I)

7th February 1945, in the amended version of 26th February 1945

Crew

Tank had been convinced from the start that a third crew member was essential. Pilot, radio operator and navigator together in one pressure cabin.

Powerplant

Two Heinkel HeS 011A turbojets each rated at 1,300kP (2,865lb) static thrust in central fuselage.

Dimensions

Span	16.00m	52ft 6in
Sweep	30° at 0.25 chord	
Wing area	50.0m²	538ft²
Aspect ratio	5.12 : 1	
Length overall	14.55m	47ft 8½in
Height overall	5.00m	16ft 4¾in

Weights

		(Amended data)	
Empty equipped		6,415kg	14,142lb
Normal loaded		11,000kg with	24,250lb with
		3,500kg (4,200 ltrs)	7,716lb (923.8 galls)
		of fuel	of fuel
	or	12,000kg with	26,455lb with
		two 600 litres	two 131 gallons
		additional fuel	additional fuel
		in external tanks	in external tanks
Max wing loading		220kg/m²	45lb/ft²
(with external tanks		240kg/m²	49lb/ft²

Performance

As per JP 011-45 of 7th February 1945, calculated with 15% additional thrust.

Max speed	900km/h	559mph
	at 6,000m	at 20,000ft
Initial rate of climb	20.0m/sec	65ft/sec
Service ceiling	14,200m	46,500ft
Endurance 2hr 40min	with 4,500kg fuel	(9,920lb)
	of which 2hr 20min with 80% thrust	
	and 20min with 100% thrust	

Armament

Two fixed forward-firing 30mm MK 108 cannon, plus two oblique (less than 80°) upward-firing 30mm MK 108 cannon, or four fixed forward-firing 30mm MK 108 cannon.

Electronic equipment

FuG 24, FuBl 3, FuG 101a, FuG 244, FuG 25a, FuG 139, FuG 218 (217) 'Neptun II' tail-warning, FuG 280, FuG 350 'Naxos' as conversion set.

Focke-Wulf night fighter with
two HeS 011 (Design III)

19th March 1945

Crew Pilot, radio operator and navigator in pressure cabin.

Powerplant

Two Heinkel HeS 011 turbojets each rated at 1,300kP (2,865lb) static thrust positioned side-by-side in fuselage.

Dimensions

Span	14.10m	46ft 3in
Sweep	30° at 0.25 chord	
Wing area	40.0m²	430ft²
Aspect ratio	0.5 : 1	
Length overall	13.52m	44ft 4in
Height overall	5.00m	16ft 4¾in

Weights (As per Focke-Wulf tender)

Empty equipped	6,170kg	13,602lb
Loaded	10,500kg with	23,148lb with
	3,750kg of fuel	8,267lb of fuel
Max wing loading*	262kg/m²	53.6lb/ft²

* 294kg/m² (60lb/ft²) according to EKH calculated comparison figures. When compared to the Arado and Messerschmitt data, the above figure may not seem all that outstanding, but it must be borne in mind that, apart from a normal cambered flap, the Focke-Wulf's wing was fitted with no additional lift devices (such as slots).

Performance

According to EHK comparison figures calculated with 4,000kg (8,818lb) fuel, take-off weight 11,750kg (25,903lb).

Max speed		945km/h at 5,500m	587mph at 18,000ft
Initial rate of climb		16.0m/sec	52ft/sec
Service ceiling		13,300m	43,600ft
Endurance	1.7 hrs	at 10,000m	32,800ft
		with 100% thrust	
	3.5 hrs	at 6,000m	20,000ft
		and 450km/h	279mph
		with one engine shut down	
Take-off run		1,200m	3,937ft

Armament

Armament and electronics as Design II.

Constructed entirely of Duraluminum, this aircraft had a reduced wing area in comparison to Design II. This gave the proposal a somewhat higher maximum speed, but at the same time increased the landing speed; a fact which was criticised by the experts at the 20th/21st March meeting.

This Focke-Wulf proposal was finally realised in the shape of the post-war Soviet MiG I-320 (or R-1) night and all weather fighter, which resulted from a specification of January 1948. The first prototype made its maiden flight in April 1949, but the type failed to enter series production.

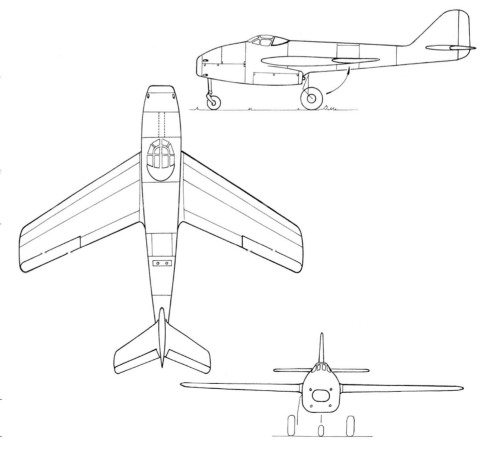

Focke-Wulf night fighter with three HeS 011 (Design IV)

19th March 1945

This tri-jet project featured a Duraluminum fuselage and wooden wings with steel spars and glue-sealed fuel cells.

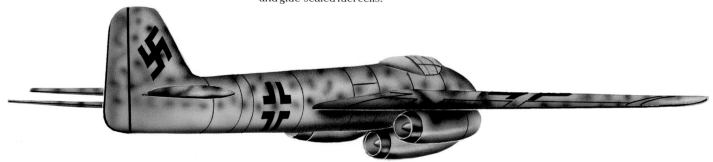

Crew

Pilot, radio operator and navigator together in one pressure cabin.

Powerplant

Three Heinkel HeS 011 turbojets each rated at 1,300kP (2,865lb) static thrust: two engines in underwing nacelles, one in forward fuselage. At least one engine could be shut down to increase endurance.

Dimensions

Span	19.40m	63ft 7in
Sweep	25° at 0.25 chord	
Wing area	75.0m²	807ft²
Aspect ratio	5.0 : 1	
Length overall	19.10m	62ft 8⅓in
Height overall	5.40m	17ft 8½in

Weights

Empty equipped	10,032kg	22,116lb
Loaded	19,600kg with	43,209lb with
	9,000kg of fuel	19,841lb of fuel
Max wing loading	261kg/m²	53.4lb/ft²

Performance

No data available; in view of the amount of fuel carried it may be assumed that the endurance would have come very close to that demanded in the specification.

Armament

Armament and electronics as Design II

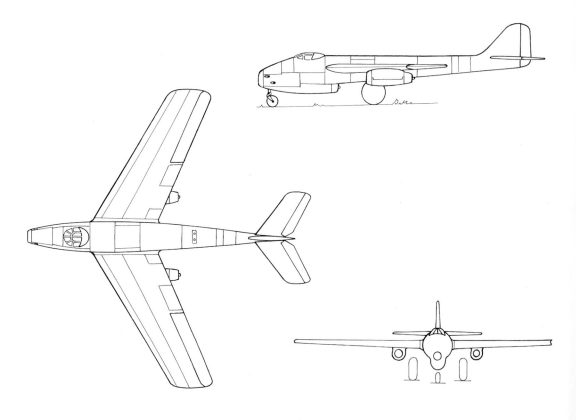

Focke-Wulf night fighter with three HeS 011 (Design V)

19th March 1945

(Construction as Design IV)

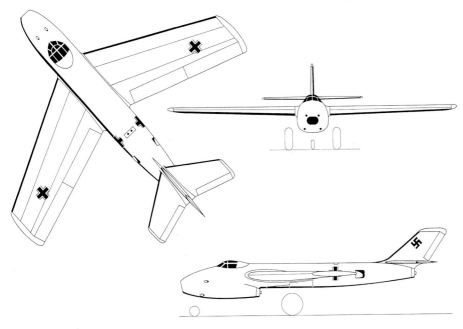

In the introduction to the report by the 'Night and All-Weather Fighter' ESK on the conference held on 20th/21st March 1945, it says of Focke-Wulf's Designs IV and V:

Every attempt to achieve the required endurance by the use of two turbojets led to unsatisfactory take-off performance due to the high take-off weights. Designs with three turbojets, which are not taken into further consideration here, resulted in loaded weights of about 19 tonnes. These should be rejected, not only on the grounds of labour costs, but also because the aircraft themselves are too cumbersome for the night and all-weather fighter roles. Operational experience with the Ju 88 has already shown that the manoeuvrability of this machine, especially about the longitudinal axis, is unsatisfactory.

Tank used every means to save weight. While he regarded an extended endurance as essential, he was not averse to paring down the armament. Not one of Focke-Wulf's night fighter projects was provided with any form of defensive armament, and even the provision of offensive weapons only partially met the specifications of 27th February 1945.

Focke-Wulf's work in this field had a great influence on Soviet aircraft manufacturers. In 1949 two night- and all-weather fighter prototypes, the Lavochkin La-200 and the above-mentioned MiG I-320, commenced flight testing. Both bore certain similarities to the earlier Focke-Wulf designs. But when the Yakovlev Yak-25 'Flashlight' was selected for the nocturnal defence of the Soviet Union, development of the two other types ceased after the completion of several prototypes and an exhaustive test programme.

Crew

Pilot, radio operator and navigator together in one pressure cabin.

Powerplant

Three Heinkel HeS 011 turbojets each rated at 1,300kP (2,865lb) static thrust: two engines side-by-side in forward fuselage, one in tail with side intakes and boundary layer suction. At least one engine could be shut down to increase endurance.

Dimensions

Span	19.30m	63ft 3¼in
Sweep	25° at 0.25 chord	
Wing area	74.8m²	80ft²
Aspect ratio	5.0 : 1	
Length overall	17.80m	58ft 4¼in
Height overall	5.50m	18ft 0in

Weights

Empty equipped	9,812kg	21,631lb
Loaded	19,392kg with	42,751lb with
	9,000kg of fuel	19,841lb of fuel
Max wing loading	259kg/m²	53lb/ft²

Performance

See notes on Design IV.

Armament

Armament and electronics as Design II.

GOTHA

When the TLR brought the Gothaer Waggon-fabrik company into the programme planning for the night fighter of the future on the strength of their previous work on the P.60, chief designer Hünerjäger decided to retain the basic concept and structure of the earlier heavy fighter. However, the project engineers completely redesigned the crew cabin. Pilot and radar operator were now accommodated sitting fully upright in tandem in a pressure cabin. This meant there was no problem in positioning the search radar in the nose. But the intended use of the FuG 240 surveillance radar did make another measure necessary: as a certain longitudinal instability could not be ruled out, the designers provided small fin and rudder assemblies at the wing trailing edges.

Similar to the 'Arado solution', Gotha also intended that these control surfaces double as wing boundary layer fences in the sensitive area between the two rudders.

When, in March 1945, the upgraded specification made the provision of a third crew member necessary, Gotha came up with an ingenious and unusual solution for the P.60C; the navigator and radar-operator were accommodated in a semi-prone position under a glazed hatch set into the wing contours to right and left of the pilot's cockpit. With a fuel load of 4,000kg (8,818lb) this variant of the P.60 had a maximum calculated endurance of 3.55 hours.

Gotha P.60C

February 1945

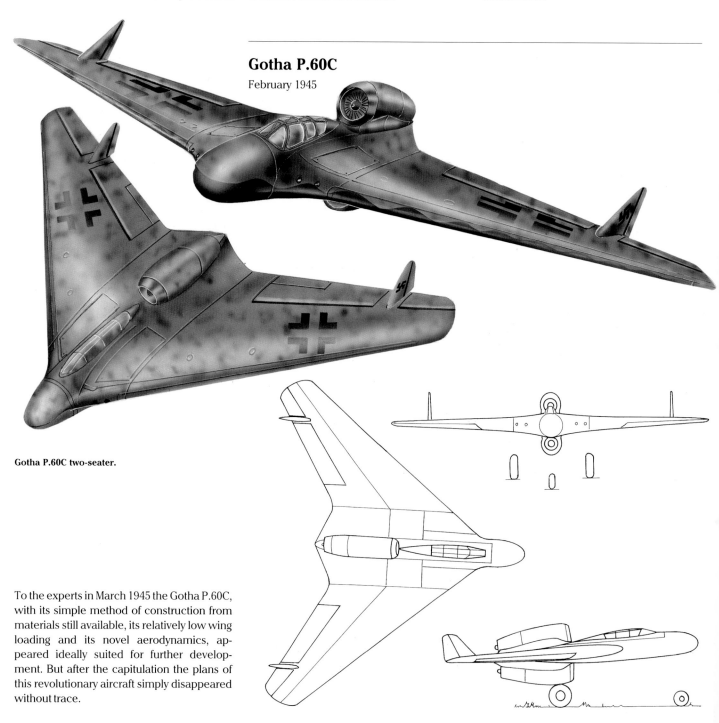

Gotha P.60C two-seater.

To the experts in March 1945 the Gotha P.60C, with its simple method of construction from materials still available, its relatively low wing loading and its novel aerodynamics, appeared ideally suited for further development. But after the capitulation the plans of this revolutionary aircraft simply disappeared without trace.

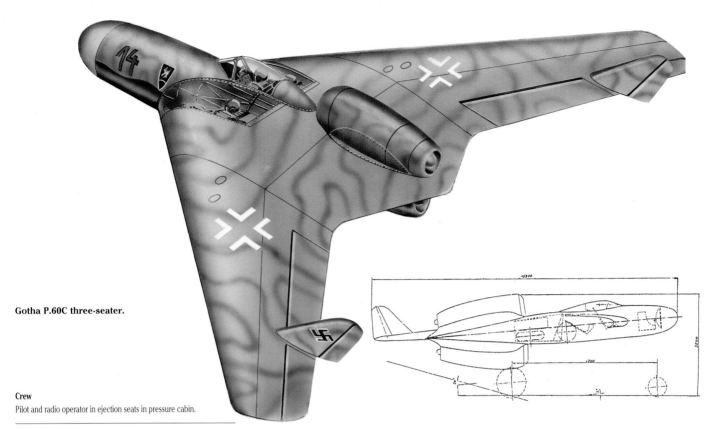

Gotha P.60C three-seater.

Crew
Pilot and radio operator in ejection seats in pressure cabin.

Powerplant
Two Heinkel HeS 011 turbojets each rated at 1,300kP (2,865lb) static thrust above and below wing centre-section; provision to be made for rocket take-off assistance.

Dimensions
Span	13.50m	44ft 4in
Sweep	45° at 0.25 chord	
Wing area	54.7m²	588ft²
Aspect ratio	3.3 : 1	
Length overall	10.90m	35ft 8¼in
Height overall	3.50m	11ft 6in

Weights
Empty equipped	5,346kg	11,785lb
Loaded	10,470kg with	23,082lb with
	3,500kg of fuel	7,716lb of fuel
Max wing loading	192kg/m²	39lb/ft²

Performance
Max speed		930km/h at 8,000m	577mph at 26,250ft
Initial rate of climb		17.5m/sec	57ft/sec
Service ceiling		13,300m	43,600ft
Time to height	7.7min	to 6,000m	20,000ft
	24.4min	to 12,000m	39,400ft
Max endurance	2.82 hrs	at 13,000m	42,650ft
		with 100% thrust	
Max range, approx		2,200km	1,367 miles
Take-off run		1,020m	3,346ft

Armament
Two 30mm MK 108 or MK 213 cannon in nose of centre-section to left and right of crew cabin, plus two oblique upward-firing 30mm MK 108 or MK 213 cannon in wing centre-section.

Electronic equipment
FuG 280, FuG 355, FuG 244, FuG 101, FuG 139, FuG 120K, FuG 130, FuG 25a, FuBl 3, EiV 125.

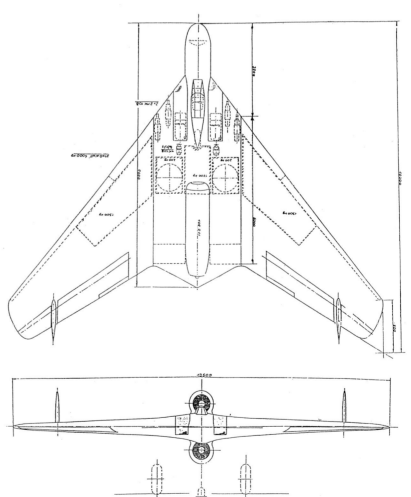

HEINKEL

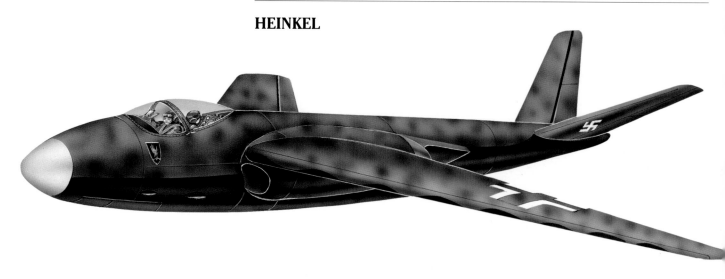

Heinkel P.1079A

The Ernst Heinkel company, which had already produced an excellent night fighter in the He 219, were to have been included in the programme to develop the night fighter of the future from its very outset in January 1945.

According to a document relating to the subsequent meeting on the subject, it is clear that by mid-February the company had still not yet received copies of the specification. In those dark days of early 1945 the route from Berlin to Vienna was beset by all sorts of obstacles. It is questionable whether Siegfried Günter, prior to his move to Landsberg on Lech in April 1945, would have had the opportunity to complete a design to meet the specification.

Despite an intensive search, no evidence has come to light in any surviving German archives that the company, already overburdened with a multitude of development projects, ever submitted a design for a night and all-weather fighter to the Commission in Berlin. It is possible that the projects department in Vienna did produce drawings and data sheets for such an aircraft under the designation P.1079, but no original documents for the period up to April 1945 have been found.

What is certain is that Günter, together with his project engineers Eichner and Hohbach, were working on the P.1079 as a set of studies of various dimensions under US supervision at Penzing near Landsberg during the summer of 1945.

The same questions and speculations apply equally to the P.1078A and 'B fighter designs and to the P.1080 ram jet fighter.

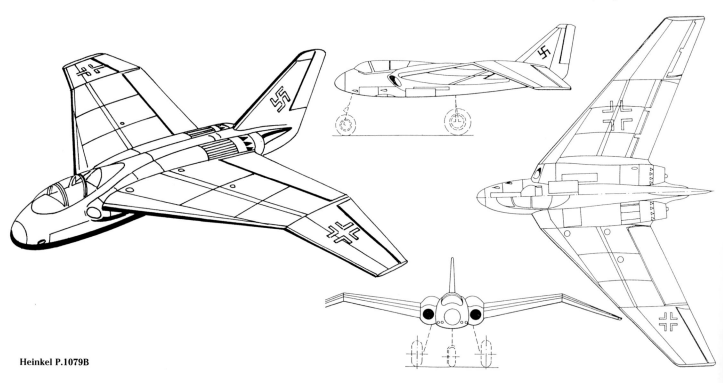

Heinkel P.1079B

JUNKERS

Like Dornier, the Dessau-based Junkers company possessed a wealth of experience in modifying bomber aircraft into three- and four-seat night fighters. The most famous among these were the 'C, 'R and 'G variants of the Junkers Ju 88, which entered operational service in large numbers. Junkers planned to replace the Ju 88 with more modern machines by introducing further developments such as the Ju 188R and, in particular, the Ju 388J. But these latter failed to gain acceptance. In the opinion of the experts they lacked manoeuvrability and sufficiently superior performance; in other words, exactly those qualities which were essential to combat the Mosquito.

It is possible that Junkers' head of development, Professor Heinrich Hertel, attempted to increase the performance of the Ju 88's successors by the addition of jet power. In September 1943 Heinkel had upgraded a He 219A by equipping it with an additional BMW 003 which resulted in an increase in speed of some 60-70km/h (37-43mph) at ground level. But none of these schemes and tests led to any practical results.

When, at the end of January 1945, the Luftwaffe began to firm up their specifications for the night fighter of the future and invited Junkers to tender, Professor Hertel based his proposal on the EF.128 fighter project, which had already made a very favourable impression on the EHK.

The result was a small, aerodynamically very ingenious proposal which did not bear the slightest resemblance to any previous Junkers night fighter designs.

At a presentation of his proposals before the EHK on 27th/28th February 1945 Hertel emphasised in particular the advantages of trailing edge fin and rudder units which, like those of Arado and Gotha, were also intended to act as boundary layer fences and improve aileron efficiency. He pointed out not inconsiderable benefits to be gained by the use of the special 'rough-surface swing-link undercarriage'. The proposed 'tactical brakes', in the shape of two large spoilers on the rear fuselage of the night fighter, were to be widely employed after the war and could be found, almost unchanged, on several US jet fighters (eg Republic F-84 Thunderstreak, North American F-86 Sabre and McDonnell F-101 Voodoo). A braking parachute was also included, to reduce the landing run.

Junkers EF.128 night fighter

Attempt at reconstruction
February 1945

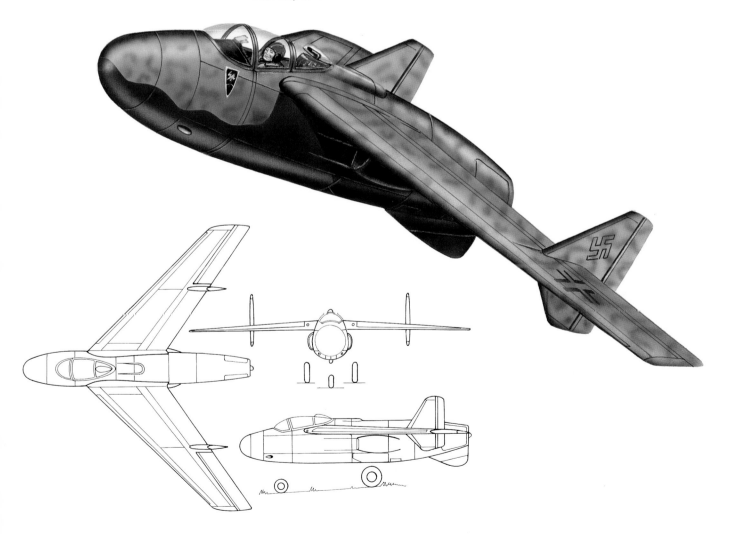

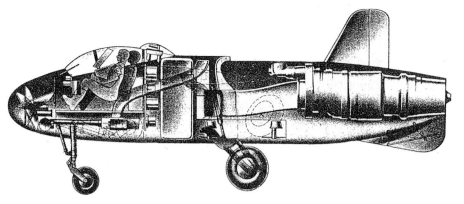

Junkers EF.128 night fighter

Crew
Pilot and radar operator slightly staggered side-by-side in cabin.

Powerplant
One Heinkel HeS 011 turbojet rated at 1,300kP (2,865lb) static thrust;
side air intakes with boundary layer suction, mid-fuselage dorsal outlet.

Dimensions

Span	9.20m	30ft 2in
Sweep	43.5° at 0.25 chord	
Wing area	19.7m²	212ft²
Aspect ratio	4.3 : 1	
Length overall	7.50m	24ft 7in
Height overall	2.95m	9ft 7½in

Weights

Loaded	5,400-5,600kg	11,904-12,345lb
Max wing loading	280kg/m²	57lb/ft²

Performance
No data available.

Armament
Two fixed forward-firing 30mm MK 108 cannon in forward fuselage
beneath cabin, plus two fixed forward-firing 30mm MK 108 cannon in
wingroots.

Electronic equipment
Included: FuG 244, FuG 350Z and FuG 101.

When the Luftwaffe upgraded the specification, the Dessau designers withdrew the EF.128 night fighter project for obvious reasons. It has not been possible to ascertain whether Junkers continued work on this modern, jet-powered night fighter. According to an Allied report, Hertel was among those attending the last meeting on night fighters at Bad Eilsen on 20th/21st March and a Junkers proposal was one of the subjects under discussion. It would be interesting to know exactly what it was about.

MESSERSCHMITT

The company's Oberammergau projects department based its work on the night fighter of the future on the 'immediate solution' Me 262B-2 and the high-speed Me 262 HG III development. Engineers Degel and Althoff opted for a further direct lineal development which, in similar fashion to Dornier, utilised existing work and models to the greatest possible extent. Messerschmitt's aim was to design an aircraft which could be produced relatively quickly, but which allowed for no compromise in terms of performance.

His proposals found little favour in official circles, however. Much of the criticism was centred around the wing loading, which was generally held to be altogether too high, a fact which the head of the 'Night and All-Weather Fighter' ESK, one Kurt Tank, was not averse to pointing out. True, an aircraft of this type would require, among other things, thoroughly trained pilots and hard surface runways, especially for night operations. Seen in this light, Messerschmitt's scheme could appear at best somewhat daring, and at worst completely unsuitable. On the other hand, the competition's proposals, while offering lower wing loadings, were either lacking in performance (Dornier and Arado), aerodynamically completely new and untried concepts (Arado, Blohm und Voss and Gotha), or expensive to produce (Focke-Wulf). One further point: the American Grumman F9F Cougar carrier-based fighter, which first flew on 20th September 1951, had a wing loading of nearly 360kg/m² (74lb/ft²). Messerschmitt's way was an undoubted pointer to the future.

Messerschmitt Me 262 night fighter with HeS 011 turbojets

12th February 1945

The head of the projects department, Dipl-Ing Voigt, was convinced that the technical specifications of 27th January 1945 could, to a large extent, already be met by a HeS 011-powered Me 262B-2. At the same time Voigt felt that, if given a swept wing and with the engines arranged in a different manner, the aircraft's performance was capable of considerable enhancement. The night fighter development of the Me 262 thus paralleled that of the day fighter version, which was also to be fitted with swept wings and to have the engines buried in the wingroots to reduce drag.

Crew

Pilot and radar operator in tandem in pressure cabin; a navigator could also be accommodated by inserting an additional centre section.

Powerplant

Two Heinkel HeS 011A turbojets each rated at 1,300kP (2,865lb) static thrust, or two Heinkel HeS 011B each rated at 1,500kP (3,306lb) static thrust, plus four 1,000kP (2,204lb) thrust Rheinmetall-Borsig take-off rockets.

Dimensions

Span	11.20m	36ft 8½in
Sweep	46.5° at 0.25 chord	
Wing area	28.7m²	308ft²
Aspect ratio	4.37 : 1	
Length overall	11.70m	38ft 4½in
Height overall	3.58m	11ft 8½in

Weights

Empty equipped	5,064kg	11,164lb
Normal loaded	8,070kg with	17,791lb with
	3,100 litres of fuel	681 gallons of fuel
Max loaded	9,106kg with	20,074lb with
	additional two	additional two
	600 litre external	131 gallon external
	fuel tanks	fuel tanks
Max wing loading	281kg/m²	57.5lb/ft²
with external fuel tanks	317kg/m²	65lb/ft²

Performance

		(With HeS 011A)	
Max speed		965km/h	599mph
		at 7,000-8,000m	at 23,000-26,250ft
Initial rate of climb		23.5m/sec	77ft/sec
Service ceiling		12,000m	39,400ft
Time to height	11.5min	10,000m	32,800ft
Endurance	2.3hr	at 10,000m	32.800ft
	4 hr	12,000m	39,400ft
		(approx) with external tanks	
Take-off run, approx		1,000m	3,280ft
		(approx) without take-off rockets	

Armament

Four 30mm MK 108 cannon in forward fuselage, plus (as conversion set) two oblique upward-firing 30mm MK 108 cannon. Weapon load: Two 500kg (1,102lb) fuselage bomb-racks could replace the external fuel tanks; rockets as optional conversion set.

Electronic equipment

FuG 24SN with ZVG 24, EiV 7, FuG 25a, FuBl 3 with AWG 1, FuG 218R with 'Bremen 0' antenna, FuG 350Zc, FuG 101a, FuG 319, FuG 280.

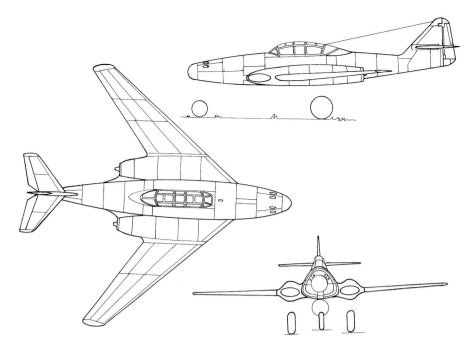

Messerschmitt Me 262 night fighter with HeS 011 turbojets

For purposes of comparison a night fighter proposal, designated P.1112, was produced at the end of February 1945. A tail-less design based on the P.1111, its aim was to reduce the wing loading as much as possible. But in this it failed, and the project did not progress beyond the initial stages. Messerschmitt returned to developing the Me 262 concept.

Three-seat night fighter with HeS011 turbojets

17th March 1945

This design, based on the 27th February 1945 specification, also tried to use as many components of the Me 262 as possible. Unlike the Me 262B-2 proposal of the same date, however, this project at least featured a new, redesigned wing centre-section.

In order to speed progress, a first step foresaw the engines mounted in underwing nacelles in the usual fashion. In addition, tests with a Me 262 HG II fitted with a 35° swept wing were imminent. This meant that reliable flight data could soon be expected.

This intended first stage featuring a swept wing with increased chord centre-section and underslung engine nacelles represents the classic layout for high-speed subsonic civil and military aircraft.

Messerschmitt did not plan to bury the engines in the wingroots until the second stage. As things turned out, that was left to the British. On 29th April 1945 Oberammergau was occupied by an American infantry unit and in the following weeks British and American specialists, among them R E Bishop of de Havilland and R J Woods of Bell, were kept busy evaluating the material found there.

The Messerschmitt proposal was neither overly heavy, nor were the surface areas too large. By using major components from the Me 262, material and production costs could be kept within acceptable limits. The basic aerodynamics of the design had been extensively tested and, in all probability, would have posed no great risk. The calculated performance data were compelling and placed the aircraft firmly among the leading group of all the designs submitted. Had the circumstances been different, and with the benefit of more powerful engines, this night fighter would undoubtedly have proven superior to the first of the American, British and Soviet jet-powered night and all-weather fighters.

Crew
Pilot, radar operator and navigator together in one cabin with optional pressurised or unpressurised canopy.

Powerplant
Two Heinkel HeS 011A turbojets each rated at 1,300kP (2,865lb) static thrust, or two Heinkel HeS 011B each rated at 1,500kP (3,306lb) static thrust, plus four 1,000kP (2,204lb) thrust Rheinmetall-Borsig take-off rockets.

Dimensions

Span	13.06m	42ft 9½in
Sweep	35° at 0.25 chord	
Wing area	28.0m²	301ft²
Aspect ratio	6.1 : 1	
Length overall	12.57m	41ft 3in
Height overall	3.58m	11ft 8in

Weights

Empty equipped	5,541kg	12,215lb
	With Doppelreiter ('double-rider') fuel fairings –	
	5,681kg	12,524lb
Normal loaded	With two take-off rockets –	
	9,176kg	20,229lb
	with 3,200 litres of fuel	with 703 gallons of fuel
Max loaded	With two take-off rockets and two	
	600 litres	131 gallons
	fuel in Doppelreiter fairings –	
	10,316kg	22,742lb

Performance

		(with HeS 011A)	
Max speed		948km/h	589mph
		at 6,000m	at 20,000ft
Initial rate of climb		21m/sec	68ft/sec
Service ceiling		12,500m	41,010ft
Time to height	12.1min	to 10,000m	32,800ft
Endurance	2.5hr	at 10,000m	32,800ft
	3.4hr	at 10,000m with Doppelreiters	
Take-off run		with two 1,000kP (2,204lb) take-off rockets –	
		800m	2,624ft
		with two 1,000hp (746kW) take-off rockets and	
		Doppelreiters –	
		1.050m	3,444ft

Armament
Four 30mm MK 108 cannon in forward fuselage, plus (as conversion set) two oblique upward-firing 30mm MK 108 cannon.
Weapon load: Two 500kg (1,102lb) bombs on fuselage racks in place of Doppelreiter fairings and two take-off rockets. Intended provision for rockets as conversion set. No initial plans for retrofitting of defensive armament at expense of fuel load.

Electronic equipment
FuG 24SE with ZVG 15, FuG 29, EiV 125, FuG 25a or 'c, FuG 120k, Peil G6 with APZ 6, FuG 244, FuG 350Zc, FuG 125, FuG 101a.

Chapter Six

Beyond the Me 262 – Designs for 1946-47

By the beginning of 1944, even though the German fighter arm was by then already committed to a hopelessly defensive role in trying to protect the beleaguered Reich in numerically, and – to a large extent – technically inferior machines, the Oberkommando der Luftwaffe (OKL – Luftwaffe High Command) was expecting yet worse to come: the advent of Allied jet fighters by the end of that year at the latest. Because official circles greatly overestimated the state of Anglo-American high speed development, they also assumed that, if this did prove to be the case, then the Me 262 would be outclassed. To add to their difficulties it was at this juncture that the shortages in skilled labour and resources, which had been growing ever more serious over the years, now began to assume catastrophic proportions.

Fighter aircraft such as the Me 262, designed years before – heavy, twin-engined and costly to produce in terms of materials and man hours – were no longer relevant to the current situation. Even the very steel which made up so much of the Messerschmitt's structure was in increasingly short supply.

A tightening up of armament procurement, authorised early in 1944 by the Reichsministerium für Rüstung und Kriegsproduktion (RfRuK – Ministry for Armament and War Production) headed by Albert Speer and Karl-Otto Saur, resulted in the widespread axing of many projects and types, which in turn, it was hoped, would lead to the freeing of capacities for fighter production.

Established on 1st March 1944, the Jägerstab (Fighter Staff) initiated a new production programme in July by issuing specifications for a single jet high performance fighter to three well known manufacturers: Focke-Wulf, Heinkel and Messerschmitt. In addition, the Hamburg-based Blohm und Voss company was also invited to participate on the strength of its wide ranging research and development activities and its unconventional approach to problems in the past.

Each of the companies named was allocated work for which it was particularly suited and which, as far as possible, carried forward preliminary studies already undertaken. The common aim was to produce a fighter powered by the most up-to-date engine then under test, the Heinkel HeS 011. It was to be easy and simple to build, economical in use of materials, while at the same time, thanks to advanced aerodynamics, offering a superior performance.

Specifically, the OKL was seeking a maximum speed of about 1,000km/h (621mph) and a 60 minute endurance at full throttle at an estimated operational altitude of 7,000 to 9,000m (23,000 to 29,500ft). The pilot was to be housed in a pressure cabin and afforded sufficient protection against the 0.5in (12.7 mm) calibre ammunition generally used by the Americans. Standard fighter equipment (including, for example the EZ 42 gunsight and an automatic pilot) was to be fitted, as was the normal radio equipment: FuG 15 ZY or FuG 16 ZY and FuG 25.

At the time the specification was issued, Heinkel's Hirth engine works at Zuffenhausen were expecting to commence delivery of the first 60 Heinkel HeS 011 prototype engines in September 1944. The pre-production HeS 011A0 series would then follow in the spring of 1945. As the problems with the somewhat complicated turbojet seemed to be neverending, these dates could not be met. The airframe manufacturers thus 'won' a little extra time – time which was allowed to slip away, however.

At a first round of meetings held at Oberammergau on 8/10th September 1944, Focke-Wulf, Heinkel and Messerschmitt put forward their first designs. Although Dipl-Ing Hans Amtmann of Blohm und Voss also attended, his company's proposal was not yet completed and he deferred submission. In order to provide a common basis for the evaluation studies, the companies' representatives agreed upon an armament of two 30mm MK 108 cannon and, no doubt at the instigation of the Messerschmitt representative, upon an internal fuel load of 830kg (1,000 litres, 1,829lb or 219 gallons).

The Luftwaffe accepted the armament suggested, but insisted on their original requirement of one hour's endurance at full throttle, which latter could only be achieved with a fuel load of some 1,200kg (2,645lb). (Note: with 830kg of fuel the endurance of the 'high performance fighter' would have been roughly the same as that of the Volksjäger which was also in the planning stage at this time.)

One aggravating problem which arose at the Oberammergau meeting could not be solved. The speeds required and the aerodynamics to be used meant that much new ground was being broken. This in turn led to each company using its own systems and methods of calculation and thus arriving at different results. It was agreed that a common formula would have to be found quickly if a proper basis for project comparison was to be achieved. This was easier said than done.

In the autumn of 1944 Junkers was also contracted to participate in the single jet high performance fighter project, by which time the other companies were either already amending their initial proposals or developing new ones.

Further discussions on progress of work together with presentation of designs took place at the Reichsluftfahrtministerium (RLM – Air Ministry) in Berlin on 15th December. There were no signs of any agreement being reached on the subject of a unified system of calculation. Siegfried Knemeyer, head of Flugzeugentwicklung (F1-E – Aircraft Development) within the Technische Luftrüstung (TLR – Technical Air Armaments Board) therefore requested that the Deutsche Versuchsanstalt für Luftfahrt (DVL – German Aviation Research Establishment) be brought in to arbitrate.

Another attempt to address the question was therefore made a few days later on 19th December at the DVL's offices at Berlin-Adlershof under the leadership of that organisation's Professor A W Quick and Dr P Höhler. They felt themselves unable to resolve the problem in the short time which had elapsed and therefore merely laid down some basic guidelines. The DVL proposed mid-January 1945 for a final comparison based on a common method of calculation.

While the scientists occupied themselves formulating uniform mathematical bases, the industry was working on new or improved designs. Arado and Henschel also took it upon themselves to throw their hats into the ring without any official invitation.

When the December meeting was reconvened in Berlin on 12/15th January 1945, a mathematical comparison of the projects submitted was at last feasible, but a decision regarding manufacturing contracts was now ruled out for an entirely different reason – immediately prior to the discussions the Luftwaffe had upgraded its requirements for the standard fighter of the future. On 11th January the General Staff suddenly demanded an endurance of two hours at full throttle at 9,000m (29,500ft) and, in principle, an armament of four 30 mm cannon. This meant an unavoidable increase in loaded weight and – of even more significance in the light of the current situation – a substantial lengthening of the take-off run.

The TLR, the bureaucratic arm of the military, doubted whether these requirements could be met.

And so it went on. It seems unlikely that any decisive or meaningful advances would have been made even had the General Staff not intervened. Promising designs from Heinkel and Messerschmitt were still incomplete. Things were anything but unanimous on the official side. At the end of January the Blohm und Voss P.212 and Junkers EF.128 projects and Focke-Wulf's Design No 3 were adjudged as being the best by the TLR. The industry's representatives on the Entwicklungshauptkommission (EHK – Main Development Commission) saw things somewhat differently: together with further development of the Junkers EF.128 they wanted above all to press on with work on the Messerschmitt P.1110.

Disagreements arose and a struggle for the upper hand promptly broke out between the individual offices.

At the beginning of February the project and design departments of all the participating companies – with the exception of Messerschmitt – were continuing work on the basis of the proposals they had submitted in January. Messerschmitt, who always tended to cut things fine, now embarked on a third set of designs.

By the end of February all parties felt that a course of action on how best to proceed should at last be decided upon. On 27th and 28th February they met for a 'final discussion'. But confusion continued to reign and no decision was in sight.

The EHK now demanded the Focke-Wulf Ta183 as an 'immediate solution', but the Luftwaffe rejected this on operational and tactical grounds. In contrast, the head of the TLR, Generaloberst Ulrich Diesing, wanted development contracts awarded to Junkers, Blohm und Voss and (an amended) Focke-Wulf project. Messerschmitt was to produce an 'optimum solution' at a later date. All this, it should be pointed out, was taking place in March 1945!

No decision regarding these suggestions could be made at the last meeting on the subject which took place at Bad Eilsen on 22nd/23rd March 1945 as Professor Willy Messerschmitt, the head of the 'Day Fighter' Special Development Sub-committee within the EHK, was not present. Nevertheless, Junkers did receive a development contract for their EF.128, although no production contract was awarded. Other companies designs were recommended for a variety of reasons: Messerschmitt's for its excellent projected performance, those of Focke-Wulf and Junkers for the advanced stage of project work already reached which would have allowed for an immediate start on production, and finally Blohm und Voss for its deceptively simple method of construction and unusually varied and high load-bearing capacity. In addition, Focke-Wulf's proposal promised an exceptional high altitude performance.

Above all, it was Focke-Wulf's and Messerschmitt's work which, after the capitulation, was to have a lasting influence on fighter development within the world's major air forces. Such influence has often been disputed, but one only has to look at the North American F-86 Sabre, the Swedish SAAB J29 and a number of Soviet types, foremost among them the MiG-15, to name but a few, to appreciate the validity of this assertion.

Messerschmitt versus Focke-Wulf: the wings of the F-86 Sabre (above) and the Soviet MiG-15.

ARADO

Following on from the unsuccessful E.580, the Arado design bureau at Landeshut in Silesia began development of a fighter incorporating the latest in aerodynamic technology. Initial work on Project E.581 dated back to November 1944. Featuring a typically Arado wing planform designed specifically for high speed flight it was originally intended for the aircraft to be powered by the BMW 003 turbojet then in production. The reasoning for this

decision is not clear, other than perhaps the desire to get an aircraft built and into the air as quickly as possible. Nor is it known whether Arado was undertaking this work on its own initiative or in response to an official contract from Berlin.

Professor Walter Blume's team based their aerodynamic concept on, among others, the E.555 long range bomber, of which there were no fewer than 14 development studies.

Most of these depicted an aircraft characterised by a short span wing with reduced outboard sweep.

The abandonment of the long range bomber project at the end of November 1944 released additional capacity for the development of the fighter. At the beginning of 1945 Arado adapted their E.581 design to conform to the on-going specifications for the high performance fighter powered by the HeS 011.

Relatively little is known of the E.581-1, '581-2 and '581-3 studies. But of the somewhat larger E 581-4 and '581-5 proposals – which differed only in detail – general arrangement drawings, weight tables, and sketches have survived.

Arado obviously ceased work on this design after the Luftwaffe issued its new requirements and concentrated instead on further development of the Ar 234 and their plans for the night fighter of the future.

Arado E.581-5

January 1945

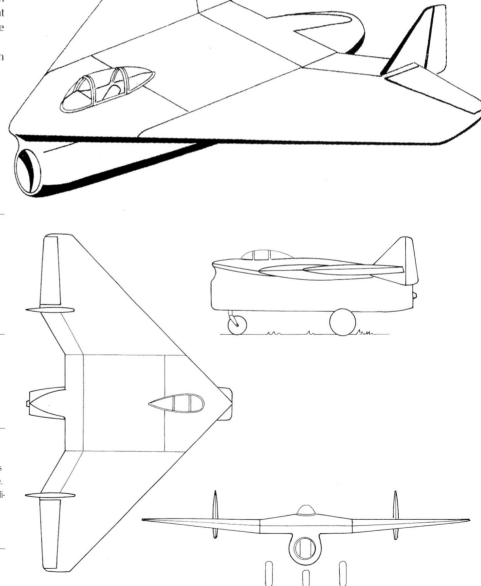

Powerplant

One Heinkel HeS 011 turbojet rated at 1,300kP (2,865lb) static thrust.

Dimensions

(E.581-4 and E 581-5)

Span	8.95m	29ft 2½in
Sweep	45° at leading edge	
Wing area	24.5m²	263ft²
Aspect ratio	3.27 : 1	
Length overall	5.65m	18ft 6in
Height overall	2.60m	8ft 6in

Weights

Empty equipped	2,454kg	5,410lb
Loaded	3,734kg with	8,231lb with
	1,400kg (1,250litres)	3,086lb (274 galls)
	of fuel	of fuel
Max wing loading	152.4kg/m²	31.2lb/ft²

Performance

No data are available. The inherent danger of duct loss from the long intake and, above all, the large surface areas with their various corners and edges would seem to indicate insufficient high speed performance. On the other hand, the low wing loading figure points to manoeuvrability and good climb and high altitude characteristics. Take-off and landing speeds should also have been superior to those of its competitors. Fuel capacity would not have sufficed for the endurance required.

Armament

Two 30mm MK 108 cannon in wing roots.

BLOHM UND VOSS

This tail-less fighter, designated P.209/01, was developed in the autumn of 1944. Its layout, typical of that favoured by chief designer Dr Richard Vogt, had its origins in the P.208 piston-engined fighter. The aircraft was apparently unsatisfactory in certain respects, but whether this was due to flight mechanics or was performance-related it has been impossible to establish.

In November 1944 the Hamburg company produced an alternative design, the P209/02. This featured a sharply forward-swept wing, but was otherwise of conventional configuration.

As the design of the wing gave rise to some imponderables, and as Dr Vogt apparently disliked putting all his eggs in one basket, he and his design team completely reworked the P.209/01 during the same month.

In December they then submitted the latter – now designated P.212/02 together with the P.209/02, as their contribution to the 'fighter comparison' being held at the DVL in Berlin.

One result of this meeting was the company's abandoning the P.209/02 and concentrating all its efforts instead on the tail-less design which, as the P.212/02, had reached an advanced study stage by the war's end.

Blohm und Voss P.209/01

September/October 1944

Tail-less low wing design of simple, all-metal construction.

In November 1944 this design underwent major modification and further development to become the P.212.

Powerplant
One Heinkel HeS 011 turbojet rated at 1,300kP (2,865lb) static thrust.

Dimensions
(Some reconstructed)

Span	7.70m	25ft 3½in
	10.65m	34ft 10in
	including outer sections	
Sweep	35° at 0.25 chord	
Wing area	13.0m²	139.9ft²
Aspect ratio	4.56 : 1	
Length overall	7.30m	23ft 10½in
Height overall	2.50m	8ft 3in

Weights

Empty equipped	3,470kg with	7.649lb with
	approx 1,200kg	approx 2,645lb
	of fuel	of fuel
Max wing loading	267kg/m²	54/6lb/ft²

Performance

Max speed	900km/h at 8,800m	559mph at 29,000ft
Initial rate of climb	25.8m/sec	84ft/sec
Service ceiling	11,200m	36,750ft
Endurance approx 1hr	at 7,000m	23,000ft
	with 100% thrust	

Armament
Two 30mm MK 108 cannon in central fuselage

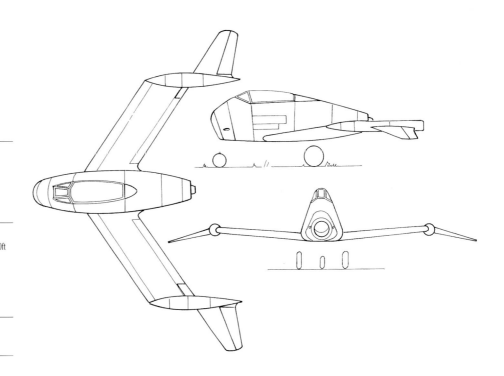

Blohm und Voss P209/02

December 1944

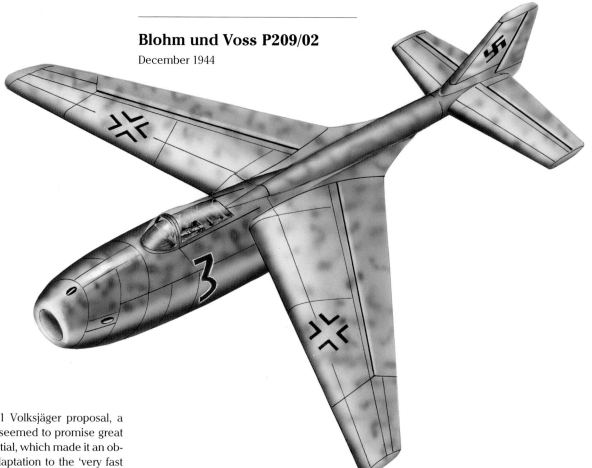

Based on the P.211 Volksjäger proposal, a design of this kind seemed to promise great development potential, which made it an obvious choice for adaptation to the 'very fast fighter' role. But as Dr Vogt explained:

The substantially higher speed meant, of course, that certain other factors had to be taken into consideration. In the first instance wing sweep had become a necessity.

It was felt that a forward-swept wing would afford the new project improved stall characteristics. The aircraft was of very simple construction designed to be built of steel and Duraluminum.

The P.209/02 did not receive a particularly favourable report from the DVL adjudicators. Above all, they felt that the 'question of deformation' of a sharply forward-swept wing

would require thorough investigation. This would have meant wind tunnel tests and an exhaustive trials and research programme and thus posed an almost incalculable development risk.

Dr Vogt decided against any further work on the P.209/02 and withdrew the proposal. He had another iron in the fire.

Powerplant
One HeS 011A turbojet rated at 1,300kP (2,865lb) static thrust.

Dimensions
Span	8.10m	26ft 6in
Sweep	-35° at 0.25 chord	
Wing area	14.0m²	150ft²
Aspect ratio	4.69 : 1	
Length overall	9.20m	30ft 2in
Height overall	3.38m	11ft 1in

Weights
Empty equipped	2,674kg	5,895lb
Loaded	4,094kg with 1,200kg of fuel	
	9,025lb with 2,645lb of fuel	
Max wing loading	292kg/m²	60lb/ft²

Performance
Max speed	988km/h at 9,000m	613mph at 29,500ft
Initial rate of climb (approx)	26m/sec	85ft/sec
Service ceiling	12,000m	39,000ft
Time to 10,000m (32,800ft)	13 minutes	
Max endurance	1.5 hours	

Armament
Two 30mm MK 108 cannon in forward fuselage, provision for fitting a third MK 108 cannon.

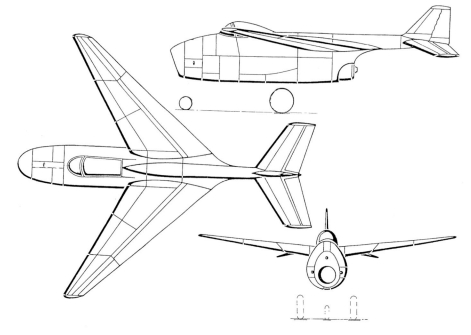

Blohm und Voss P.212 Design III

February 1945

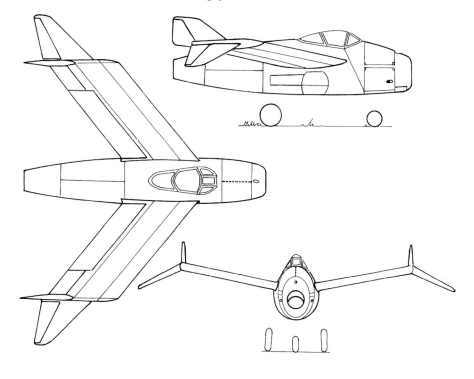

Powerplant
One HeS 011 turbojet rated at 1,300kP (2,865lb) static thrust.

Dimensions
Span	7.00m	22ft 10½in
	9.50m	31ft 2in
	including outer wing sections	
Sweep	40° at 0.25 chord	
Wing area	14.0m²	150ft²
Aspect ratio	3.5 : 1	
Length overall	7.40m	24ft 3½in
Height overall	7.15m	23ft 6in

Weights
Empty equipped, normal	2,710kg	5,974lb
Loaded – normal	4,180kg (9,215lb) with 1,250kg (2,755lb) of fuel and two MK 108	
– overloaded*	5,030kg (11,089lb) with 1,850 litres (406 galls) fuel, two MK 108 and one SC 500	
Wing loading	359kg/m²	73.5lb/ft²

* Loaded weight (without overload) of the enlarged wing version would have been between 4,340 and 4,860kg (9,567 and 10,714lb) depending on the fuel and armament carried.

Performance
Max speed	965km/h at 7,000m	599mph at 23,000ft
Initial rate of climb	21.3m/sec	70ft/sec
Service ceiling	12,400m	40,500ft

No precise data available for endurance, but at 2,700 litre (593 gallon) max fuel capacity (2,100 litre plus two 300 litre in auxiliary tanks) flights of up to four hours endurance would certainly have been possible.

Armament
Optional: Two, three, five or seven 30mm MK 108 cannon, or two 30mm MK 103 cannon, or one 55mm MK 112 cannon, or two MK 103 plus two 15mm MK 151 cannon, or one MK 112 plus two MK 108 cannon, or three MK 108 plus one SC 500 bomb semi-recessed in fuselage. Special weapon load: 22 R4M unguided air-to-air rockets plus two MK 108 cannon. Armament normally grouped in nose, but cannon could also be fitted in mid-fuselage or beneath the engine.

After exhaustive preliminary wind tunnel and structural tests, it was intended for three prototypes to be built starting in February 1945: the first was to make its maiden flight in August 1945. The TLR was not unfavourably disposed towards this plan, as is indicated by a note to the effect in that body's official war diary. But in the light of the then prevailing situation, talk of such a timescale was just one more meaningless declaration of intent.

Based upon the P.208, P.210 and P.209/01, the Hamburg firm's definitive proposal for the single jet high performance fighter with the Heinkel HeS 011 evolved in three stages commencing in November 1944.

The company was able to submit its P.212/02 study together with the P.209/02 at the 19th/21st December 1944 meeting. Compared to the initial studies, the redesigned fuselage and shoulder-mounted wing were immediately apparent. In a report issued on 9th January 1945 the two leading officials from the Institute of Flight Mechanics of the DVL, Professor Quick and Dr Höhler, said of the P.212/02 that they regarded the provision of some form of vertical rudder as essential. This led to the Hamburg-Finkenwerder bureau's producing the definitive P.212-03 featuring yet further redesign of the fuselage and a midwing with the required rudder assemblies mounted at its extremities. In order finally to dispel any concerns about flutter arising from the concentrations of mass at the wingtips,

the wingspan was shortened by 2.5m (8ft 2½in) when compared to the P.212/02 and the sweep was reduced from 45° to 40°. The designers also built in the option to increase the wing chord by fairly simple means from 2m to 2.2m or 2.4m (6ft 6in to 7ft 2in or 7ft 10½in). The higher take-off weight thereby achieved would allow for the accommodation of 2,400 litres (527 gallons) of (internal) fuel, or for a more extensive weapon load to be carried.

Dr Vogt departed somewhat from the idea of all-metal construction; provision being made for the wings to be built of wood, steel or aluminium. Initially, however, the wings were to be of his usual stressed skin steel construction. The fuselage structure, too, was a typical Blohm und Voss design, the kinked steel air intake duct also serving as the fuselage inner load-bearing member. Immediately ahead of the engine this tubular member widened into a double crossbeam with the wing being attached to its face and with the powerplant mounted at the rear. The armament was grouped ahead of the pilot's pressure cabin, which was itself positioned above the intake duct.

Blohm und Voss Ae 607/P.217

February 1945

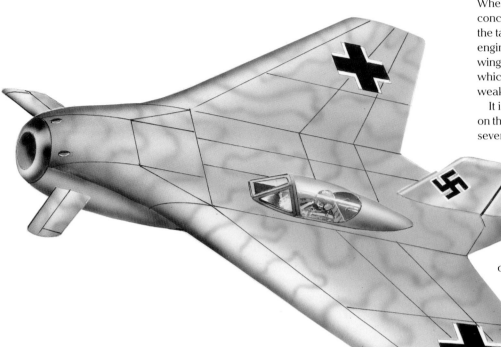

When the DVL adjudicators began voicing concerns about the flutter characteristics of the tail-less designs, the aerodynamicists and engineers came up with a short span swept wing project, minus horizontal tail surfaces, which was intended to eliminate this possible weakness from the outset.

It is interesting to note the canard winglets on the nose, which have since reappeared on several of today's high speed tail-less aircraft. Their purpose was primarily to improve angle of incidence and low speed stability. The unusual undercarriage would undoubtedly have posed forward visibility problems for the pilot during take-off and landing.

Unfortunately there are no weights or performance data available for this study. It may be assumed that take-off weight was in the region of 4,000 to 4,200kg (8,818 to 9,259lb). In terms of performance the P.217 (project number not confirmed) should have had a short take-off and landing run and displayed excellent climb and high altitude capabilities.

Powerplant
One Heinkel HeS 011 turbojet rated at 1,300kP (2,865lb) static thrust.

Dimensions

Span	8.00m	26ft 3¼in
Sweep	45° at 0.5 chord	
Wing area	26.0m²	280ft²
Aspect ratio	2.46 : 1	
Length overall	7.05m	23ft 2in
Height overall	2.90m	9ft 6in

Armament
Three 30mm MK 108 cannon in forward fuselage.

The P.217 was consigned to the files when further development of the P.212 succeeded in eradicating most of the latter's shortcomings.

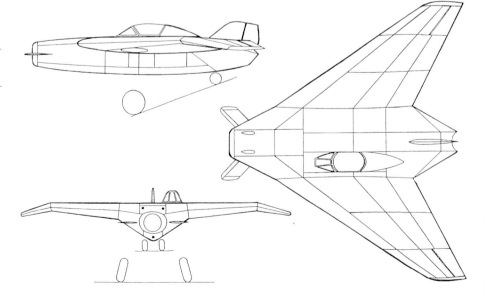

FOCKE-WULF

When, in July 1944, Focke-Wulf was awarded a development contract for a single jet fighter, the company was able to refer back to extensive studies, much preliminary work and almost finished examples of just such an aircraft. In effect, Berlin's requirements corresponded almost exactly to work already undertaken.

When it became clear in the autumn of 1944 that the performance of this machine, known in-house as the Flitzer (Dasher or Whizzer), did not match up to the competition and could not be significantly improved upon,

Professor Kurt Tank decided in October 1944 to resurrect and update his '5th design' of the previous January, which featured sharply swept wing and tail surfaces.

The design department carried out a series of modifications and improvements right up until the war's end. Designated the Ta 183, the aircraft was to have been built as the 'immediate solution', in other words to fill the gap pending the advent of the 'optimum solution' from Messerschmitt. Should the Heinkel HeS 011 still not have been ready by the end of 1945, provision was made for the prototypes –

and, in an emergency, the early production models – to be fitted with the less powerful Jumo 004 turbojet.

Tank also proposed a more 'moderate' alternative to this somewhat daring design, submitting both to Berlin in January 1945. The former was basically very similar to the Ta 183 in layout, but featured slightly reduced wing sweep and a conventional tail unit. A design team including, among others, Multhopp, Mittelhuber and Quenzer, worked on this alternative proposal up until about the end of February.

Flitzer single jet fighter

July/September 1944

Based on previous experience gained from the Fw 189 and the BMW 803-powered fighter project of June 1941 and April 1943, Focke-Wulf's design department began work in December 1943 on a single jet twin-boom fighter (4th design). The following month this proposal underwent considerable improvement when the aerodynamics were refined and the Heinkel HeS 011 powerplant was fitted. Retaining the original design's optional use of additional rocket power, it was possible by July 1944 to offer the fighter in three different operational modes:

1 – Jet fighter with booster rocket power for fast climb to high altitudes.
2 – Jet fighter with booster rocket power, but reduced rocket fuel, sufficient for fast climb to medium altitudes.
3 – Pure jet fighter without rocket assistance with approximately two hours endurance at about 10,000 to 11,000m (33,000 to 36,000ft).

By using additional rocket power Tank's aim was drastically to reduce the fighter's approach times and thus enable it to engage enemy bombers before they arrived over the target area and released their deadly loads. Another valuable advantage of rocket assistance was a not inconsiderable reduction in the length of the take-off run.

During the course of 1944 Focke-Wulf carried out a series of wind tunnel tests, worked on detailed design plans and produced a finished mock-up. At the 8/10th September 1944 meeting held at Oberammergau to compare the various project studies, Focke-Wulf's 'single jet fighter with rocket power' was presented as almost ready to enter production.

But this meeting, attended by six leading members of the Focke-Wulf design team,

already marked the beginning of the end for the project. Of the three original operational proposals, only the pure jet fighter (operational mode 3) remained. What counted for more now was a design that was as simple and uncomplicated as possible, and which made limited use of resources, particularly of those 'premium materials' which were becoming increasingly scarce. All of Focke-Wulf's extensive preliminary work had, to a large extent, been totally in vain.

The data overleaf have been taken from the transcript of 10th September 1944 (1) and from specification No.280 in its extended draft form of 15th September 1944 (2). The all-metal fighter had a 52% steel content.

Powerplant

Heinkel HeS 011 turbojet rated at 1,500kP (3,306lb) static thrust, plus additional jettisonable booster rocket to improve take-off and climb capability in the interceptor role.

Dimensions

Span		8.00m	26ft 3in
Sweep		32° at 0.25 chord	
Wing area		17.0m²	183ft²
Aspect ratio		3.77 : 1	
Length overall		10.55m	34ft 7in
Height overall		2.35m	7ft 8in

Weights

Empty equipped		2,730kg	6,018lb
Loaded	(1)	3,660kg with	8,068lb with
		830kg of fuel	1,829lb of fuel
	(2)	4,350kg with	9,589lb with
		1,250kg of fuel	2,755lb of fuel
Max wing loading	(1)	215kg/m²	44lb/ft²
	(2)	256kg/m²	52lb/ft²

Performance

Max speed	(1)	965km/h at 7,000m	599mph at 23,000ft
	(2)	955km/h at 7,000m	593mph at 23,000ft
Initial rate of climb	(1)	21.2m/sec	69ft/sec
	(2)	18.2m/sec	59ft/sec
Service ceiling	(1)	13,800m	45,000ft
	(2)	13,000m	42,500ft
Time to 10,000m (33,000ft)		11.5 mins (1)	14.5 mins (2)
Endurance	(1)	75 minutes to 10,000m with 100% thrust	
	(2)	110 minutes at 10,000m with 100% thrust	

Armament

(1) Two 30mm MK 108 cannon in forward fuselage beneath the cockpit.
(2) Two 30mm MK 103 cannon in fuselage and two 20mm MG 151 cannon in wings .

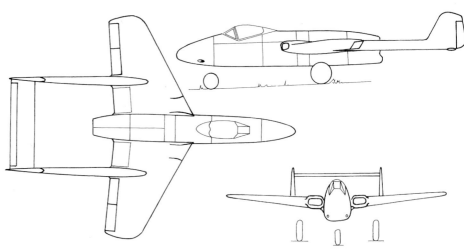

Focke-Wulf Flitzer single jet fighter.

The calculated maximum speed of the Flitzer was inferior to that of both the Heinkel and Messerschmitt designs. One reason for this was undoubtedly the aircraft's relatively large surface area. The design department therefore attempted to decrease the overall size of the airframe by reducing the wing area to 14.0m² (150ft²). The cost of modifying the completed aircraft was to be kept to a minimum. But not even this measure, as laid down on 3rd October 1944, achieved the required result. Tank had no other option but to scrap the design and replace it with a new proposal.

Below left and right: **Wind tunnel half-model of the Focke-Wulf Flitzer of July/September 1944.**

Bottom left and right: **Mock-up of the Focke-Wulf Flitzer jet fighter.**

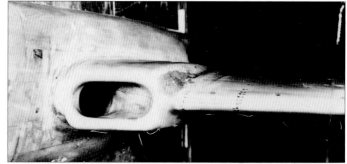

Focke-Wulf Ta 183, single jet fighter with HeS 011

February 1945

The Ta 183 described here was the end result of months of development which brought with it a whole series of modifications but which, at the same time, never lost sight of the basic concept.

Although the tail unit with its 'rearward canted and upwardly drawn' rudder gave rise to a certain amount of criticism and prompted some discussion regarding flutter, Hans Multhopp remained true to his design until the end.

It was not until Tank himself developed the basic Ta 183 concept into the Instituto Aerotecnico IAe 33 Pulqúi II jet fighter in post-war Argentina that an aerodynamically more satisfactory and statically very efficient version of this rudder was finally produced.

At the beginning of March 1945, with the award of a contract to build a prototype, the aircraft received the RLM type number 8-183. (The '8' suffix denoting an aircraft or a missile, the '183' a sequential allocation – the Ta 183's

'neighbours' being the Bücker Bü 182 Kornett (Cornet) advanced piston-engined trainer of 1938 and the Flettner Fl 184 autogyro of 1936.)

The fuselage and vertical tail were to be constructed of steel and Duraluminum; the wings and horizontal tail surfaces of wood. The data are taken from specification sheet JP. 011.018a 'Single jet fighter with HeS 011A' of 18th February 1945.

Full model of the Ta 183 inverted in the wind tunnel at the end of 1944.

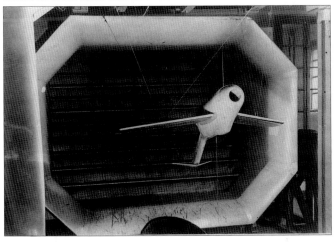

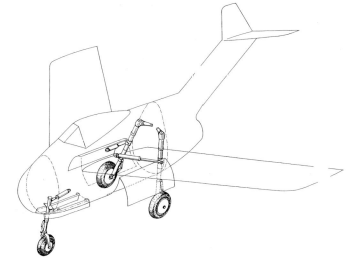

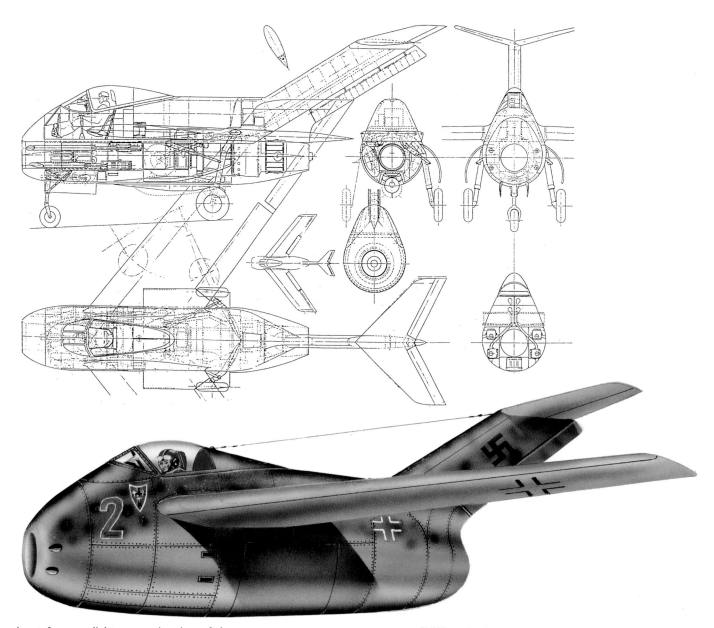

Ta183 production model powered by the HeS 011 engine (1945).

Apart from a slight over-estimation of the achievable maximum speed, the Ta183 possessed an excellent performance, which would have afforded it wide operational capabilities. The low wing loading offered good prospects for future development. This latter, plus the extensive preliminary work already undertaken and the advanced stage of detailed planning which would have allowed for short term completion dates, prompted the powers-that-be to award a contract for the production of prototypes.

Focke-Wulf began with the construction of the Ta183 V1. Powered by the Jumo 004, this first prototype was also to be used to test the Design III tail unit. The maiden flight of this aircraft was scheduled for May/June 1945. If a production contract followed, Focke-Wulf planned to have the first production machines completed by October 1945. On 8th April 1945 British troops took over Focke-Wulf's design department at Bad Eilsen.

Powerplant

One Heinkel HeS 011A turbojet rated at 1,300kP (2,865lb) static thrust.

Dimensions

Span		10.00m	32ft 9⅝in
Sweep		40° at 0.25 chord	
Wing area		22.5m²	242ft²
Aspect ratio		4.45 : 1	
Length overall		9.20m	30ft 2in
Height overall		3.86m	12ft 8in

Weights

Empty equipped		2,980kg	6,569lb
Loaded	(1)	4,300kg with	9,479lb with
		1,200kg of fuel	2,645lb of fuel
	(2)	5,100kg with	11,243lb with
		2,000kg of fuel	4,409lb of fuel
Max wing loading	(1)	191kg/m²	39lb/ft²
	(2)	227kg/m²	46lb/ft²

Performance

Max speed		962km/h at 7,000m	597mph at 23,000ft
Initial rate of climb		24.2m/sec	79ft/sec
Service ceiling		14,400m	47,000ft
Endurance		at 7,000m	23,000ft
at 100% thrust	(1)	1.1 hr	
Max, 40% thrust	(1)	2.25 hr	
Max,40% thrust	(2)	4.25 hr	
Range		at 7,000m	23,00ft
at 100% thrust	(1)	990km	615 miles
Max, 55% thrust	(1)	1,300km	807 miles
Max, 55% thrust	(2)	2,150km	1,335 miles
Take-off run		665m	2,181ft
Landing speed		166km/h	103mph

Armament

Designed from the outset for four 30mm MK 108 located in the forward fuselage to left and right of the cockpit. Weapon load: 500kg (1,102lb) including SD 500, SC 500 or BT 200 possible with reduced fuel load.

Single jet fighter with HeS 011, Design III

February 1945

Powerplant

One Heinkel HeS 011 turbojet rated at 1,300kP (2,865lb) static thrust.

Dimensions

Span	9.50m	31ft 2in
Sweep	35° at 0.25 chord	
Wing area	20.0m²	215ft²
Aspect ratio	4.5 : 1	
Length overall	9.10m	29ft 9½in
Height overall	3.65m	11ft 11in

Weights

Loaded	4,150kg with	9,149lb with
	1,200kg of fuel	2,645lb of fuel
Max wing loading	207.5kg/m²	42.5lb/ft²

Performance

Max speed	965km/h at 7,000m	599mph at 23,000ft
Initial rate of climb	25.3m/sec	83ft/sec
Service ceiling	14,600m	48,000ft
Endurance with 100% thrust	1.1 hr at 7,000m	23,000ft
	2.03 hr at 13,000m	42,500ft
Range with 100% thrust	990km at 7,000m	615 miles
	1,740km at 13,000m	1,081 miles
Take-off run	720m	2,362ft

Armament

Two 30mm MK 108 cannon in forward fuselage.

Note: the classification of Focke-Wulf projects was based very much on the company's own terminology and usage. There was hardly any system to speak of. Design I, for example, referred to the Flitzer project. Design II was the later Ta 183, and Design III was an alternative proposal to Design II. This form of nomenclature had nothing in common with the design designations of late 1943/early 1944. To complicate the issue further, the DVL was still identifying the later Ta 183 as Focke-Wulf Design 1 and the alternative Design III as Design 2!

There are two known studies of Design III, which differed only in detail. While that of January 1944 shows a curvilinear sweep of the fuselage into the vertical tail surfaces, the 'definitive' drawing 0310 25215 of February 1945 displays a straight dorsal profile. This meant that the tail unit of Design III was interchangeable with that of the Ta 183. The design and layout of Design III was otherwise similar to the Ta 183.

The adjacent data table is taken from specification sheets JP.011.037a and 039a of 18th February 1945.

After 27/28th February 1945 Focke-Wulf ceased further work on this project. Although Ta 183A-1 production aircraft were to be fitted with the Design II tail unit, the Ta 183 V1 prototype was to be used to test both Design II and III tail configurations. By the war's end the Focke-Wulf aircraft had reached the most advanced development stage of all the single jet fighter with HeS 011 projects.

Development of the design was continued post-war in both Argentina and the Soviet Union. The parallels to the MiG-15 are more than just pure chance.

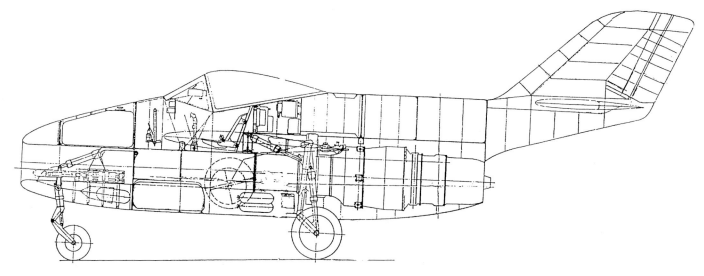

Single jet fighter with HeS 011, Design III,
of February 1945.

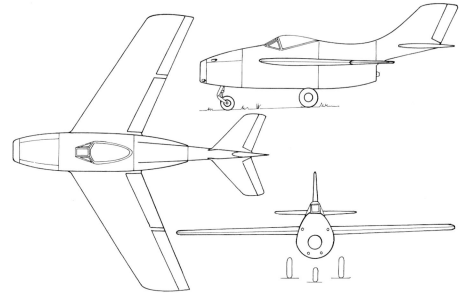

I-310 prototype of the Soviet MiG-15 clearly
showing the influence of Tank's design work.

HEINKEL

For their preliminary work in response to this specification, Heinkel again turned to their Project P.1073 of July 1944, just as they had done for their initial designs for the He 162. The first proposal was thus very similar to the Volksjäger (People's Fighter), although Dipl-Ing Siegfried Günter was to alter the design several times in the weeks that followed. Heinkel participated in the 19th/21nd December 1944 study comparison meeting, chaired by the DVL, by submitting an 'He 162 further development'. When it became clear that a proposal of this nature was not really viable, despite the fact that the He 162 was already flying, Günter came up at the beginning of January 1945 with a radically new, tail-less proposal designated P.1078. It is not certain whether this project relates to the P.1078A and 'B studies which were carried out by Günter, Hohbach, Eichner and others during their internment at Penzing near Landsberg in the summer of 1945; but much would point to this being the case.

The uncertainties and confusion which surround Heinkel's final projects were brought about by the technical design department's decision to vacate Vienna on 31st March 1945 for Bad Gandersheim. All those files which could not be taken with them were destroyed. As Bad Gandersheim itself was no longer considered wholly safe, the department split into two groups; one heading for Rostock, the other, led by Günter, finally arriving – via a circuitous route and only after several diversions – at Landsberg am Lech, some 30km (18.6 miles) south of Augsburg, on 14th April 1945. It was here, beginning in June 1945, that the team continued with their research and design work for the Americans. This activity ended on 7th October 1945 when all documentation was handed over to the United States Army Air Force. In the 1950s the US returned part of these files to Heinkel.

Heinkel fighter based on the P.1073

10th September 1944

Heinkel naturally wanted to use as many components from their existing He 162 project as possible in the 'pure jet fighter' proposal. Apart from the change of powerplant, this present design differed primarily from the Volksjäger in the intended use of a swept wing and 'V' tail.

As well as the swept wing as initially envisaged, Heinkel also carried out exploratory wind tunnel tests on a forward-swept wing. Not only was this idea rejected, but the original 'V' tail was also replaced by a more orthodox twin tail unit similar to that of the He 162.

It was in this form that Heinkel submitted the design to the first study comparison meeting of 19th/21st December 1944.

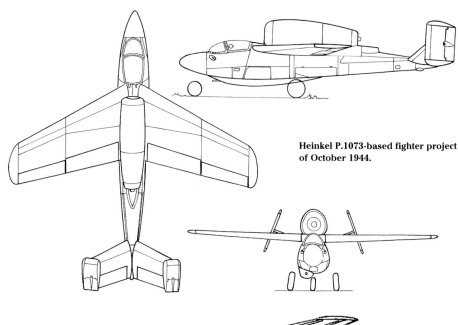

Heinkel P.1073-based fighter project of October 1944.

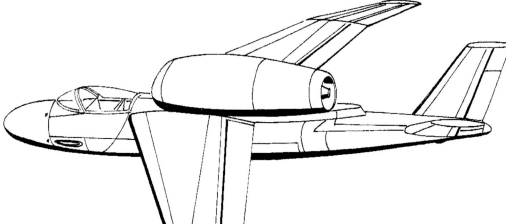

Derivative of the P.1073 with cranked wing and V-tail.

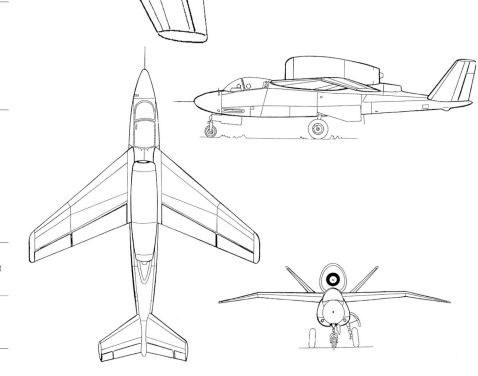

Powerplant

One Heinkel HeS 011 turbojet rated at 1,300kP (2,865lb) static thrust.

Dimensions

Span	8.00m	26ft 2½in
Sweep	35° at 0.25 chord	
Wing area	14.0m²	150ft²
Aspect ratio	4.57 : 1	
Length overall	9.30m	30ft 6in
Height overall, approx	2.80m	9ft 2in

Weights

Empty equipped	2,674kg	5,895lb
Loaded – as per Heinkel's tender		
with two MK 108 (1)	3,604kg and	7,945lb and
	830kg of fuel	1,829lb of fuel
with two MG 213 (2)	4,060kg and	8,950lb and
	1,250kg of fuel	2,755lb of fuel
Max wing loading (1)	257kg/m²	52.6lb/ft²
(2)	290kg/m²	59.4lb/ft²

Performance

Max speed*	(1)	990km/h at 6,000m	615mph at 20,000ft

* From Heinkel's calculations. No further details available.

Armament

Two 30mm MK 108 or two 30mm MG 213 cannon, plus one 20mm cannon in forward fuselage.

Heinkel P.1078

February 1944

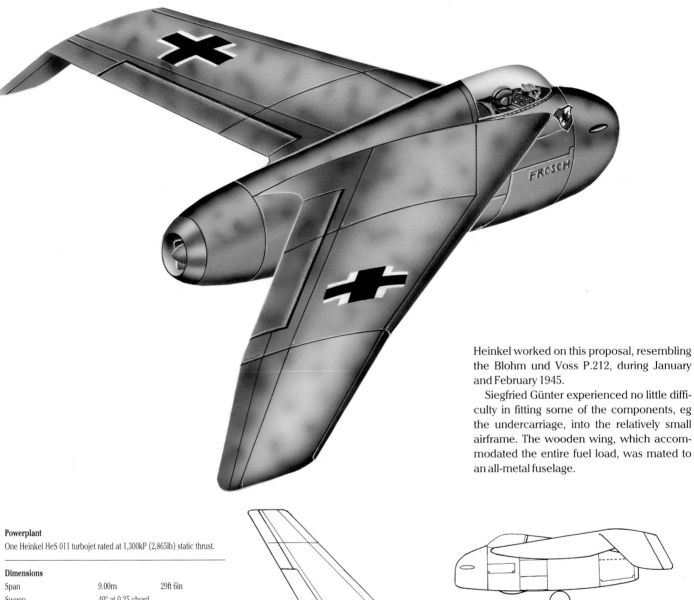

Heinkel worked on this proposal, resembling the Blohm und Voss P.212, during January and February 1945.

Siegfried Günter experienced no little difficulty in fitting some of the components, eg the undercarriage, into the relatively small airframe. The wooden wing, which accommodated the entire fuel load, was mated to an all-metal fuselage.

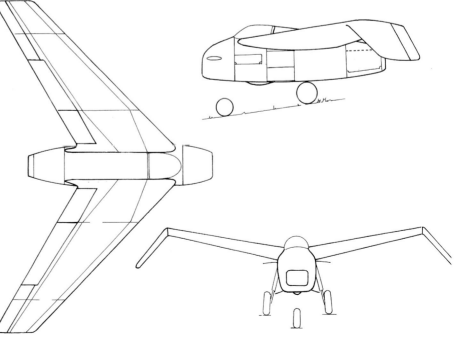

Powerplant
One Heinkel HeS 011 turbojet rated at 1,300kP (2,865lb) static thrust.

Dimensions

Span	9.00m	29ft 6in
Sweep	40° at 0.25 chord	
Wing area	17.8m²	191ft²
Aspect ratio	4.55 : 1	
Length overall	6.10m	20ft 0in
Height overall	2.35m	7ft 8in

Weights

Empty equipped	2,454kg	5,410lb
Loaded	3,920kg with	8,641lb with
	1,200kg of fuel	2,645lb of fuel
Max wing loading	220kg/m²	45lb/ft²

Performance

Max speed	1,050km/h	652mph
	at 7,000m	at 23,000ft
Initial rate of climb	29.8m/sec	98ft/sec
Take-off run	700m	2,296ft
Landing speed	182km/h	113mph

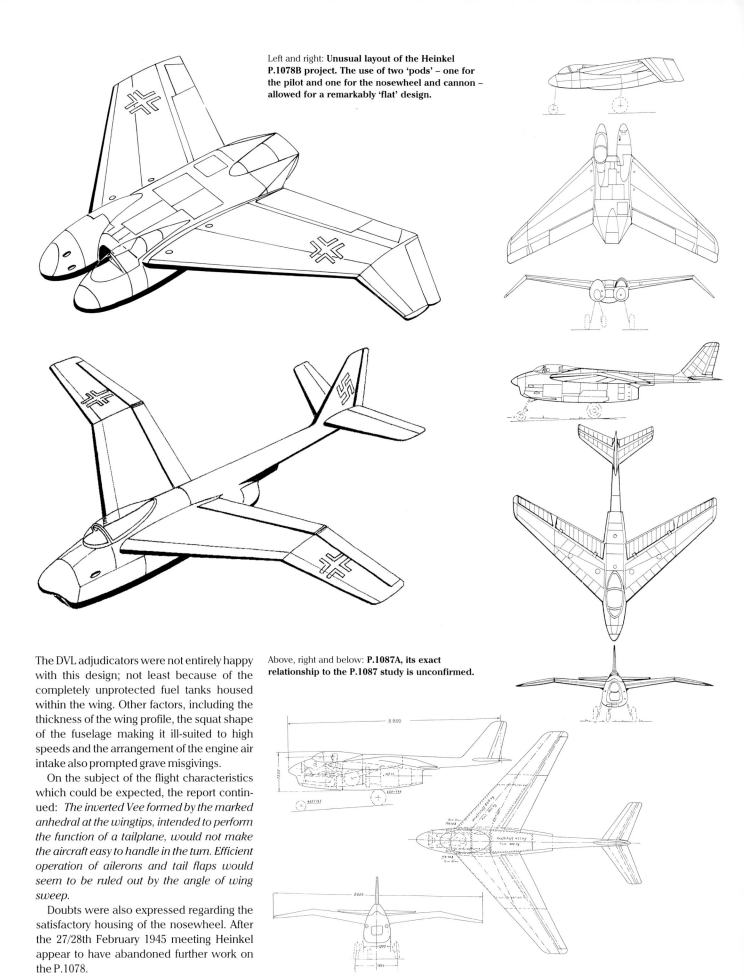

Left and right: **Unusual layout of the Heinkel P.1078B project. The use of two 'pods' – one for the pilot and one for the nosewheel and cannon – allowed for a remarkably 'flat' design.**

Above, right and below: **P.1087A, its exact relationship to the P.1087 study is unconfirmed.**

The DVL adjudicators were not entirely happy with this design; not least because of the completely unprotected fuel tanks housed within the wing. Other factors, including the thickness of the wing profile, the squat shape of the fuselage making it ill-suited to high speeds and the arrangement of the engine air intake also prompted grave misgivings.

On the subject of the flight characteristics which could be expected, the report continued: *The inverted Vee formed by the marked anhedral at the wingtips, intended to perform the function of a tailplane, would not make the aircraft easy to handle in the turn. Efficient operation of ailerons and tail flaps would seem to be ruled out by the angle of wing sweep.*

Doubts were also expressed regarding the satisfactory housing of the nosewheel. After the 27/28th February 1945 meeting Heinkel appear to have abandoned further work on the P.1078.

HENSCHEL

In the autumn of 1944 Henschel had contacted Arado, from whom they learned of the advantages to be gained from a swept wing incorporating reduced outboard sweep. The development work of Dr Alexander Lippisch was not entirely unknown to Henschel's designers in Berlin-Schönefeld either; Henschel having been entrusted with the building of Lippisch's experimental Delta VI. Utilising this knowledge, the design bureau under Dipl-Ing Friedrich Nicolaus began work on their own initiative at the beginning of 1945 on a project to meet the Luftwaffe's requirements. This was then submitted to the official bodies in February 1945.

Henschel P.135
February 1945

The design of this aircraft warrants closer examination. Despite certain risks, Dipl-Ing Nicolaus opted for an aircraft without any horizontal tail surfaces. A problem with this type of tail-less configuration when compared to a more normal aircraft is the limited permissible movement of the centre of gravity occasioned by changing loads (eg ammunition, fuel) and the retractable undercarriage. This factor also makes any further development that much more difficult.

The five-part, wooden wing featured a double cranked leading edge similar to that employed years later by the Swedish SAAB J35 Draken double-delta fighter. The compound sweep of the wing decreased from 42° inboard to 38° at the centre section with the tips being reduced by a further 15° to improve stall characteristics. The undersides of the wing featured split flaps ahead of the rudders. To enhance low speed flight performance even further, it was intended to carry out trials using the type of leading edge flap proposed by Ludwig Bölkow which was to become a standard feature of post-war high performance aircraft. The outboard rudders acted as both elevators and ailerons (elevons); the inner rudders solely as ailerons, which extended upwards when landing. Wing profile thickness decreased from 12% at the root to 10% outboard.

It was intended for the first prototypes to be powered by the BMW 003. The V-setting of the outboard wing sections were adjustable in flight to ensure the optimum manoeuvrability so important in air-to-air combat.

The aerodynamically clean fuselage and large vertical tail surfaces were of all-metal construction. The pilot, sitting in an ejection seat, would adopt an almost supine position with head tilted slightly forward during combat; in normal flight he sat half upright.

After painstaking tests with the aid of a mock-up, Henschel had come to the conclusion that this cockpit arrangement offered the best solution. Something similar may be seen today in the General Dynamics (now Lockheed Martin) F-16 Fighting Falcon.

The characteristic 'kinked' leading-edge of the Swedish SAAB J35 Draken's double-delta wing.

Henschel P.135

Powerplant
One Heinkel HeS 011 turbojet rated at 1,300kP (2,865lb) static thrust.

Dimensions	Data according to Dipl-Ing Fiecke (Henschel).	
Span	9.20m	30ft 2in
Sweep	37.5° (mean) at 0.25 chord	
Wing area	20.0m²	215ft²
Aspect ratio	4.13 : 1	
Length overall	7.75m	25ft 5in
Height overall	4.20m	13ft 8½in

Weights		
Loaded	4,100kg	9,038lb
	with 1,200kg	with 2,645lb
	(approx 1,500 litre)	(approx 329 gallons)
	of fuel	of fuel
Max wing loading	200kg/m²	41lb/ft²

Performance		
Max speed	984km/h	611mph
	at 7,000m	at 23,000ft
Initial rate of climb	21.2m/sec	69ft/sec
Service ceiling	14,000m	46,000ft
Range, approx	1,000km	621 miles
Endurance	1 hr	at 7,000m at 100% throttle
Take-off run	690m	2.263ft
Landing speed	155km/h	96mph

Armament
Four 30mm MK 108 cannon in nose and wing roots.
Provision for 500kg (1,102lb) jettisonable load.

The adjudicators criticised both the high-set cockpit, which could cause shock waves at high speeds, and the length of the engine air intake. They also recommended that the vertical tail surfaces should be swept.

At the 27/28th February meeting the Henschel project obviously met with the approval of the EHK. At the beginning of March they advocated its acceptance as the 'secondary solution' to Messerschmitt's 'optimum solution'. Even at this late stage of the proceed-ings, just weeks short of the final collapse, the powers-that-be could not be dissuaded from making such decisions, which did nothing but add to the expense and confusion of an already hopeless situation.

According to Dipl-Ing Nicolaus the final wind tunnel tests of the P.135 showed very favourable results. A contract at least for the construction of prototypes now seemed pos-sible, and design work on this undoubtedly very advanced aircraft was well under way.

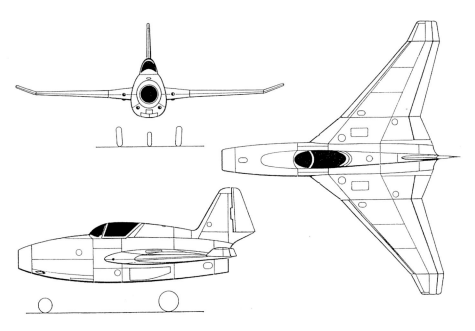

JUNKERS

Model of the EF.128

The Junkers company had no great tradition in the field of fighter production, but were among the leaders in aerodynamic research. In the autumn of 1944 they were awarded a development contract for the single jet high performance fighter.

In December 1944 Junkers submitted their EF.128 proposal, a design which was to remain under development until the war's end.

Over the course of the months, the forward fuselage and in particular the shape of the air intakes, which were similar to those to be seen on Messerschmitt designs, underwent a number of modifications and improvements. Despite this, between December 1944 and February 1945 take-off weight rose only marginally from 3,900 to 4,077kg (8,597 to 8,988lb). Dr Backhaus carried out extensive tests of the EF.128 design at the company's own wind tunnel facility using both partial and complete models. The greatest care was taken to ensure that the final form of the air intakes offered the least resistance.

By March 1945 work on the project had reached a stage which would have permitted construction to have begun immediately.

Junkers EF.128

February 1945

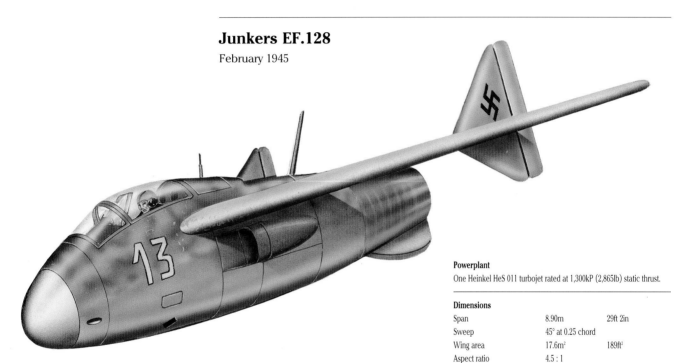

Indicative of the advanced aerodynamics of this design, Professor Heinrich Hertel and Dipl-Ing Gropler made provision for the boundary layer build-up ahead of the air intakes to be drawn off by suction. This was intended to guarantee a perfect duct flow of air to the powerplant. In contrast to Messerschmitt, however, there was no special extraction fan. The 'separated' air simply exited via a faired dorsal outlet aft of the cockpit. The aircraft was constructed 'according to standard specifications' with an all-metal fuselage and wooden wing.

The data are taken from Technical Report TB 139/45 of the Upper Bavarian Research Institute Oberammergau (ie Messerschmitt) of 26th February 1945.

Powerplant
One Heinkel HeS 011 turbojet rated at 1,300kP (2,865lb) static thrust.

Dimensions

Span	8.90m	29ft 2in
Sweep	45° at 0.25 chord	
Wing area	17.6m²	189ft²
Aspect ratio	4.5 : 1	
Length overall	7.05m	23ft 1in
Length of fuselage	6.48m	21ft 2¼in
Height overall	2.65m	8ft 8in

Weights

Empty equipped	2,607kg	5,747lb
Loaded	4,077kg with	8,988lb with
	1,250kg of fuel	2,755lb of fuel
Max wing loading	231kg/m²	47lb/ft²

Performance

Max speed	990km/h	615mph
	at 7,000m	at 23,000ft
Initial rate of climb	22.9m/sec	75ft/sec
Service ceiling	13,750m	45,000ft
Take-off run	700m	2,296ft
Landing speed	186km/h	115mph

Armament
Two 30mm MK 108 cannon in forward fuselage beneath the cockpit, plus provision for two additional MK 108.

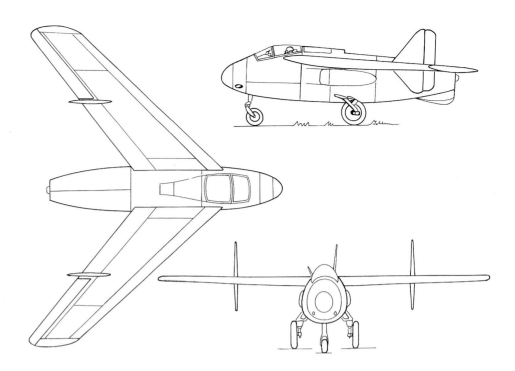

In the adjudicators' opinion there were some uncertainties contained in the calculated performance data arising out of the estimated duct loss caused by the unusual intake arrangement, even to the extent of 'technical failures' not being entirely ruled out. Problems were also foreseen with the leading edge split flaps, which had not yet been tested in practice and which would eventually have to be replaced by normal slats. The DVL evaluators expressed concern, too, about the rotational stability (torsion) of the wing; it being feared that the combination of large lateral proportions and tail-less fuselage layout could, at high speeds, result in a reversal of aileron forces.

The serious accidents suffered during high speed flight by the British de Havilland DH.108 would seem to substantiate such reservations. The wing of this tail-less experimental aircraft also featured 45° sweep and a length of 15ft 2in (4.64m). At 27lb/ft^2 (133kg/m^2), however, the wing loading was appreciably lower.

In the EF.128's favour were the calculated maximum speed and a number of technical features (such as an enclosed weapons bay, advanced target search and gunsight, etc).

Very optimistically, Junkers planned for series production to commence in mid-1945. Following the meeting of 22nd/23rd March 1945 the war diary of the TLR noted:

Fl-E chief*, with the assent of the Führer's Plenipotentiary for Jet Aircraft, SS-Obergruppenführer Kammler, has awarded Messrs Junkers a development contract for the EF.128.

In the light of the risks described above, the uncertainties and the limited performance potential of the design, just why this development contract was awarded is somewhat hard to fathom. All the files relating to the project fell into the hands of the advancing Soviets, who continued work on it for a while and reportedly constructed a mock-up. However, the EF.128 appears to have had no obvious influence on subsequent Soviet fighter aircraft development.

*Head of the Aircraft Development Commission, Oberstleutnant Siegfried Knemeyer.

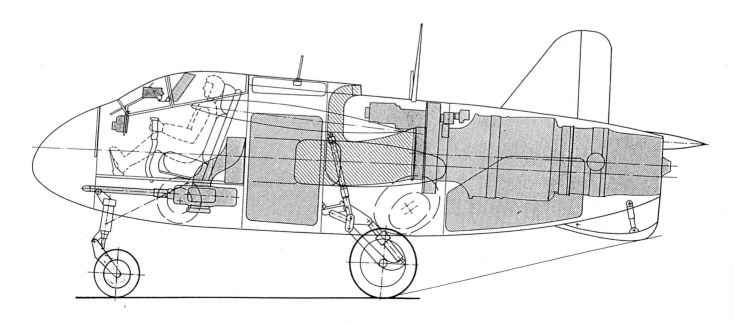

MESSERSCHMITT

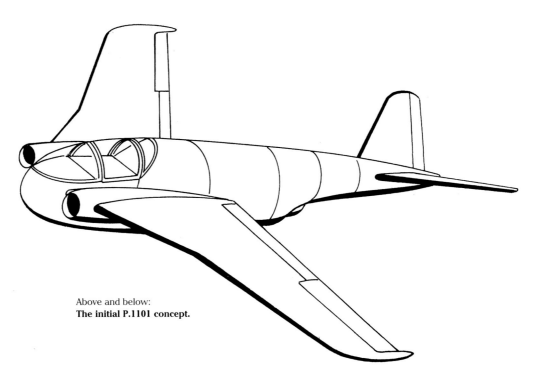

Above and below:
The initial P.1101 concept.

In response to this specification the south German company produced no fewer than five projects together with dozens of variants, comparison and subsidiary studies.

In keeping with the design philosophy which Professor Willy Messerschmitt had championed for years past, his project bureau endeavoured throughout to produce an aircraft which combined the smallest possible airframe with the most powerful engine in order to achieve maximum performance.

Another characteristic of Messerschmitt's project activity was his consistent use of the most up-to-date method of construction and a continual awareness of the latest developments in aerodynamic research.

The only danger in this techno-scientific method of working was that military requirements, which sometimes called for constant modifications to be made during the development stage, could often prove to be incompatible with work in progress. This may have been one of the reasons for the comprehensive nature of the project work which went to make Messerschmitt one of the founding fathers of the modern day lightweight jet fighter. Only a few days after receipt of the development contract, Dipl-Ing Hans Hornung, head of preliminary project studies, submitted his first design, designated P.1101.

This initial proposal, presented in diagram form, not unnaturally, proved unsatisfactory. Hornung therefore amended, redesigned and by the closing days of August 1944 had produced a project for submission in the proper form as required by the authorities.

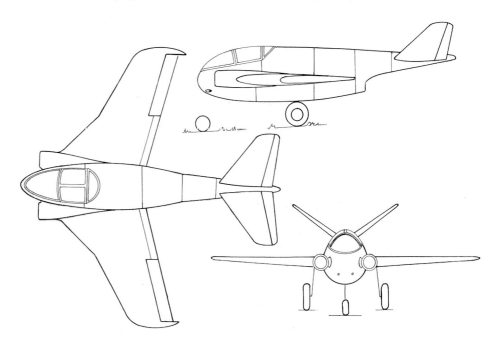

Messerschmitt P.1101

30th August 1944

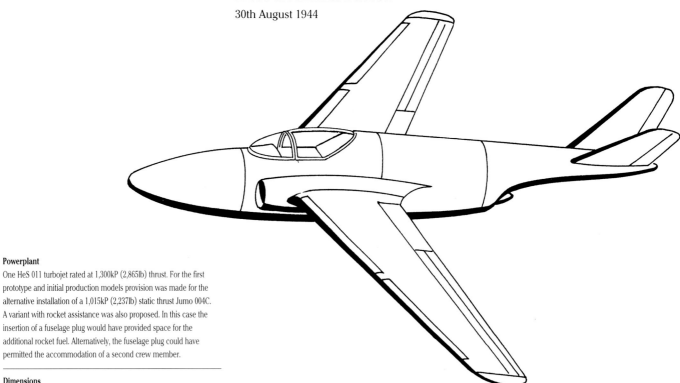

Powerplant

One HeS 011 turbojet rated at 1,300kP (2,865lb) thrust. For the first prototype and initial production models provision was made for the alternative installation of a 1,015kP (2,237lb) static thrust Jumo 004C. A variant with rocket assistance was also proposed. In this case the insertion of a fuselage plug would have provided space for the additional rocket fuel. Alternatively, the fuselage plug could have permitted the accommodation of a second crew member.

Dimensions

Span	8.16m	26ft 9in
Sweep	40° at 0.25 chord	
Wing area	13.5m²	145ft²
Aspect ratio	4.94 : 1	
Length overall	9.37m	30ft 9in
with 'plug'	10.02m	32ft 10½in
Height overall	3.08m	10ft 1in

Weights

Empty equipped		2,624kg	5,784lb
Loaded weight	(1)	3,554kg (7,834lb) with 830kg (1,830)lb fuel and two MK 108	
Max loaded weight	(2)	4,050kg (8,928lb) with increased armament or 1,330kg (2,932lb) of fuel including 600 litres (131 gallons) in external tanks.	
Max wing loading	(1)	263kg/m²	53.8lb/ft²
	(2)	approx 300kg/m²	approx 61lb/ft²

Performance

According to Messerschmitt data of 18th August 1944, configuration (1).

Max speed at 7,000m	approx 1,080km/h	671mph at 23,000ft
Initial rate of climb	30m/sec	98ft/sec
Service ceiling	14,800m	48,500ft
Time to 7,000m	4.6 minutes	
Endurance at 7,000m	0.85 hr with 100% thrust	
Range at 7,000m	700km (434 miles) with 100% thrust	

These data projected by the Messerschmitt team were undoubtedly a little too high. At the September meeting new figures, based on other methods of calculation, indicated a maximum speed of between only 965 and 1,000km/h (599 and 621mph) and an endurance with 1,000 litre (219 gallons) fuel at an altitude of 7,000m (23,000ft) of just 30 min.

Armament

Two 30mm MK 108 cannon in fuselage (1) plus space for a third MK 108, or one 30mm MK 103 plus one 20mm MG 151 cannon, or one 55mm MK 112 cannon, or oblique upward-firing armament.

The aircraft discussed at the meeting on 8/10th September 1944 featured an all-metal fuselage with a wing derived from the Me 262 albeit swept at an angle of 40°. Hornung intended for the fighter to be fitted with a V-tail, an arrangement preferred and proposed time and time again by Messerschmitt.

After this meeting Messerschmitt, Waldemar Voigt and Hornung decided to start work on a new design. Messerschmitt himself participated in the preparation of the new plans; offering numerous suggestions and sketches. He it was who, in October 1944, ordered the construction of an 'experimental aircraft' based upon the P.1101. This purely test machine was to be employed in researching the flight characteristics in general, and in establishing the optimum angle of wing sweep in particular. For this purpose the aircraft, which was almost completed by the war's end, possessed a variable wing sweep adjustable on the ground between 35° and 45°.

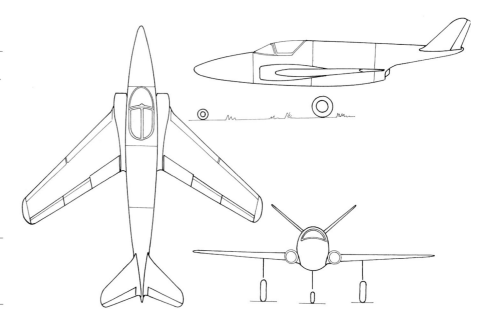

Messerschmitt P.1101

14th December 1944

Powerplant

One Heinkel HeS 011 turbojet rated at 1,300kP (2,865lb) static thrust; alternatively as immediate or emergency solution: one Junkers Jumo 004B turbojet rated at 890kP (1,962lb) static thrust, plus intended option of two take-off assistance rockets each rated at 500kP (1,102lb).

Dimensions

Span	8.08m	26ft 6in
Sweep	40° at 0.25 chord	
Wing area	13.6m²	146ft²
Aspect ratio	4.8 : 1	
Length overall	8.92m	29ft 3½in
Height overall	3.72m	12ft 2in

Weights — With HeS 011

Empty equipped		2,567kg	5,659lb
Loaded	(1)	3,863kg with	8,516lb with
		1,300 litre of fuel	285 gallons of fuel
Max loaded	(2)	4,453kg	9,817lb
		with take-off assistance and external load	
Max wing loading	(1)	284kg/m²	58lb/ft²
	(2)	327kg/m²	67lb/ft²

Performance — Messerschmitt calculations, configuration (1).

Max speed		1,050km/h	652mph
		at 7,000m	at 23,000ft
Initial rate of climb		25m/sec	82ft/sec
Service ceiling		13,500m	44,000ft
Time to height	10min	to 10,000m	33,000ft

Armament

Two 30mm MK 108 in forward fuselage to left and right of cockpit.

The project bureau designed this aircraft almost from the outset as a multi-purpose weapons system. In addition to the standard daylight fighter role powered by the Jumo 004 or HeS 011, other proposed variants included night and all-weather, interceptor and tactical reconnaissance aircraft.

P.1101 V1 'experimental aircraft'.
Photo taken at the Upper Bavarian Research Institute at Oberammergau shortly after the capitulation of 8th May 1945.

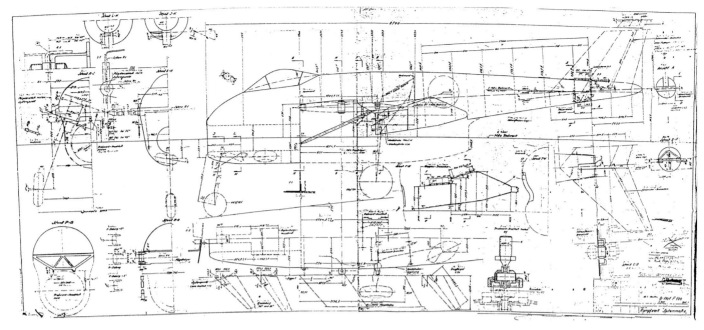

One of the very few surviving original construction drawings of the P.1101 'experimental aircraft'.

The required endurance of one hour at full throttle at 7,000m (23,000ft) would hardly have been feasible with the amount of fuel carried. The project bureau therefore worked out a new proposal, re-arranging the major components in an attempt to gain more space and a better performance for less expenditure. This persuaded Messerschmitt to defer the P.1101 production aircraft on 20th December 1944 in favour of the new P.1106 project. Construction of the P.1101 derivative 'experimental aircraft', on the other hand, forged ahead with all speed.

The P.1101 V1 at the Bell factory at Buffalo, New York state during investigations for the X-5 project. Trial installation of an Allison J35 turbojet was considered for the P.1101 airframe.

The world's first variable geometry aircraft, the Bell X-5, which relied heavily on the company's experience of the Messerschmitt P.1101.
Jay Miller collection

Powerplant

One Heinkel HeS 011A0 turbojet rated at 1,300kP (2,865lb) static thrust; intended provision for take-off assistance rockets.

Dimensions

Span	8.25m	27ft 0in
Sweep	40° at 0.25 chord	
Wing area	15.25m²	164ft²
Aspect ratio	4.29 : 1	
Length overall	9.18m	30ft 1in
Height overall	3.71m	12ft 2in

Weights

Empty equipped	2,594kg	5,718lb
Loaded	4,065kg with	8,961kg with
	1,250kg of fuel	2,755lb of fuel
Max wing loading	256kg/m²	52lb/ft²

Performance

Max speed	980km/h	608mph
	at 7,000m	at 23,000ft
Initial rate of climb	22.2m/sec	73ft/sec
Service ceiling, approx	14,000m	46,000ft
Time to 10,000m, approx	9.5 minutes	

Armament

Four 30mm MK 108 cannon to left and right of nose intake.

Messerschmitt P.1101
22nd February 1945

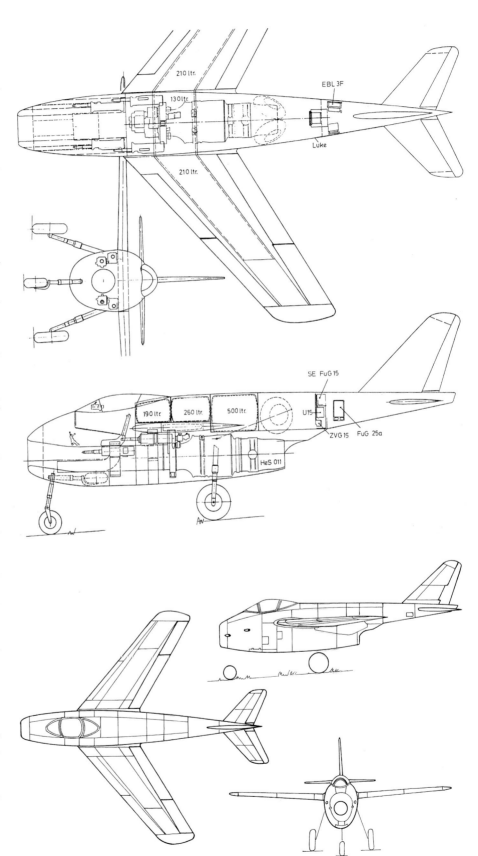

With the construction of the P.1101 test aircraft all but complete by the beginning of 1945 and only awaiting delivery of a serviceable Jumo 004 engine, Messerschmitt decided to offer the authorities an improved version of the P.1101 of December 1944. The time lead advantage which the P.1101 V1 gave the company was used as a weighty argument to press their case.

On 27th and 28th February 1945 Messerschmitt submitted three very different designs to the single jet fighter specification: the P.1101, the P.1110 and the P.1111. In contrast to the initial model, the P.1101 now featured an almost completely new wooden wing which no longer bore any relationship whatsoever to that of the Me 262. Whereas the fuselage and pilot's pressure cabin were constructed of Duraluminum as before, the tail unit was made almost entirely of wood. Fuel capacity, armament and other equipment matched those of the competition.

In this form the P.1101 received no special recommendation, although emphasis was laid on the minimum risk design of the aircraft. Despite, or perhaps precisely because of this aspect, the proposal – like the Ta 183 – was to have a great influence on future jet fighter development.

The P.1101 'experimental aircraft', which immediately prior to the capitulation the EHK had ordered to be completed and tested as quickly as possible, was subsequently used in the USA as the model for the world's first variable geometry aircraft, the Bell X-5.

Messerschmitt P.1106

11 January 1945

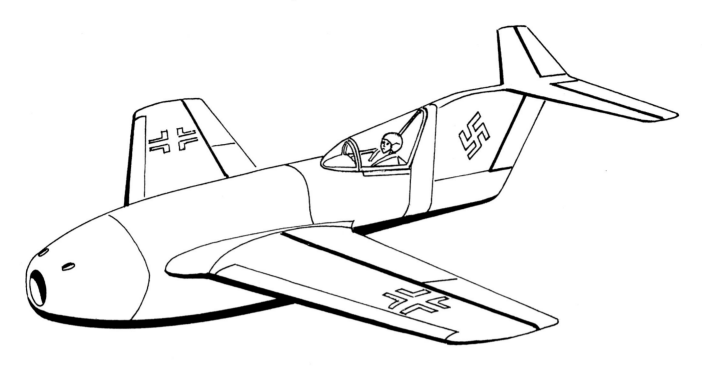

Somewhat unusual in appearance due to the regrouping of the major components, this aircraft was to have been simpler and cheaper to build than the P.1101. The designers also expected a marked improvement in performance. As Dipl-Ing Waldemar Voigt explained on 20th December 1944:

The structural shape of the P.1106 offers the best performance we have yet been able to find for the single jet fighter.

Messerschmitt's P.1106 project as of 12th December 1944, with T-tail and cockpit integral with the fin.

Powerplant
One Heinkel HeS 011 turbojet rated at 1,300kP (2,865lb) static thrust.

Dimensions

Span	6.65m	21ft 9½in
Sweep	40° at 0.25 chord	
Wing area	13.17m²	147ft²
Aspect ratio	3.38 : 1	
Length overall	9.19m	30ft 1⅛in
Height overall	3.37m	11ft 0in

Weights

Empty equipped	2,300kg	5,070lb
Loaded	4,000kg with	8,818lb with
	1,200kg of fuel	2,645lb of fuel
Max wing loading	303.7kg/m²	62lb/ft²

Performance

Max speed	993km/h	617mph
	at 7,000m	at 23,000ft
Initial rate of climb	21.2m/sec	69ft/sec
Service ceiling	13,300m	43,500ft

Armament
Two 30mm MK 108 cannon in nose.

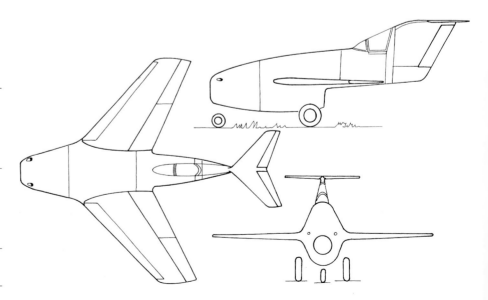

Above and below:
P.1106 of 11th January 1945.

Several studies were developed between 4th December 1944 and about the middle of February 1945, two of which found their way to Berlin-Adlersdorf for submission to the DVL adjudicators at the meetings held on 19th to 21st December 1944 and those from 12th to 15th February.

In order to improve the aerodynamics, the pilot's cabin was positioned slightly more forward of the V-tail than it had been on the initial version. The wing structure was of wood with this version.

The specialists criticised the P.1106 for its unsatisfactory visibility, the V-tail arrangement and, in particular, for the high wing loading. The concept appeared to have reached the end of its development potential. For this reason, and the other shortcomings mentioned, a new design seemed called for. Hornung did make an attempt in mid-February to rescue the P.1106 by embarking on a new study featuring a normal tail unit. But in the end Messerschmitt withdrew the project in favour of his P.1101, P.1110 and P.1111.

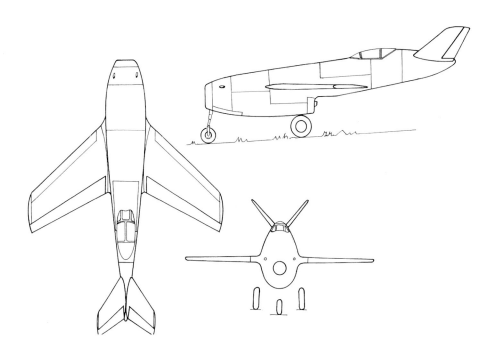

Messerschmitt P.1110

12th January 1945

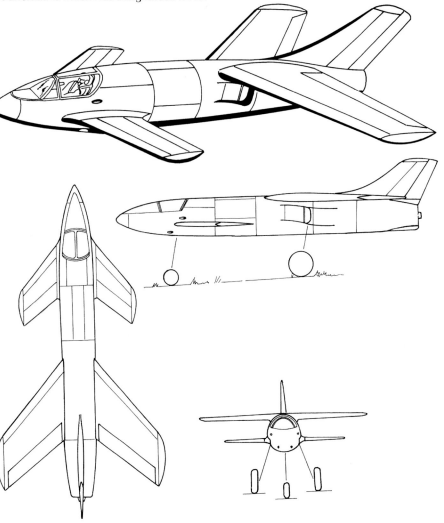

After the first criticisms of the P.1106 had been voiced, a new design appeared on the drawing boards at Oberammergau at the beginning of January 1945. The intention was to reduce the cross section and surface areas even further. By arranging the major components in line one behind the other it was hoped to achieve the ideal fuselage shape with the smallest possible cross section. The greatest problem posed by such a fuselage layout was to find the optimum intake arrangement for the rear-positioned engine. As an aircraft powered by the HeS 011 would not be exactly 'overmotorised', every percentage point was important. Like Junkers, Messerschmitt invested a great deal of research and wind tunnel work on this point.

This proposal was not quite finalised when presented for comparison to the fighter project study session of 12/15th January 1945. The design retained the wing of its predecessor. Nor was Messerschmitt yet ready entirely to forgo the V-tail arrangement, although this was now set wider apart at the roots. Engine air was delivered via a mid-fuselage annular slot intake. To reduce suction loss, boundary layer air ahead of the intake was to be drawn off by a fan mounted on the engine shaft.

Although the aircraft was adjudged very favourably on the whole, here too the very high wing loading naturally gave rise to some concern. The specialists were above all afraid that manoeuvrability would be impaired. The DVL advised Messerschmitt generally to increase the wing area and redesign the suspect air intake arrangement.

While reworking the P.1110, the project bureau also embarked on a new design; a tailless alternative which was designated P.1111.

In the middle of February Hornung's team investigated another possible solution. But this somewhat unusual proposal, known as the 'P.1110 Canard' (Ente, or Duck) disappeared almost as soon as it was mooted. Despite the promise of considerable advantages in the low speed flight envelope, these did not outweigh concerns regarding the high development risks and the problems of directional stability.

Powerplant

One Heinkel HeS 011 turbojet rated at 1,300kP (2,865lb) static thrust.

Dimensions

Span	6.65m	21ft 9½in
Sweep	40° at 0.25 chord	
Wing area	13,17m²	141ft²
Aspect ratio	3.36 : 1	
Length overall	9.67m	31ft 8in
Height overall, approx	2.70m	8ft 10in

Weights

Empty equipped	2,580kg	5,687lb
Loaded	4,000kg with	8,818lb with
	1,200kg of fuel	2,645lb of fuel
Max wing loading	304kg/m²	62.2lb/ft²

Performance

Max speed	1,000km/h	625mph
	at 7,000m	at 23,000ft
Initial rate of climb	26m/sec	85ft/sec
Service ceiling	13,100m	43,000ft
Take-off run	830m	2,723ft
Landing speed	180km/h	111mph

Armament

Three 30 mm MK 108 cannon in nose.

Messerschmitt P.1110

22nd February 1945

At the beginning of February 1945 the P.1110 was given the new wooden wing ('Wing A') which had been designed around the turn of the year 1944-45 and which was also employed by the reworked P.1101. On the former, however, Hornung added highly swept wing root leading edge extensions to increase the angle of incidence. At the same time, while retaining boundary layer suction, new intakes resembling those of the Junkers EF.128 were provided. In response to the DVL's reservations, the designers replaced the V-tail with a normal wooden tail unit. The aircraft also employed area rule to reduce drag at high speeds. The entire fuel load was housed in protected tanks located in the all-metal fuselage between the pilot's cabin and the powerplant.

The adjudicators' assessment was generally very good despite certain reservations again concerning the high wing loading and, in particular, the intake arrangement which was regarded as 'definitely risky'. The P.1110 offered a good platform for further development and Dipl-Ing Hornung incorporated all the experience gained on this design into Messerschmitt's final 'comprehensive' proposal, the P.1112 V1.

Powerplant

One Heinkel HeS 011 turbojet rated at 1,300kP (2,865lb) static thrust; boundary layer suction fan coupled directly to engine shaft.

Dimensions

Span	8.25m	27ft 0in
Sweep	40° at 0.25 chord	
Wing area	15.85m²	170ft²
Aspect ratio	4.29 : 1	
Length overall	10.36m	33ft 11in
Height overall	3.18m	10ft 5in

Weights

Empty equipped	2,812kg	6,199lb
Loaded	4,290kg with	9,457lb with
	1,230kg of fuel	2,755lb of fuel
Max wing loading	271kg/m²	55.5lb/ft²

Performance

Max speed	1,000km/h	621mph
	at 7,000m	at 23,000ft
Initial rate of climb	21.5m/sec	70ft/sec
Service ceiling, approx	14,000m	46,000ft
Endurance 1.8 hr	at 10,000m (33,000ft) with 100% thrust	
Take-off run	790m	2,591ft
Landing speed	178km/h	110mph

Armament

Three 30mm MK108 cannon in nose, provision for two additional MK108.

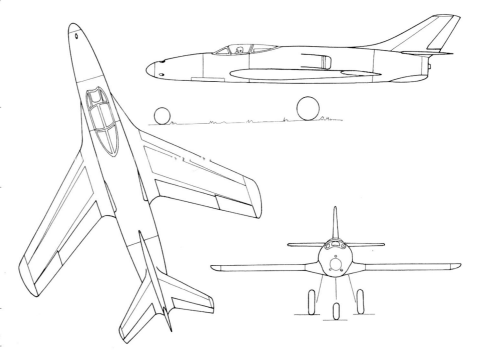

Messerschmitt P.1111

22nd February 1945

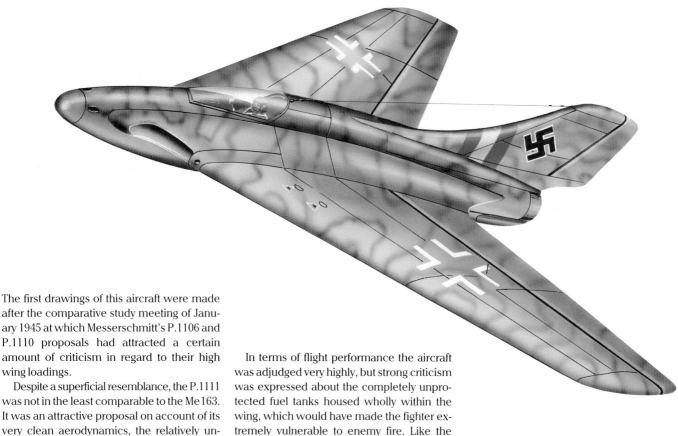

The first drawings of this aircraft were made after the comparative study meeting of January 1945 at which Messerschmitt's P.1106 and P.1110 proposals had attracted a certain amount of criticism in regard to their high wing loadings.

Despite a superficial resemblance, the P.1111 was not in the least comparable to the Me 163. It was an attractive proposal on account of its very clean aerodynamics, the relatively uncomplicated intake arrangement and wide track undercarriage.

In terms of flight performance the aircraft was adjudged very highly, but strong criticism was expressed about the completely unprotected fuel tanks housed wholly within the wing, which would have made the fighter extremely vulnerable to enemy fire. Like the P.1110, the P.1111 also provided much of the groundwork for the ultimate P.1112.

Dimensions

Span	9.16m	30ft 0in
Sweep	45° at 0.41 chord	
Wing area	28.0m^2	301ft^2
Aspect ratio	3.0 : 1	
Length overall	8.92m	29ft 3in
Height overall	3.06m	10ft 0in

Weights

Empty equipped	2,740kg	6,040lb
Loaded	4,281kg with	9,437lb with
	1,250kg of fuel	2,755lb of fuel
Max wing loading	153kg/m^2	31lb/ft^2

Performance

Max speed	995km/h	618mph
	at 7,000m	at 23,000ft
Initial rate of climb	23.7m/sec	77ft/sec
Service ceiling, approx	14,000m	46,000ft
Endurance 1.8hr	at 10,000m (33,000ft) and 100% thrust	
Take-off run	600m	1.968ft
Landing speed	155km/h	96mph

Armament

Two 30mm MK 108 cannon in nose, plus two 30mm MK 108 cannon in wing root/fuselage section.

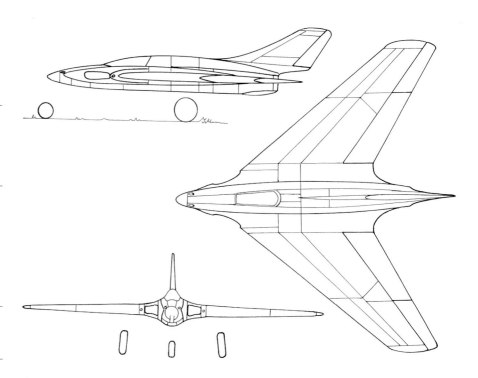

The project bureau combined all their previous hard-won experience into this one design producing arguably the 'optimum solution'. After several preliminary studies of tail-less layouts, there finally emerged a very modern looking 'normal' (ie conventional) aircraft featuring a V-tail. The controversy regarding the pros and cons of tail-less designs versus aircraft of more orthodox configuration had still not been resolved by the war's end.

Other characteristics of the P.1112 project included a new wing incorporating the leading edge root extensions of the P.1110, re-designed side 'ramp intakes', a pilot's cockpit which was fully faired into the fuselage contours and an increased fuel capacity. Entry of Allied troops into Oberammergau on 29th April 1945 signalled the end of this project too.

Messerschmitt P.1112

30th March 1945

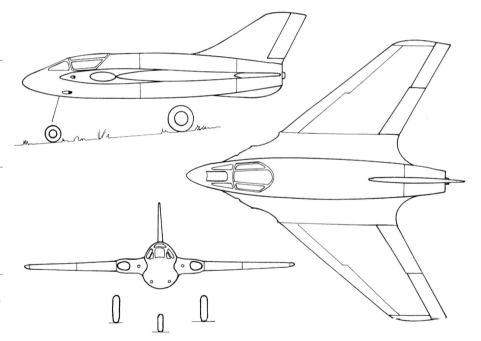

Powerplant

One Heinkel HeS 011A0 turbojet rated at 1,300kP (2,865lb) static thrust, later to be replaced by the more powerful HeS 011B0 rated at 1,500kP (3,306lb) thrust.

Dimensions

Span	8.16m	26ft 8¼in
Sweep	40° at 0.25 chord	
Wing area	19.0m²	204ft²
Aspect ratio	3.5 : 1	
Length overall	9.24m	30ft 3¼in
Height overall	2.84m	9ft 4in

Weights

Empty equipped	2,290kg	5,048lb
Loaded	4,673kg with	10,302lb with
	1,900 litres of fuel	417 gallons of fuel
	provision for increasing fuel capacity to	
	2,400 litres	527 gallons.
Max wing loading	246kg/m²	50lb/ft²

Performance

Complete performance data had not been made available by the war's end; but speeds in excess of 1,000km/h (621mph) must be assumed. Endurance would certainly have been more than two hours at full throttle at 7,000m (23,00ft). Other data would presumably have been slightly superior to those of the P.1110.

Armament

Armament studies for this aircraft also bore the designation P.1110W (W – Weiterentwicklung; further development).Standard armament: Four 30mm MK 108 cannon to left and right in forward fuselage, or two 30mm MK 108 cannon plus two 30mm MK 103 cannon likewise in forward fuselage. Weapon load: Maximum of 500kg (1,102lb) possible. Special armament (for anti-bomber Pulkzerstörer role): one 50mm MK 214 cannon in upper forward fuselage with barrel protruding through cockpit canopy, or one 55mm MK 112 cannon offset in lower forward fuselage area.

The head of the project bureau, Dipl-Ing Waldemar Voigt, estimated that this aircraft could commence flight testing by mid-1946 at the latest. Immediately prior to the occupation of Oberammergau the workshops had begun construction of a mock-up of the forward fuselage to establish armament arrangements and the layout of the pilot's cabin. In May 1945 the Americans took possession of all the files relating to this project.

The direct influence which the P.1112 exerted, particularly on post-war carrier fighters of the US Navy, is unmistakable. Even to this present day, a number of the design features first introduced by Messerschmitt remain an integral part of the most modern military aircraft.

The P.1112 S-1 as of 27th March 1945.

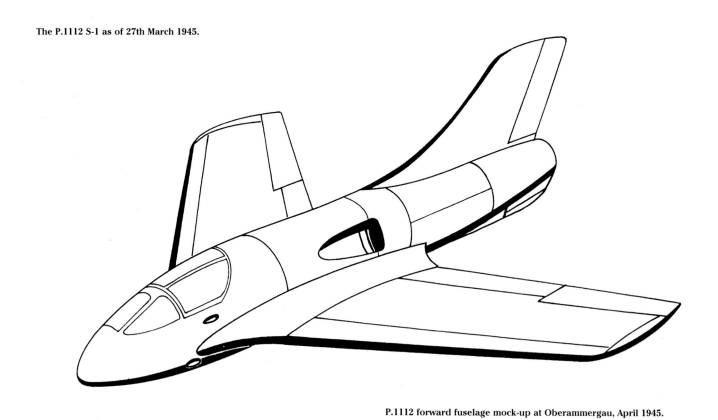

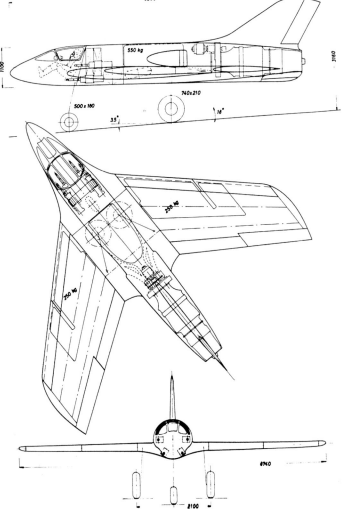

P.1112 forward fuselage mock-up at Oberammergau, April 1945.

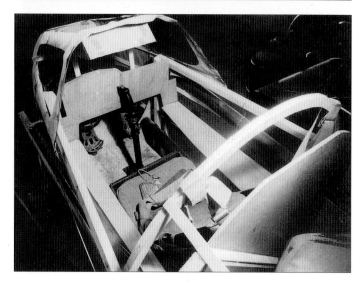

'Optimum solution',
the Messerschmitt P.1112 V1
high performance fighter of
30th March 1945.

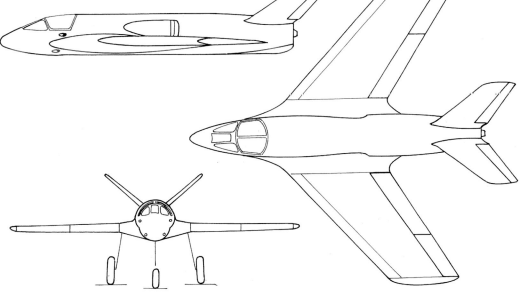

INDEX

OKB SUKHOI
A history of the design bureau
and its aircraft

Vladimir Antonov et al, with Jay Miller

A team of authors have thoroughly documented the products of this famous Soviet aircraft design bureau, thanks to extensive access to the company records and photo files. A huge amount of unpublished information and illustrations are included. Each aircraft type is reviewed in detail, also prototypes, testbeds and projects, some of which never saw the light of day. Appendices detail test pilots and major personalities.

Hardback, 280 x 216 mm, 296pp
645 photos/illusts plus 23 in colour
and 104 3-views and line drawings
1 85780 012 5   **£29.95/US $49.95**

OKB MiG
A history of the design bureau
and its aircraft

Piotr Butowski, Jay Miller

Beginning with a comprehensive overview of Soviet military aviation, the text methodically moves from the births of Mikoyan and Gurevich through to the founding of the MiG design bureau during 1939, its war years, and the period of greatest importance, beginning with the advent of the MiG-15 and the Korean War and continuing via the MiG-17, -19, -21, -23, -25 and -27 to the MiG-29 and MiG-31 era. A highly acclaimed work.

Hardback, 280 x 216 mm, 248pp
800 photographs, over 100 drawings
0 904597 80 6   **£24.95/US $39.95**

LOCKHEED MARTIN'S SKUNK WORKS
The First Fifty Years (Revised Edition)

Jay Miller

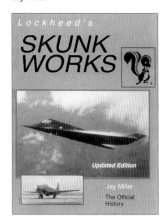

An updated edition of the original 1994 'Lockheed's Skunk Works' – written with the total co-operation of Lockheed Martin's Advanced Development Company. In a major 'pulling back' of the veil of secrecy, official histories of such products as the U-2, A-12, D-21, SR-71, and F-117 are finally brought to light.

This is the closest thing yet to a definitive history of this most enigmatic aircraft design and production facility.

Softback, 305 x 229 mm, 216 pages
479 b/w and 28 colour photos
1 85780 037 0   **£19.95/US $29.95**

We hope you enjoyed this book . . .

Aerofax and Midland Publishing titles are edited and designed by an experienced and enthusiastic trans-Atlantic team of specialists.

Further titles are in preparation but we always welcome ideas from authors or readers for books they would like to see published.

In addition, our associate company, Midland Counties Publications, offers an exceptionally wide range of aviation, spaceflight, astronomy, military, naval and transport books and videos for sale by mail-order around the world. For a copy of the appropriate catalogue, or to order further copies of this book, and any of the titles mentioned on this or the facing page, please write, telephone, fax or e-mail to:

Midland Counties Publications
Unit 3 Maizefield,
Hinckley, Leics, LE10 1YF,
England

Tel: (+44) 01455 233 747
Fax: (+44) 01455 233 737
E-mail: 106371.573@compuserve.com

US distribution by Specialty Press –
see page 10.

SPECIALTY PRESS

Midland is pleased to act as a distributor for selected titles published by Specialty Press (who also act as trade distributor in the United States for Midland's aviation books).

GERMAN JETS VERSUS THE US ARMY AIR FORCE
Battle for the Skies over Europe

William N Hess

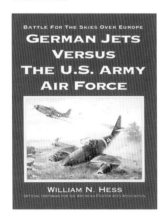

In the summer of 1944, radical new German jet fighters appeared over Europe, striking fear into allied airmen. Chief amongst these was the excellent Messerschmitt Me 262 a twin jet that had previously suffered from Hitler's desire to make it a fighter-bomber. Air combat interviews with German and American pilots produce a vivid account of the then 'new' aerial warfare. He recounts the strengths and weaknesses of the new jets, and dwells on what might have been.

Softback, 228 x 153 mm, 176 pages
52 black/white photographs
0 933424 63 9   **£14.95/US $19.95**

FINAL TOUR OF DUTY
North American's T-28 Trojans

Robert Genat

North American's potent T-28 Trojan trainer is somewhat unsung, yet it is without doubt one of the most technically advanced propeller driven military aircraft ever designed. The T-28 can outclimb and out-turn the legendary P-51 Mustang, has performed a close air support role in conflicts worldwide, prepared thousands of pilots for jet flight and continues to be active as a popular 'warbird'.

This heavily illustrated work takes a close look at the technical and operating aspects of the aircraft (as would be expected from the author, who is an active T-28 pilot) and reviews each of the models in turn. The photographic coverage includes a selection of air-to-air, and cockpit, engine and other detail close-ups.

Softback,184 x 223 mm, 144 pages
145 colour photographs
0 933424 61 2   **£19.95 / US $28.95**

B-17 NOSE ART NAME DIRECTORY
Wallace R Forman
Includes Group, Squadron and Aircraft Serial Numbers and photo availability

Wally Forman has been a resource to aviation historians for decades with his collection of aircraft data by name, unit and serial number, in many cases with matching photographs.

Starting with *A Bit O' Lace* and concluding with *'Zootie Cutie'*, the author has assembled data on over 8,200 B-17 aircraft into one concise reference that coordinates the aircraft name with its group, squadron and serial number.

A photo section illustrates 32 rare views of combat Fortresses.

Softback, 280 x 216 mm, 96 pages
32 b/w photographs
1 883809 14 2   **£9.95 / US $14.95**

In 1982, American author Jay Miller published his first major book, the AeroGraph on the F-16, since when there has been a flow of widely acclaimed books from the Aerofax line.

After many years acting as the European distributors for Aerofax, Midland Publishing has acquired the rights to this series, and many new titles are in preparation, compiled by a talented team of internationally known authors.

Some of these continue to be produced for Midland by Jay Miller in the USA, but are now augmented by others originated in the UK.

These softback volumes are full of authoritative text, detailed photographs, plus line drawings. They also contain some colour and cockpits, control panels and other interior detail are well illustrated in most instances.

The previous categories of AeroGraph, DataGraph, MiniGraph, and Extra are being dropped; all new titles are to be simply published as 'Aerofax' books.

The first two new-style 'Aerofax' titles were updated 'Extras', namely:
Lockheed-Martin F-117 (Jay Miller)
1 85780 038 9   **£7.95/ US $12.95**
Northrop B-2 Spirit (Jay Miller)
1 85780 039 7   **£7.95/ US $12.95**
Other new titles in the series are outlined alongside and below.

A listing of earlier titles still in print is available upon request.

Aerofax
CONVAIR B-58 HUSTLER
The World's First Supersonic Bomber

Jay Miller

Instantly recognisable with its delta wing and 'coke bottle' area-ruled fuselage the B-58 was put into production for the US Air Force in the 1950s. First published, in 1985, this revised edition, which takes a retrospective in-depth look at this significant aircraft, from design studies, through development and comparatively short service life to, and beyond retirement, includes yet more amazing material, and 80 new illustrations.
Due for publication 1997 (3rd qtr)

Softback, 280 x 216 mm, 152 pages
415 b/w, 14 colour, 100 line illusts.
1 85780 058 3 **£16.95/ US $27.95**

Aerofax
GRUMMAN F-14 TOMCAT
Leading US Navy Fleet Fighter

Dennis R Jenkins

Entering US Navy service in 1972, the Tomcat is still one of the classic jet fighters of all time. It remains a formidable weapon system and is still in widespread frontline use with America's carrier air wings. This work describes all variants, including the so-called 'Bombcat' attack version and the very capable F-14D. Colour schemes, aircraft production details, squadrons and markings, are all covered, also close-up details of cockpits and weaponry.
Due for publication 1997 (3rd qtr)

Softback, 280 x 216 mm, 88 pages
151 b/w, 39 colour, 22 line illustrations
1 85780 063 X **£12.95 / US $21.95**

Aerofax
BOEING KC-135
More Than Just a Tanker

Robert S Hoskins III

The highly readable text follows the development and service use of this globe-trotting aircraft and its many and varied tasks. Every variant, and sub-variant is charted, the histories of each and every aircraft are to be found within; details of the hundreds of units, past and present, that have flown the Stratotanker are given. This profusely illustrated work will interest those who have flown and serviced them and the historian and enthusiast community.
Due for publication 1997 (3rd qtr)

Softback, 280 x 216 mm, 224 pages
c185 b/w and 50 colour photos
1 85780 069 9 **£24.95/US $39.95**

Aerofax
YAKOVLEV'S
V/STOL FIGHTERS

John Fricker and Piotr Butowski

The story of Russia's programme to achieve a supersonic VTOL jet fighter can now be revealed, from the earliest Yak-36 'Freehand' experiments through the carrier-operated Yak-38 'Forger' and astonishing Yak-141 'Freehand', on to the agreement between Yakovlev and Lockheed Martin to help produce JAST, the USA's next generation fighter.

Using material never before seen in the West, this book tells the story of a programme that has to an extent, until recently, been shrouded in secrecy.

Softback, 280 x 216 mm, 44 pages
90 b/w photos, diagrams etc
1 85780 041 9 **£7.95/US $12.95**

Aerofax
MiG-21 'FISHBED'
Most widely used Supersonic Fighter

Yefim Gordon and Bill Gunston

The ubiquitous MiG-21 is unquestionably one of the greatest fighters of the post-Second World War era. It was Russia's first operational Mach 2-capable interceptor, and a stepping stone for many nations to enter the age of supersonic air combat. Access to the files of the MiG design bureau and other previously inaccessible sources reveal the secrets of the fighter that has flown and fought in more countries than any other supersonic jet.

Softback, 280 x 216 mm, 144 pages
335 b/w and 46 col illusts, plus colour artwork and scale plans.
1 85780 042 7 **£16.95/ $27.95**

Aerofax
MIG-25 'FOXBAT' and
MIG-31 'FOXHOUND'

Yefim Gordon

This book takes a detailed, informed and dispassionate view of an awesome aeronautical achievement – the titanium and steel MiG-25. Its follow-on was the similar-looking MiG-31 'Foxhound', very much a new aircraft designed to counter US cruise missiles and in production from 1979. Includes a large amount of previously unpublished material plus lavish illustrations and extensive full colour artwork.
Due for publication 1997 (3rd qtr)

Softback, 280 x 216 mm, 96 pages
c110 b/w and colour photos plus 91 line and colour airbrush illustrations
1 85780 064 8 **£12.95/ US $21.95**

Aerofax
TUPOLEV Tu-95/Tu-142
'BEAR'

Yefim Gordon and Vladimir Rigmant

During the 'Cold War' Tupolev's Tu-95 'Bear' strategic bomber provided an awesome spectacle. It was the mainstay of the USSR's strike force, a reliable and adaptable weapons platform. Additional roles included electronic/photographic reconnaissance and maritime patrol, AEW and command and control.

The author has had unparalleled access to the Tupolev OKB archives, taking the lid off a story previously full of speculation.
Due for publication 1997 (3rd qtr)

Softback, 280 x 216 mm, 128 pages
c220 b/w and colour photos, diagrams
1 85780 046 X **£14.95/US c$24.95**